Alfred Ollivant

Owd Bob: The grey dog of Kenmuir

Alfred Ollivant

Owd Bob: The grey dog of Kenmuir

ISBN/EAN: 9783337814892

Printed in Europe, USA, Canada, Australia, Japan

Cover: Foto ©ninafisch / pixelio.de

More available books at **www.hansebooks.com**

OWD BOB:

THE GREY DOG OF KENMUIR

BY
ALFRED
OLLIVANT

CONTENTS

PART I: THE COMING OF THE TAILLESS TYKE

CHAP.		PAGE
I.	THE GREY DOG'S CA'.	11
II.	A SON OF HAGAR	20
III.	CUTTY SARK	31
IV.	IN THE DEVIL'S BOWL.	38
V.	FIRST BLOOD	45

PART II: THE LITTLE MAN

VI.	A MAN'S SON	53
VII.	A LAD'S FATHER	62
VIII.	THE WHITE WINTER	70
IX.	M'ADAM AND HIS COAT	79

PART III: THE SHEPHERDS' TROPHY

X.	RIVALS	91
XI.	IN THE PASS	99
XII.	WE TWA	105
XIII.	THE FIGHT IN THE FLOOD	111
XIV.	RED WULL HOLDS THE BRIDGE	120
XV.	THE PASSING OF THE CUP	130

RED AND GREY

RED AND GREY	139

PART IV: THE BLACK KILLER

XVI.	A MAD MAN	148
XVII.	DEATH ON THE MARCHES	155
XVIII.	THE BLACK KILLER	163
XIX.	IN THE FOG	172
XX.	THE WITCH'S LAP	178

CONTENTS

CHAP.		PAGE
XXI. THREATS OF A STORM		190
XXII. THE STORM BREAKS		200
XXIII. HORROR OF DARKNESS		208

PART V: OWD BOB O' KENMUIR

XXIV. A MAN AND A MAID.		216
XXV. THE CHASE IN THE DARK		229
XXVI. A SHOT IN THE NIGHT		237
XXVII. THE SHEPHERDS' TROPHY		246

PART VI: THE BLACK KILLER

XXVIII. RED-HANDED		260
XXIX. FOR THE DEFENCE		270
XXX. THE DEVIL'S BOWL		279
XXXI. THE DEVIL'S BOWL		287
XXXII. THE KILLER AT BAY		294
POSTSCRIPT		307

Part I

The Coming of the Tailless Tyke

Chapter I

THE GREY DOG'S CA'

WITHOUT, the slow rich stillness of a summer's morning; the wickering m-a-a-a of sheep; the stealthy hail of curlews; the hum of bees; and the whole sleepy murmur of a sluggard summer day.

Within, a cold dead room, uncared, unkempt, barren with all the bleak discomfort of a womanless home; and on the floor, huddled his length, a little man.

Lying there in the dust and deadness, on the edge of a slant sunbeam, he slept noisily. His shirt, open at the neck, discovered a meagre throat; one careless arm shrouded his face; and the black mask of a bottle, glinting from his pocket, betrayed him. At his head, lying in a pond of sun, absorbing light as only a dog knows how, was a veteran collie, whose grey-flecked muzzle lay along the boards, while her eyes blinked large, eternal love, as they rested on their God, Hero Ideal of the Perfect Being, thus sleeping off his debauch.

From without there came the sound of stealthy feet. The old dog's ears leaped to attention.

The door gaped softly, and a fair young face peered in. Another moment and a boy had entered. His shoes were in his hand, and he stole across the floor, naked-footed, frowning a warning at the old dog, who lay, motionless yet alert, eyeing the intruder with cold hostility.

Contempt sat all conspicuous on the boy's frank features as he bent over the sleeper.

"Artna' 'shamed, peg? and afoor yer dog and a'!" he muttered, rootling at the prostrate figure with his toe. "A pretty piece to call a man's father!" And bending, he smote the prone form with his slipper.

The drunkard in the dust opened one eye, and frowned portentous.

"That's ree'! hit a man when he's doon—Englishmen a'!" he muttered mistily. Then, glaring up cornerwise—"Davie!" he wailed, in grieved wonder-tone; "Davie! oh, wae is me! Ha' ye no reshpec' for yer father? Oh, peetiful! peetiful!" He wept a tear, and was again asleep.

When all was still, the boy advanced afresh. But a low-grumbled protest from the old dog halted him.

"Fool, Cutty Sark!" he hissed. "Does ta' think it's a fit?" But Cutty Sark made no reply. Hers was to deal with consequences; others might inquire the cause. This chronic ill overtook her master. As often as it held him, it was for her to see no harm befell him. And loyally she did her part, and her love bated no wit.

Outside the door the boy resumed his shoes. Then he launched into the light and ran down the hill, making for the Muir Pike and Stony Bottom; blithely whistling as he pierced the morning from very joy in his young limbs, the air, the sun, his exploit.

And within the dead room the little man and nobler brute were left together.

* * * * *

Away in the West, over the Marches, the thin air sweltered in the Pass. On the other hand, through the village, the Mere turned a lazy silver side like a salmon dozing. Linking the two, a thin-drawn wire lying along the lowest hollow of the Dale, ran the Wastrel. The stream pattered between the village on the one side and the bluff bald face of the Muir Pike upon the other; between squat alders, many-shimmering birch; until, a mile from the Mere, a plank-bridge spanned it.

There, half-hidden behind the swell of the ground, a hoar farmhouse lay in the staring silence; solemn stacks peered over the brink and frowned at the stream flirting in the meadow-bottom; while a long array of out-buildings reflected the sombre glare of the opposing Pike.

In the stackyard two men were deeply engaged in idleness. One, perched high upon a ladder, wren-like, was craning over the crest of a rick into the distance, his old nut-face glowing with excitement. The other, on a lower level, was a solid Dalesman of huge hands, hairy arms, and an immutable melancholy.

In the distance were three figures on the lowland lips of the Pike: a grey dog and a black-faced ram engaged in fateful duel, and on a mound, something apart, the tall form of a man watching, motionless.

"Noo, Bob!" screamed the veteran on the ladder, and held his breath as the warrior ram made a last huge onslaught. "Stan' till her! Heart oop, lad! Noo, noo he's comin'! Ma wud! a despart fratch! . . . Ah-h-h!" —smiting the ladder in red-hot ecstasy—"Weel done, oor Bob! See owd Staggy run, Sam'l! see un' 'op! Ma sarty, if that doesna bang a'! . . . Ah, if iver I seed a good tyke. . . . He's a reet 'un! He's a rare 'un! A proper Grey Dog, I's uphod thee! A reg'lar—reg'lar—Rex, son o' Rally!"

The other's resolute melancholy refused to be thus dissipated.

"And what coom to Rex, son o' Rally?" he asked, in dismal, grave-deep tones.

Tammas clucked irritably.

"Hod tongue o' thee, Sam'l Todd!" he ordered. Art' niver 'appy without thoo's makin' thysel miser'ble. I niver see thy like—nor niver wush to. Coom, Sam'l, coom! Man thyself!"

"What coom to Rex, son o' Rally?" the other pursued, dogged as a fell tip.

"He won Cup, did Rex, that's what he did!" Tammas replied, as stubborn. "Twice he won it, did Rex; the last o' the Grey Dogs as browt Shepherds' Trophy to Kenmuir—eh, dearie! fifty year sinsyne—fifty year!" lachrymose in his turn, as he looked back along the years.

Sam'l was not to be outdone.

"Gay weel thoo kens what coom to Rex," he cried, righteously wrath; "but thoo's far ower cowardly to say it. Took he was—took in the pride of his prime, ower the 'ills and far away." He chanted the words like a death-song, rolling his eyes in unctuous enjoyment of his misery. "And mark me, Tammas Thornton! Oor young Bob—poor Bobbie! . . . he'll gang same gate—gang 'ome—ower the 'ills, and "—

Tammas turned.

"Thoo lives in graves, Sam'l Todd!" he cried furiously. "Wilt' niver be 'appy, for sure, till thoo's dead; and then it's like thoo'll be grumblin'." He struck at the big man's face with his booted heel.

"Thoo 'carse-'orse, thoo! thoo wormy willain! thoo melancholy maggot!"

"Gie owre, Tammas Thornton!" bellowed the other querulously. "Let be wi' yon girt 'oof o' thine! Let be, I say, or I'll brong thee seccan a dander as'll like to be t' end o' thee."

The old man ceased suddenly, and fell upon his work.

A tall, gaitered man, with cold, lean, austere face and the steel-blue eyes of the hill-country, strode into the yard; and trotting soberly at his heels, a Grey Dog of Kenmuir.

No man can mistake the type. A Grey Dog of Kenmuir is as little indistinct as a Raphael's Madonna. Outside a radius of twenty miles from Kenmuir he is never met. Money cannot win one, neither love; for a Moore would as soon think to sell his child as part with a Grey Dog.

But should you, while wandering in the wild sheep- and about the twin Pikes, happen on moor or in market upon a very perfect gentle knight clothed in dark grey habit, splashed here and there with rays of moon; free by right divine of the guild of gentlemen, strenuous as a prince, lithe as a rowan, graceful as a girl, with high king-carriage, motions and manners of a airy queen; should he have a noble breadth of brow, an air of still strength born of right confidence, all unassuming; last, and most unfailing test of all, should you look into two snowcloud eyes, calm, wistful, inscrutable, their soft depths clothed on with eternal sadness—yearning, as is said, for the soul that is not theirs—know then you look upon one of the line of most illustrious sheep-dogs of the North.

Such is one; such are all. And such was Owd Bob o' Kenmuir—owd, young though he was, by reason of that sprinkling shower of snow upon the dome of his head

"If you worked as mickle as ye talked it's like I'd be better sarved," said the tall man sternly.

Tammas, with the privilege of long service, put the rebuke aside.

"A proper mak' o' Grey Dog!" he mused, gazing down into the sweet, sagacious face uplifted. "His father's own get, surely; his varra spit and pictur'; sma' yet big, leet to get aboot on backs o' his sheep yet not owre leet, cannie yet cantie; and wi' them sorrerful eyes on him as niver gangs but wi' a good 'un. Amaist he minds me o' Rex, son o' Rally."

Sam'l groaned; but the old man continued.

"Did ye hear tell o' him and that lil gob o' wiciousness, Adam M'Adam, Maister?" he inquired.

The Master of Kenmuir shook dissent.

"Whey," Tammas pursued, "it seems t' lil by-spel coom sneakin' around the farm to catch David. But the lad see his father, slipped ahint stack, and set Bob here on till him."

James Moore's brow lowered as he hearkened.

"I wunna ha' M'Adam lay in wait for t' lad at Kenmuir," he said in hard incisive tones. "If he mun beat t' poor boy it shallna be on ma land, and that's plain."

The plank-bridge below rang to the patter of feet.

"Here is t' lad!" said Tammas, glancing round. "Late this morn an' a'; it's like he's bin havin' a bit of an hay-bay wi's dad."

A fair-haired boy spurred up the slope, his face rosy as the morning. The young dog dashed off to meet him. Together the two raced back into the yard.

"Morn', Maister Moore! Morn', Tammas! Morn', owd Worrit-t'-worms!" panted the boy, raced across the straw-strewn yard, round the stables, and into the house.

In the kitchen a frail-faced woman was bustling about
 morning business. To her skirts clung a sturdy
y; while at the central table a girl with soft brown
es was seated at her morning meal.
'Whey, Davie! where's ta bin the morn?" the
man cried, and greeted him with a tender, motherly
utation. "I thowt ye couldna be comin'. Noo clap
on beside Maggie." And soon he, too, was engaged
 a task twin to the girl's.
'Did thy father beat thee last night, Davie?"
iggie inquired in low voice, after a long munching
use; and a shade of anxiety clouded the soft eyes.
'Nay," the boy answered; "he fain wud, but he was
 ower fou o' lear to catch me."
"What for was he goin' to bang thee, Davie?" asked
rs. Moore from the outer kitchen.
"What for?" the boy cried, and laughed bitterly—
Vhy, for comin' home thro' Kenmuir, and for the fun
 seein' me squiggle."
"Ye shouldna speak so o' yer dad, David," reproved
 other, as severely as was in her nature.
"Dad! a famish dad! I'd dad him an I'd the
ance," the boy muttered. Then turning, "Us should
 startin', Maggie," he said, and going to the door,
3ob! Owd Bob, lad! art' coomin' along?"
The grey dog came plunging up, and the three started
 school together. Mrs. Moore stood in the doorway,
lding the child Andrew by the hand, and watched
em go.
"Poor bit laddie!" she murmured softly.

. . . .

Six hours later. A slumberous silence held the farm.
Of a sudden, like a thunderclap in a vault, a deep
emendous "Wough!" woke the stillness.

Straightway the whole farm leaped from its sleep. Scuttling feet; bangings of hurrying men: the whole disorder of a startled community.

"Ma wud! The Grey Dog's Ca'!" came Tammas's shrill scream. And any fool can tell you that 'tis not for nothing that a Grey Dog calls.

James Moore started to his feet, and hurled out into the yard.

"This gate!" yelled Tammas. "In t' coo-hoose."

Hard behind, the Master followed. As he crossed the yard, from the building in front there came a shower of curses, clash of steel, and slatter of slight evasive feet.

Then a quivering scream jagged the air.

"Come on, ye devil!

> 'Scots, wha hae wi' Wallace bled,
> Scots, wham Bruce has aften led'—

Come on, Englishmen a'! Ye sall hae a taste o' the steel—

> 'Welcome to your gory bed,
> Or to victorie'!"

The Master swung round the doorpost. Glaring into the half darkness, he caught the glint of steel; and then discerned a small dark figure at bay upon a truss of straw, jabbing madly with a pitchfork, and sloganing forth his shrill war-cry; while, right in the very flash of the steel, with the light heart and gay demeanour that has always characterised a Grey Dog in time of peril, was Owd Bob, baying him dumbly.

"M'Adam!" called the Master, in his hard voice. "Come oot of it."

"Then call aff the grey devil!" panted a small, uneven voice.

"Bob, lad, coom in!" and as the grey dog obeyed—"Noo, M'Adam."

Out the intruder shuffled, blinking for the light: a little miserable man, bonnet awry, weapon still in hand. He was shaking, his face was blenched, but the light of battle yet enthused his eyes; while about him still clung the wretched heat and circumstance of a late debauch.

"What was ta' doin' in theer?" the Master asked, eyeing him sternly.

"Fightin' for ma life agin yon grey devil!" the little man replied furiously; and turning all in a crack, he lunged at Owd Bob. The dog lightly evaded the thrust, and James Moore had wrenched away the weapon ere it could be repeated.

"Ha' a care, M'Adam!" he ordered, his eyes flashing. "I've tell't thee afoor a Grey Dog'll bide no bang but a' a Moore. Noo, what was ta' doin' in coo-hoose?"

The little man calmed slowly. Soon a smile wreathed his lips.

"I e'en thocht to surprise the dear lad," he replied softly. "Hide in byre and then loup out on him like an angel unawares, and say, 'Davie, dear lad, I've somethin' for ye—he! he!'" He giggled as he spoke, and bending, picked up a long ash-plant which was lying at his feet.

A dark flush heated the Master's cheek.

"An' that's what ye come for, M'Adam," he said—"you gang!" He pointed to the gate.

The little man turned.

"I'm aff," he said vindictively; "and ye may tell David I'm awaitin' him."

He backed out of the yard, his eyes never lifting from the grey dog, who followed him with cold courtesy to the gate.

Safe outside he paused.

"James Moore," he called earnestly, "that dog has a evil! I see it first time iver I clapp't een on him."

CHAPTER II

A SON OF HAGAR

IT is a lonely country, that about Wastrel-dale. Parson Leggy Hornbut will tell you that his is the smallest church in the biggest parish north of Trent; and that his cure numbers more square miles than parishioners. Of fells and ghylls it consists, of screes and crag; with here a scattered hamlet and there a hill sheep-farm. It is a country in which sheep are paramount. Every other Dalesman is engaged in that profession which is old as Abel. And the talk of the men of the land is of wethers and gimmers; of tup-hoggs, ewe-tegs-in-wool; of four-crops, two-tooths; and ever of the doings or misdoings, the intelligence or stupidity, of their subalterns, the sheep-dogs.

Of all the Dale-land the country from the Black Water to Grammoch Pike is the wildest. Above Wastrel-dale the Muir Pike nods. Westwards, the Mere Marches, from which the Sylvesters' great estate derives its name, reach away in mile on mile of sheep-infested, curlew-haunted heather-land. Beyond this bleak moor barrier is that twin Dale where flows the Silver Lea. And it is there, in the paddocks behind the Dalesman's Daughter, that in the late summer months the famous sheep-dog Trials of the North are held: there that the battle for the Dale Cup, the world-known Shepherds' Trophy, is fought out.

Past the inn the turnpike road leads to the market-[ce]ntre of the district, Grammoch-town. Behind the [lit]tle alehouse, at foot of the paddocks, a plank-bridge [cr]osses the Lea; and beyond, the Murk Muir Pass [cr]awls up the sheer side of the Scaur on to the Marches. At its neck, just before debouching on to the wind-[sw]ept moors, the Pass swells and droops into that [sn]ake-hooded hollow, shuddering with gloomy possi[bil]ities, the Devil's Bowl. In the centre of the Bowl, [rig]ht beneath the shadow of the Red Screes, lies the [Lo]ne Tarn.

It was beside that black water, across whose frozen [su]rface the storm was swirling in white snow-wraiths, [th]at many, many years ago (and not in this century) [ol]d Andrew Moore came upon a collie, heavy in whelp [an]d nigh spent.

He carried her home over the Marches and nursed [he]r tenderly. It was of no avail. She died; but not [til]l she had paid her debt of gratitude, and earned her [im]mortality as mother of the Grey Dogs of Kenmuir.

In the North everyone who has heard of the Muir [la]ke—and who is there has not?—has heard of the [Gr]ey Dogs of Kenmuir; everyone who has heard of the [Sh]epherds' Trophy knows their fame. In that country [of] good dogs and jealous masters the pride of place [ha]s long been held, unchallenged. Whatever line may [cla]im to follow, the Grey Dogs always lead. And there [is] a saying in the land: "Faithfu' as the Moores and [th]eir tykes."

On the dresser to the right of the fire in the kitchen [at] Kenmuir lies the family Bible. At the end you will [fin]d a loose sheet—the pedigree of the Grey Dogs; at [th]e beginning, pasted on the inward side, a similar [sh]eet—the family register of the Moores of Kenmuir.

These two yellow sheets should be studied together, side by side. For since the days of Grey Grip, first of the line, the history of the Moores would be no true history without that of their dogs, so deeply have the two been dove-tailed.

If you can induce James Moore to take down that well-thumbed volume and comment on the entries, you will hear many a tale to kindle your blood and rouse the man within you. Only, twice you will come upon a name so indelibly erased that nothing but a great black blot tells of some dog's sin. Of that James Moore will not speak, and do not ask him. There are things best left unexplained; and the Moores have always held the good name of their dogs second only to that of their blood. And in the code of sheep-dog honour there is written a word in stark black letters; and opposite it another writ large in the colour of blood. The first is Sheep-murder; the second Death. Every sheep-dog knows it, and every shepherd.

Running your eye on past those ill blots, once, twice, and again it will be caught by a small red cross beneath a name; and beneath the cross the one word, Cup. Lastly, opposite the name of Rex, son of Rally, are two of those tell-tale badges. The Cup is the renowned Dale Cup; Champion Challenge Dale Cup, open to the world, aptly called the blue riband of the heather. Had Rex won it but once again, the Shepherds' Trophy, which many men have lived to win and died still striving after, would have stayed for ever in the hoar farmhouse below the Pike.

It was not to be, however. Comparing the two sheets, you read beneath the dog's name a date and a pathetic legend; and on the other sheet, beneath the name of Andrew Moore, the same date and same gend. From that day James Moore had been Master Kenmuir.

So past Grip and Rip and Rex and Rally, past Beck d Brock and Tup and Tally and a hundred more; til at the foot of the page you come to that last name— b, son of Battle, last of the Grey Dogs of Kenmuir.

Now any shepherd will tell you that the son of a eep-dog is a sheep-dog from his birth. Training is as perfluous as to teach a duck to swim. It is in the ood. And so it proved with Owd Bob, scion of a ndred sires.

From the first he took to his work in a manner to aze even James Moore. Rarely had such fiery élan en seen on the Pike; and with it the young dog mbined a strange sobriety, an admirable patience, that stified, indeed, the epithet Owd. Silent he worked d resolute as the Grey Dogs always have; quick and shing, as one whose labour lies amongst the wild ack-faces of the fells must be; while already he had at famous trick of tact of his—seeming to coax the eep to do his wishes—which later made his name a usehold word through half two kingdoms. In short blended, as Tammas the phrase-maker put it, " t' ains of a man and t' way of a woman."

Parson Leggy, who was reckoned the best judge of a eep 'twixt Trent and Tweed, summed him up in the e word—" Genius." And James Moore himself, nnie man, was more than pleased. While even David 'Adam, who was at that age when criticism of everying, from a sermon to a sow, is possible and necessary, knowledged himself as satisfied.

" Ay, ay," he replied to an anxious inquiry of aggie's; " reck'n he's better'n some I've seen. And ye n tell yer father I said it."

In the village the Dalesmen, who took a personal pride in the Grey Dogs of Kenmuir, began to nod sage heads when "oor" Bob was mentioned. Jim Mason, the postman, whose word went as far with the villagers as Parson Leggy's with the gentry, reckoned he'd never seen a young un' as so took his fancy; and others—for every Dalesman is competent to judge in such a matter —corroborated the report.

That winter, when they had gathered of a night round the fire in the Sylvester Arms; the wind in the chimney, the gale without; it was a rare thing but Rob Saunderson must inquire—

"Weel, Mr. Thornton, and what o' oor Bob?"

Whereat Tammas would always make reply, shaking his head in maiden diffidence,

"Oh, ask Sam'l theer. He'll tell thee better'n me," and was waist-deep in a yarn ere the big man had time to groan.

And the way in which, as the story proceeded, Tupper of Swinsthwaite winked at Ned Hoppin of Fellsgarth, and Long Kirby, the smith, nudged Jem Burton, the publican, and Sexton Ross said, "Ma wud, lad!" spoke more eloquently than many words.

One man only never joined in the chorus of admiration. Sitting alone in the cold background, little M'Adam would hearken with an incredulous smirk upon his face. Sometimes he would content himself with the oft-muttered comment: "The dog has a devil!" more often he mocked in opener fashion.

"Lost all his sheep in the market-place, I onderstand, Mr. Thornton, and then found them agin—found them all but the maist part o' them! Oh, ma certes! The devil's in the dog! It's no' cannie ava!" Whereon Tammas would arise and smite; and for awhile was chaos.

In the Dale-land it is rare to see a stranger's face
[w]andering in the wicked land about the twin dales,
[wi]th shy curlew for comrade, the black-cock's bubble-
[no]te for company, the heather beneath you, and a hen-
[ha]rrier soaring speck-large in the blue above, you might
[ha]ve met at the time of this story Parson Leggy strid-
[in]g along, varmint terriers at heel, and Cyril Gilbraith,
[wh]om he was teaching to tie flies and fear God, beside
[hi]m ; or Jim Mason, postman by profession, poacher by
[pr]edilection, honest man and sportsman by predestina-
[tio]n; hurrying along mail-bag on shoulder, rabbit in
[po]cket, and the faithful Betsy her measured yard
[be]hind. Besides these, you might have hit upon a quiet
[sh]epherd and a wise-faced dog ; Squire Sylvester going
[hi]s rounds ; or — had you been lucky — sweet Lady
[El]eanur bent on some errand of mercy.

It was while the Squire's lady was driving through
[th]e village on a visit to Tammas's slobbering, week-old
[gr]andson, that M'Adam, standing in the door of the
[Sy]lvester Arms, a twig in his mouth, a sneer fading
[fro]m his lips, made his ever-memorable remark.

" Sall ! " he said, speaking in a low, rapt voice. " 'Tis
muckle wumman ! "

" What ? Whatsta' sayin,' man ? " cried Jem Burton,
[st]artled from a beery muse.

M'Adam turned sharply on the publican.

" I said the wumman wears a muckle hat ! " he
[sn]apped.

Deleted as it was, the observation still remains — a
[tr]ibute of honest admiration. Doubtless the Recording
[A]ngel did not pass it by. That one statement anent the
[ge]ntle Lady of the Manor is the only personal remark
[ev]er credited to little M'Adam not born of malice and all
[un]charitableness. And that is why it is ever memorable

The little Scotsman with the sere, sardonic face had been the tenant of the Grange these many years; yet he had never grown acclimatised to the land of the Southron. With his shrivelled body and weakly legs, he looked among the sturdy, straight-limbed sons of the hill-country like some brown wrinkled leaf holding its place amidst a galaxy of green. And as he differed from them physically, so he did morally. He neither understood them, nor attempted to. The north-country character was to him an unsolved mystery still, and that after ten years' study of it. "One half o' what ye say they doot, and they let ye see it; t'ither half they disbelieve, and they tell ye so," he once declared. And therein lay the explanation of their mutual relations.

From the first he had stood apart; for his was one of those natures which isolate themselves and then are prone to think they are being isolated. Yet, during his wife's life, his aloofness had been less patent. It was not till a while after her death that he had drifted into such an apartness from his fellow-men that now he could honestly declare, and not without a certain touch of proud defiance, that they were all agin him.

He stood entirely alone: a son of Hagar, mocking. His sharp ill-tongue was rarely still and always bitter. There was hardly a man in the land, from Langholm How to the market-cross in Grammoch-town, but had at one time known its sting, endured it in silence, for they are slow of speech these men of the fells and dales, and was nursing his resentment till a day should bring that chance which always comes. And on an occasion Tammas's epigrammatic summary — " Drunk, wilent sober, wicious," met with an applause to gratify the blasé heart of even Tammas Thornton.

Yet it had not been till his wife's death that the little
[ma]n had allowed loose rein to his ill-nature. With her
[o]nly gentle hand no longer on the tiller of his life,
[his] spleen had burst into fresh being. And alone in the
[wo]rld with David, the whole venom of his vicious
[te]mperament was ever directed against the boy's head.
[It] was as though he saw in his fair-haired son the
[un]conscious cause of the ever-living sorrow of his life.
[All] the more strange this, seeing that during her life
[the] boy had been to poor Flora M'Adam as her heart's
[cor]e. And the lad was growing up the very antithesis
[of] his father. Big and hearty, with never an ache or ill
[in] his sturdy young body; of frank open countenance;
[whi]le even his speech was slow and burring like any
[da]le-bred boy's. And the fact of it all, and that the
[lad] was palpably more Englishman than Scot,—ay, and
[g]ried in it,—exasperated the little man, a patriot before
[eve]rything, to blows. While, on top of it, David evinced
[an] amazing pertness such as to have tried a better man
[tha]n Adam M'Adam.

On the death of his wife, kindly Elizabeth Moore
[ha]d more than once offered such help to the lonely
[litt]le widower as a woman only can give in a house
[tha]t knows no mistress. On the last of these occasions,
[aft]er crossing the Stony Bottom and toiling up the
[hil]l to the Grange, she had met M'Adam in the door.

"Ye mun let me fettle up yer bit oddments, Maister,"
[she] had said shyly; for she feared the little man.

'Thank ye, Mrs. Moore," he had answered, with the
[que]r smile the Dalesmen knew so well; "but ye maun
[thi]nk I'm a waefu' cripple." And there he had stood,
[gri]nning sardonically, opposing his small bulk in the
[ve]ry centre of the door.

Mrs. Moore had turned down the hill, abashed and

hurt at this reception of her offer; and her husband, proud to a fault, had forbidden her to repeat it.

Nevertheless her motherly heart went out in a great tenderness for the little orphan David. She knew well the desolateness of his life, his father's aversion to him, and its inevitable consequences. It became an institution for the boy to call every morning at Kenmuir, and trot off to the village school with Maggie Moore. And soon the lad came to look on Kenmuir as his true home, and James and Elizabeth Moore as his real parents. His greatest happiness was to be away from the Grange. And the ferret-eyed little man there noted the fact, bitterly resented it, and vented his ill-humour accordingly.

It was this, as he deemed it, deliberate trespass on his authority which was the motive of his animosity against James Moore. The Master of Kenmuir it was at whom that sneer of his was aimed—" Masel', I aye prefaire the good man who doesna go to Church, to the bad man who does. But then, as ye say, Mr. Burton, I'm peculiar."

The little man's treatment of his son, exaggerated as it was by eager credulity, became at length such a scandal in the Dale that Parson Leggy felt called upon to intervene.

Now M'Adam was the Parson's pet antipathy. The sturdy old minister with his bluff manner and big heart would have no truck with a man who was always in liquor and never in church; who never spoke well of his neighbours and always did ill by his son. While the little Scotsman with his mocking face and satirical replies had the knack of irritating the old man, quicker of temper than tongue, almost to blows. And, indeed, in this case the interview had barely been in progress two minutes ere the Parson found his fingers already itching.

"You, Mr. Hornbut, wi' James Moore to lend ye a hand, see to the lad's soul; I'll tend his body."

The little man was standing in the door of the Grange, sucking his eternal twig; while Cutty Sark glared out from between the crooked arch of her master's legs.

The Parson's passions were rising fast.

"And which d'you think the more important, soul or body? Oughtn't you, his father, to be the first to care for both? Answer me, Sir!"

The little man sniggered.

"Ye're right, Mr. Hornbut, as ye aye are. But my argiment is this: that I get at the lad's soul best thro' his leetle carcase."

The Parson brought down his stick with an angry thud.

"M'Adam, you're a brute, sir! a brute!" he shouted.

The little man leant against the door, shaking with inward merriment.

"A fond dad first, a brute, aiblins, afterwards. Ah, Mr. Hornbut, ye 'fordme vast diversion, ye do, indeed, my lov'd, my honour'd, much respected friend!'"

"If you paid as much heed to your boy's welfare as you do to the poetry of that profligate ploughman"—

The little man stopped him.

"D'ye ken what blasphemy is, Mr. Hornbut?" he asked smoothly.

For the first time in the altercation the Parson was about to score, and was calm accordingly.

"I should do; I fancy I've a specimen of the breed before me now. And d'you know what impertinence is, M'Adam?"

"I should do; I fancy I've a—I wad say it's what

gentlemen aften are unless their mammies whipped 'em as lads."

The Parson strode forward.

"M'Adam," he roared, "I'll not stand your insolence!"

The little man turned, scuttled indoors, and in a moment came running back with a chair.

"Permit me!" he said, bowing over it like a hairdresser to a customer.

The other turned away. At the gap in the hedge he paused.

"I'll only say one thing more, M'Adam. When your wife, whom, I think, we all loved, lay dying in that room above, she said to you in my presence"—

It was the other's turn to be indignant. He took a step forward with burning face.

"Aince and for a', Mr. Hornbut," he cried passionately, "onderstand I'll not ha' you and yer likes lay yer tongues on ma wife's name whenever it suits ye! Say what ye will o' me—lies, sneers, snash; and I'll say naethin'. I think ye might let her bide where she lies in the kirkyard yonder. *She* never harmed ye, puir lass. Tho' she is dead, she's mine."

Standing there with flushed face and burning eyes, the little man looked almost noble in his indignation. And the Parson, striding down the hill, was conscious that with him was not the victory.

CHAPTER III

CUTTY SARK

SAM'L'S gloomy forebodings came to nought. Owd Bob lived and prospered, and his fame went [a]road. Tammas, whose stock of tales anent Rex, son [of] Rally, had, after fifty years' hard wear, grown thread[ba]re despite annual alterations and repairs, found no [stoc]k of new material now.

Of market-days there was always a cluster of Dales[m]en in the door of the Border Ram at Grammoch-town [wa]tching this, the latest of the Grey Dogs, handling his [flo]ck; gentle, judicious, slow to anger, quick to action: [a] grey commanding figure motionless on the back of [th]e hindmost sheep, or running lightly over the woolly [backs] or to whisper a stern command in the ear of some [pa]triarch of the flock.

They thought well of him, these men who loved the [G]rey Dogs, yet not so well as did James Moore, who [wa]s father to them every one.

"Happen he'll mak' summat yet," was all he would [al]low, cannie man; but, of late, a certain silver Cup, [cr]adled in shepherds' crooks, a Cup which he [re]membered to have handled reverently in childhood, [ha]d risen very instant to his view.

Only M'Adam never tired of spiteful depreciation of [th]e grey dog. And this ever-living resentment served [fo]r a while to alleviate David's lot; for the heat of his father's animosity against the grey devil of Kenmuir distracted his attention from its habitual butt. Indeed, for a while there was almost peace at the Grange. The father's interdict against his son's visits to Kenmuir seemed withdrawn. The long-enduring guerilla warfare betwixt sire and son seemed flickering to its decline. Soon, however, it was to flame into fresh being. And Owd Bob, as he had been the unconscious cause of the some-time armistice, was to prove an equally innocent occasion of renewed hostilities. For David, heartened by long immunity, made bold on his return from school of evenings to invite the young dog's company to the very doors of the Grange, ostentatiously advertising the event the while.

For some time his father endured the unspoken insult, strangely patient. Standing with Cutty Sark upon the hilltop, he would watch the two climbing towards him from the Stony Bottom. No word would he utter; only a flickering light in the dim eyes and a droop of the thin lips betrayed him. It almost seemed that he was learning the habit of restraint from his antipathy. For on these occasions Owd Bob's attitude was a perfect lesson in the art of conduct amongst enemies. No cur expression of spleen marred his bearing. To the man he never wavered in shy courtesy; neither avoiding nor seeking, making no advance, desiring none, only requiring as his due that measure of toleration which one gentleman demands as his right from another. While to Cutty Sark he bore himself with a tender deference that befitted his yet young years and her grey hairs—an unfeigned respect that won the old lady's all-unwilling heart; for well she knew her master's sentiments, and held herself guilty accordingly.

But this was not to last. David, indeed, thinking

that his action had failed of its sovereign purport of annoyance, was on the brink of desistance, when the hardy veto fell.

"David, ye're no' to bring yon grey dog with ye o' neets." His father spoke in calm small voice, with none of the furious insistence of his wont.

"Why?" the boy asked.

"I dinna like the look of him."

"Then ye can look anudder way." And he parted, and into the house.

For two more nights the boy persisted in his wrong. On neither did his father appear to enforce obedience. On the third, as he entered the house, a smooth, deadly voice called from the kitchen—

"David!"

"What?"

"Ye brought that grey devil alang?"

"What if I did!"

"I'll no' thole it, that's a'. Mind, ma lad, I'm in earnest."

"What for not?"

"The dog has a devil."

The boy scoffed.

"Aweel, Davie," carelessly. "But, see here, ma lad"—he shot a look across his shoulder—"ye'll bring him aince ower aften gin ye bring him aince agin." He spoke calmly; but there was a faint shiver in his voice and a cruel green-glint in the dim eyes that David knew well.

At least he was enough impressed to render obedience for the nonce. For five successive days he dismissed his escort at the Bottom; for five successive days M'Adam, standing in the darkness of the door with Cutty Sark's eyes two yellow disks in the black behind,

On the sixth, as the boy entered the house, he met his father.

A wry smile of contemptuous triumph wreathed the sardonic face. The eyelids drooped to hide a jeer; the lips, eloquent in silence, sneered—" Ye daurna."

"Wait till t' morn!" the boy muttered savagely; and passed on, braced to battle.

The following evening Owd Bob crossed the barrier.

No sooner was the thing accomplished—his father defied—the daring done—than a sense of dread overwhelmed the boy. He glanced around, suspecting all things. The evening was far spent. Dusk was shrouding the land. The night was full of flitting shadows. Peering forward, he thought to see a little secret form retreat before him into the doubtful darkness.

A sudden fear clapped on him.

"Hie away home, lad!" he cried in startled whisper. The young dog paused, looked up at his comrade as if loth to desert him in his peril, then turned and swung back into the night.

David held on, his heart at gasp; probing the darkness, fearful of he knew not what.

A great while it took him to the house. As he passed the window of the kitchen, the room flamed into light. Close at his elbow, his father's face loomed against the pane, peering out, haunted, it seemed to the boy, with a terrible fear; and withdrew.

David entered the house. As he opened the door something brushed against him. He checked a scream on the verge of his lips; then entered.

The door into the kitchen was ajar. Praying to escape attention, he crept by.

It was not to be.

"David!" called a husky voice.

The boy entered. Across the room his father was sitting, a bottle beneath his hand. It still seemed to David that a horror held the little man. His face was blenched. He shook.

"Ha' ye onythin' to say for yersel'?" his father asked, in ghastly whisper.

David remained dumb.

"Yer school ended-d-d at four o' the clo-ck; it's noo after s-six." His stutter rendered the whisper more fearful still. "David, ye walk slowly!"

David pursed his lips. It was the old quarrel cropping up again, it seemed.

"Aiblins I could stimulate ye!" His father pointed with tremulous forefinger to the familiar strap upon the wall.

David reached it down.

"Aff wi' yer coat! noo yer shirt!" And again the boy obeyed.

M'Adam fingered the strap, yet made no motion to rise. He spoke on again at large—slow, dropping nonsense. It was plain his soul was in his ears. Listening—listening—listening. He was talking against time. He knew not what he said. And the wet stood on his face like the dew on the Pike without.

David, his coat slung about his naked shoulders, thought to escape.

"Dinna gang!" There was almost entreaty in the tone. He stayed, wondering.

The little man still talked on, all disconnected, in snatches; talked for company.

David was himself again.

"I hear Andra' Moore's to school noo."

The boy's tongue was in his cheek.

A pause.

"They're sayin' that—that—I'm forgettin' what."
"Weel done!" in ironical applause.
Another interval.
"I'm tell't—it's like that—that we s'll ha' rain."
"Famish-h!"
A sudden resolution seized the little man. He leaped to his feet.
"It's no' too late!" he gasped with prayerful earnestness.
A stifled groan from beneath the window answered him.
The little man clapped back into his chair, his face ghastly.
"Ma God forgie me!"
In the heat of hate and liquor he had done this thing—he who had a tenderness for the brute creation exceeding his love for his own begotten; and now he was a murderer, self-abhorrent.
Another of those awful groans beneath the window; a long, moaning sob; then piteous whines and scrabbling nails, as of one entreating sanctuary.
David was beside himself.
"Father, let me gang see!" he begged, in a tremble of tears.
M'Adam was emptying the bottle down his throat. Then he flung it away, leaped to his feet, and raved round the room, screaming prayers, drinking-songs, entreaties in horrible medley; his fingers in his ears, sealing the gateways to his soul, smothering sound.
Outside, the night groaned with horror: long-drawn moans as of dead men beneath the weight of earth; tiny, whimpering notes of suffering children; huge gasps of giants in agony; the deathly struggle of a spirit warring with the trammelling clay.

David, his head buried in his coat, cowered in a
corner, stamping to help overwhelm the sound.

At length—a long, long at length—was silence.
But still the little man raved about with blind eyes,
dead ears, drowning with his uproar noises that were
not.

At length he stayed, and, fingers yet in ears, looked
into his son's eyes, his own all murder-haunted.

"Is it finished?"

The boy nodded.

The little man withdrew his sealing fingers warily,
and listened, on edge. Then he lit a candle, his hand
shaking as with a palsy, and went out, locking the door
behind.

From the window David watched, his coat about his
naked shoulders.

The door of the house opened fearfully. He saw his
father peering forth, his face ghastly in the twittering
flame. He saw him plunge into the black, the yellow
flame swaling in the night. He saw him stoop, light
held low. He saw a dark body at foot.

Then the candle quenched as though dropped.

A flash of revealing summer lightning; a little erect
figure battering his head; a glimpse of a stricken face
uplifted: and such a scream in his ears as shocked him
from the window.

"God! Ma God! Ma sin has found me out!"

For at his father's feet lay Cutty Sark—dead.

CHAPTER IV

IN THE DEVIL'S BOWL

A dour man was M'Adam for long thereafter. No jest crossed his lips. He shunned his fellow-men, glowering from downward eyes. Parson Leggy declared the curse of Cain was on him.

In the Dale they gave him sympathy; for in such a sorrow even Adam M'Adam had their hearts. But little might be said. His seemed a wound that would endure no touch. And did they dare to compassionate him, he turned and snarled upon them with such dumb-glaring savagery as compelled their silence.

Only David dimly guessed the tragedy behind, and, wise for once, kept silence. And well he did; for in the North 'twere better to attempt the shepherd's life than the dog's. Only at Kenmuir he told of lonely passions in the night; of hour-long steps pacing far into the morning; of a little voice raised in an agony of tears—"Eh, Cutty Sark, Cutty Sark! forgie me! And me wha lo'ed ye as ma life."

But the Master suspected nothing; and, one of few who dared it, crossed the Stony Bottom to offer the bereaved man a whole-souled sympathy.

"M'Adam," he said, in the short, cold manner that served to cloak a warm heart, "I'm grieved for thee."

The little man turned as though to rend him.

"Why lee, James Moore? why lee?" he cried, with

sudden, surprising animosity. "D'ye think I dinna ken that my sorrow is your joy? D'ye think I'd no' ha' bin blithe as a lavrock gin the same had fallen on yon grey devil?" And he was seized with such a sudden, shaking frenzy as his eyes fell on Owd Bob, who stood a little apart, regarding him with soft, womanly compassion, that the Master was amazed.

Another moment, and the little man was outwardly himself again.

"James Moore," he said, with queer flickering smile, "next time that dog comes on ma land, he marches aff agin—a corp."

The Master's eyes steeled; for next to their blood the Moores have always loved their dogs. But he answered nothing, thinking the other's balance overset by his great grief, and withdrew.

Now a shepherd without a dog is like a cart without wheels. The one is to the other indispensable. And so M'Adam set himself, perforce, with aching heart and bitter tongue to repair his doggy widowhood.

In the choosing of his dog, a shepherd must exercise as fully fastidious a care as in the choosing of his wife. For the one may be his better, but the other is his business half. In pair-harness they have to earn their daily bread; share ambitions, perils, sorrows, joys, sun, and snow; and in the end they grow to be rather one divided than two conjoined.

Discretion in the matter is, then, to be applauded. But with M'Adam to see was to reject. He loathed the obligation of his task. He revolted against each new offering partner, as some late widow who, in the night season, compares a new and heart-hated lord with her lion love of old. As he handled each succeeding candidate, a veteran lady, regarding him with clouded reproachful eyes, loomed instant on his view; and forthwith the sneer deepened on his face, his tongue shot its forked sting with hateful zest, and the dim eyes joyed in their all-ill-revealing stare. And at length, little loved as he had been aforetime, he became the target of a single-hearted resentment in the countryside; and Tammas, whose forte lay in alliteration and invective, apostrophised him as "a wenomous one!" and "a wirulent wiper!" to the applause of clanking pewter.

Having rejected every aspirant within his own near neighbourhood, M'Adam on a day crossed the Marches to Grammoch-town to inspect another claimant to the invidious honour.

This proved a hopeful customer: a workman, young, yet not lacking of experience, with brains and character, mirled in colour, and with orthodox wall-eye. For two hours his owner expatiated on his virtues; and for two hours more. And still M'Adam made no sign, seeming for once all acquiescent.

Early in the fifth he turned away.

"Ay, ay, a braw tyke enough; but he's no' for me."

The drover was astounded; wished to be struck dead; blasphemed at large; and finally inquired the cause.

M'Adam prevaricated; lied glibly; and at last out it came: he didna haud wi' grey dogs.

The drover hoped he might die! Why, s'op his Sammy! there was only one good colour, and that mirl-grey; hard, fashionable, workmanlike. There never yet was a wall-eyed mirled 'un but he was a good 'un. Why, bless his blue eyes! weren't the very dogs of Kenmuir grey?"

At that M'Adam turned.

"Ay, ay," he said, "ye're there the noo. Good-day to ye!"

Then at last the drover spoke his whole mind.

M'Adam heard him out, nodding in critical approval at the more purple passages; then he took his turn and withered his luckless adversary with that stream of mordant irony that had made for him an enemy of every man between the Pike and the market-cross; calmly sucking his twig the while, picking his words, revelling on in scathing intellectual debauch till it was time for the police to intervene.

In all he was in a happier frame of mind than ever since the catastrophe, when he turned out of the Dalesman's Daughter on his homeward journey.

That is at any time a heart-dulling tramp: over the Silver Lea, up the never-ending Pass, through the Devil's Bowl, and on to the Marches. To the weary, little man it seemed eternal, as he toiled up the white, strait way wreathed in the windless glare; the gaunt Scaur reaching up from his right hand, the naked void to left, and, above, the molten blue.

As he topped the last pitch and entered the Devil's Bowl, which forms the ante-room to the Marches, he was panting.

There he paused, mopping his brow, and looked around. Before him the hollow swelled out cobra-hooded-wise, darkling still despite the sun-glare. All around low hillocks squat in hag-like circle, and croon the whole day through of murder done. The Lone Tarn lifts a leprous face as one long dead; and the Red Screes sheers up from the water in abrupt, black pinnacle against the sky; while all the year through the ghastly water whines about the shore, seeking absolution for its crimes.

It is a hollow which cries aloud of tragedy. Each lichened boulder tells a bloody tale. The rushes shiver as they listen, and the hags around crouch closer. No smile ever lights its gloom; no laugh of children has it heard; only everlastingly the death-long ripple of the Tarn, and croaking of the ravens of the Reiver's Lowp. Even the unimaginative sheep shun the spot for the taint of blood is in the air; preferring, it seems, the deathlier incline of the Red Screes slanting, though it does, down into those black-glass deeps, and upwards into that sheer curtain of rock they call the Reiver's Lowp.

Across the tragic hollow M'Adam flitted, tightening his heart-strings. For though he was no cur, this Devil's Bowl ever clutched him with the cold fingers of fear; a shadowy harbinger, it sometimes seemed to him, of some dread fate awaiting him there in time to come.

So he fled fastly; now glancing fearfully at the dead Tarn beside him, now at the scarred face of the Screes dotted here and there with smut-faced sheep.

A curlew hailed him; a sheep began its fool ma-a-a-ing; and he thanked them for their company. And then again the eternal silence of the moors.

He seemed alone in a huge oven-like void; around him the skinny hillocks; above, the brazen blue; beside him the blind face of the Tarn; and afar, the long-reaching Marches with here a screen of coppice-wood against the sky and gloomy pine, solitary, sentinel.

As he gripped his sense of loneliness to smother it, over the brim of a hollow on his right there came bowling a wind-battered hat. It trundled towards him with drunken, devious course, lurched hard by him, rolled into the black water and stayed.

M'Adam was half-aghast, so weird, sudden, and unaccountable seemed this strange thing rolling out of nothingness, all unpropelled.

Almost unwillingly he turned, and mounted the ridge to see.

There below him, in a scoop of the ground, crouched a hump-backed boulder in hideous deformity; huge, grey, uncouth, like the back of some stranded Leviathan, flinging a deathly shade far across the green. And as he looked he was aware of a black form fluttering about it; the creak of wings, and muffled grunt and cackle of a raven in excess of agitation.

All around the boulder fluttered the ominous bird, stabbing, darting, retreating, croaking, like a witch flirting. M'Adam could see the shut-shears beak, the little lusty eye, the low head screwing round to gaze at him, and hunching shoulders; and he wondered.

Then something arose, flapped, and fell again. It was the lappet of a man's coat. Staring intently, he now discerned a long, prone, ragged figure beneath the grey-glooming boulder.

Such a resemblance to the dead had the sleeper, that for a moment a sudden dread fell on him. And as the evil bird stooped lower and fluttered furiously, eager to strike and yet afraid, he yelled—

"Houts, awa' wi' ye, blasphemin' corbie!" and advanced to wake the sleeper.

There was no need. The beggar had his guard.

As the bird stooped, a tiny yellow bomb burst from the sleeper's rags, and the bird wheeled away in hideous bustle.

The guardian dragged back to his position with drooping tad-pole head, tongue out, and the heavy legs of puppyhood; and a bloody gash upon his neck revealed that the unequal combat had been long sustained.

The little man advanced with alluring thumb and

finger to coax the puppy to him. But the fire-eyed defender, cornering back among the rags, would have none of him; and, as his antagonist drew nearer, he bared his little teeth, raised his little bristles, and growled a hideous menace—type of brute baby at bay.

Finally, as this fresh assailant still drew on, he dashed out, but fell, pitifully spent; and lay watching, his head along his paws, too weak to move, but resolute while he had life to fulfill his charge.

M'Adam bent and raised him tenderly. The puppy gurgled and slobbered in desperate fury, and then hung limp. A few weeks' baby, yet like his master an outcast, more wolf than dog: large, wicked head, cropped ears, and for tail a yet raw red button — no more; while the stark ribs and jagged spine were wearing through their owner's yellow coat.

"Why, wee one!" cried M'Adam with wrathful pity, "ye're nigh to starvit." And turning on the shred-robed sleeper at his feet—

"Man!" he called angrily, "hoo daur ye starve yer dog? Ha' ye no peety? Wak', man!" and he kicked him in the ribs.

The man's arm fell away and discovered his face. And then M'Adam knew there was no more waking for the gaunt starveling at his feet; knew by the evidence of a nibbled crust that this drawn-faced dead had given his last to the puppy, and died for want of the wherewithal to feed himself.

In the ground beside him was a cleft stick; and in the cleft a paper. On it, in the hand of one whose grim humour forsakes him not in death—

"Beware the dog!"

And that, as any man in the Dale-land could tell you, is the story of the coming of the Tailless Tyke.

CHAPTER V

FIRST BLOOD

"YOU and I, Wullie, you and I. You for me; I for you—it's clear ordered." And so the puppy seemed to think; for he resigned himself forthwith, recognising perhaps his destiny.

Thenceforth Adam M'Adam and his Red Wull grew as it were together. Theirs was the comradeship of a common misanthropy; jaundiced their outlook on the world; genial their mutual surliness.

The two became inseparable; for the wee dog had transferred his fealty utterly whole-hearted, and bristled defiance over his new lord as he had done over the lately dead. Once even in the Sylvester Arms he attacked Long Kirby with a cold-blooded fearless fury that routed his big antagonist and afforded Tammas and his brother topers a side-shaking topic for a week.

Many were the stories David told at Kenmuir of the truculent mite; of his savagery, his devotion to his master, his already deathless hate for him (David). Very soon this mutual antipathy led to the inevitable event. For on a morning the boy woke to find himself pinned murderously by the nose, and a smutty red face scowling into his. He yelled, and freed himself with difficulty. Red Wull, bent on blood, attacked again. A scuffle ensued, and in the middle M'Adam burst in, all disarrayed. Straightway he flew into a frenzy caught up the puppy, clouted David up and down; and finally, as a more effectual penance, imposed perpetual interdict on the lad's visits to Kenmuir.

It was on the day succeeding this affair that James Moore first encountered Red Wull. He was crossing the plank-bridge below the farm, Owd Bob and a pack of sheep before him, when midway between banks the grey dog paused, peered over the side, and stiffened in cold displeasure.

The Master followed suit, and beheld M'Adam lying in the shadow of the bridge, at play with a red puppy.

"What arta' doin' theer, M'Adam?" he asked sharply, resolved that the little man should deviate no inch from the public path which crosses Kenmuir.

M'Adam looked up, benignly smiling.

"Waitin' for the dear lad," he answered.

"I thought ye'd forbad him to come this gate?"

"So I have: flat forbade him. That's why I'm here."

The Master was puzzled; and his face betrayed it.

"It's vera simple," the other continued. "When I wush to tryst wi' Davie, I say, 'Davie, positeevely I forbid ye to be at sic-and-sic a place at sic-and-sic a time.' And then a while afore I go and hide there, and when he comes, I hop oot, a smile on my gab, the lovelight in my een, a stick in my hand, and cry, 'Weel, Davie, and hoo's a' wi' ye the day?' And then whiles I argie wi' him." He smiled tenderly as at some sweet reminiscence, and suppled the ash-plant between his fingers.

James Moore affected not to understand.

"Is yon the dead man's dog?" he asked, nodding at Red Wull, who had climbed to the top of the bank, and now stood scowling at Owd Bob and the flock on the meadowside above.

FIRST BLOOD 47

"Na," the little man replied, sucking his twig.

"Hoo did ye coom by him then?"

"Found him in ma stockin' on ma birthday. A present from ma leetle Davie for his auld dad, I doot."

"Liar agin!" came a shrill voice from up the slope.

M'Adam rose to his feet and looked about; but no one could be seen.

"Thank ye, dear lad, thank ye!" he called kindly. "I'll no' forget ye, niver fear. . . . Ah, James Moore"—turning to the Master—"I'll leave ma mark on ma son if ever dad did."

But James Moore was now far away up the slope, speeding to his subaltern's assistance; for the flock above was in sudden commotion. The sheep clustered in very act to break, in fearful head-proud disorder; while all amongst them scoured a small insidious figure, red-rocket-wise, snapping, snatching, snarling. But for the authority of their grey leader, his quick prescience, his commanding presence, panic must have seized the pack.

"M'Adam!" the Master tossed across his shoulder, "your dog's amang t' sheep."

"Niver fash," the little man replied, sucking his eternal twig, "he'll tak' no hurt."

At the moment, a tup broke away down the hill. Hard behind, the tailless puppy scurried in red wrack. An instant's interval; the Master's voice in sharp command; and a grey figure foamed against the green. In a flash this third of the three had caught the pursuer, shot past him, and was already on the heels of the pursued as he rattled over the plank. Another moment and he had rounded off the fugitive and herded him back to the bridge. But there now a wee red warrior was awaiting, resolute to hold passage against all comers.

M'Adam was chuckling.

"I'll lay the grey dog dinna get him ower in face o' ma wee Wull!" he cried.

"A pity to make ill blood atween 'em, and they neighbours," the Master replied.

"Ah-h! douce man, James Moore."

The sneer stung the other into unwilling acquiescence.

"As ye will. But mark me! a Grey Dog doesna forget."

"And mark me! Red Wull dinna forgie."

"So be it then."

Thus lightly was enterprised that feud which was to endure for years; to break one heart and crack two others; thus was begun that long vendetta whose bloody trail may yet be traced in the bleak moorland.

Tammas and Sam'l had now joined the other pair; along the wall above was a row of heads—David, Maggie, and others: all silent, intent on the contest in the green arena beneath.

The challenge accepted, the duel began.

At the bridge-head the tup paused and looked away. Red Wull snarled defiance and made as though to attack. The tup essayed retreat. In vain: the grey dog held him forward, gentle, implacable withal as smothering snow.

At length the compulsion from behind grew irresistible. With myriad misgivings the tup made his attempt; was attacked forthwith by the bomb in yellow; and turned, whimpering dismay.

M'Adam was in ecstasy.

"I tell't ye! I tell't ye! Good for you, Wullie! Keep him aff, lad! 'Come on!' says he. 'All o' ye, ony o' ye, Englishmen a', come on!' .. Weel done Wullie—he! he!"

FIRST BLOOD

Thrice the grey dog drove his charge at the obstacle; [t]ice the woolly cur refused. At the third failure Owd [Bo]b abandoned his tactics, and took the bridge in [per]son.

M'Adam's ecstasy found pause.

'He'll no' hurt ma wee Wull; he daurna!" he [u]ttered, on tip-toe of apprehension.

' He's far ower kind," said the Master.

' He's far ower coward," snapped the other.

The grey dog swirled across the bridge, swept up the [ti]ny obstacle as a yacht-prow lifts the opposing sea, [an]d cantered up the slope; patient, tender, magnani[mo]us as a great-souled woman, while Red Wull, in [ar]dent ignominy, cursed like a vixen baby in its [mo]ther's arms.

Tammas was convulsed; the Master grimly amused; [wh]ile on M'Adam's face sat a dangerous calm.

The grey dog cantered up and laid his burden at the [litt]le man's feet. For all answer M'Adam struck at [hi]m viciously; but the Master, ever-alert, frustrated [the] intent.

"It's yer own doin', M'Adam," he reminded him. ['F]air's fair a' the world thro'." And the little man [stee]lered himself with difficulty.

The grey dog now set himself afresh to the business [in] hand. Rounding up the tup, he took him hot-foot at [the] Rubicon. But there again, right in the way, stood [the] warrior of the bridge petrified now in fell frenzy of [pa]ssion.

"Ye'll beat him yet, Wullie! He's fear't o' ye! Keep [o]n aff, lad! Death or victorie!" came the burning [vo]ice from the hillside, heating him on to huge [teme]nerity.

Again the grey dog trotted on to the plank.

James Moore was grimly silent, Tammas winking to himself, Sam'l groaning; while M'Adam was shivering on a tempest's abrupt brink.

"Hands aff, ye devil!" he muttered, his fingers working. "Wad ye daur touch ma Wullie? Na, na; ye haena the spunk, tho' he is no bigger nor yer ain pat."

His face was blazing; his emotions scarcely bridled.

"Mind, M'Adam, it's yer own doin'!" came the Master's hard voice at his elbow.

Red Wull was now backing up the hill, teeth to the foe. As well Achilles might defy the lightning. The grey dog swooped, parried a thrust, overset his enemy, gathered him, motherly, and turned, captive in mouth, for the stream.

For a moment M'Adam looked; then loosed himself.

"Devil!" he yelled, hurling down the hill in hot pursuit. "Ye black-hearted murderer, drap him! James Moore!" he flung the words over his flying shoulder—"Call him aff, man! Call him aff, curse ye!"

The grey dog galloped on to the plank-bridge, halted in the middle, leant over, and dropped his burden.

The far-thrown protest of the stream was drowned in a roar of derisive applause from the on-lookers above; and that again was lost in a hollow resounding souse as M'Adam in a whirlwind of spray and oaths leaped out into the stream.

A moment, and he had rescued the puppy and was wading back, the waters surging about his waist, Red Wull limp as a wet rag in his hand. His bonnet was gone; his face ran; his clothes betrayed the meanness of his manhood; and his eyes were as red-hot embers.

He sprang on to the bank, and in cyclone fury stormed down on the grey dog.

"Stan' back, or ye'll have him at yer throat!" shouted [th]e Master, thundering up. "Stan' back, I say, tha fule!" [a]nd as the other still came madly on, he reached forth [a] lean brown hand and hurled him backward; and [si]multaneously buried the other hand down in the sea-[de]ep depths of Owd Bob's neck. And well he did; for [if] ever the flame of battle flared in grey eyes, 'twas in [th]e grey dog's then.

The little man tottered, toppled, and crashed down. At the shock, the blood spouted from his nostrils, and [r]ound his chin about with vague, red, dripping streamers; [wh]ile Red Wull, jerked afar, lay still.

For a second he sat erect, leaning on his arms; then [he] leaped to his feet, his face motleyed grey and ghastly, [th]e running red about his jaw.

"Curse ye!" he howled, and flung at the Master. "Curse ye, for a cowardly Englishman!"

But Sam'l interposed.

"Easy, lil man!" he said, holding him off with large [re]nding hand. "Eh, but art' a tearin' spit-cat, surely!"

James Moore stood breathing deep, his hand still lost [in] the grey dog's depths.

"If thoo'd touched him," he panted, "he'd ha' mauled [th]ee afoor iver I could ha' had him off. It's bad for any [m]an but a Moore to handle a Grey Dog to his hurt."

"Ma wud! that it be!" corroborated Tammas, speak[in]g from the experience of sixty years. And, indeed, it [is] notorious that a Moore may flay a Grey Dog alive [w]hile another may not so much as flout him.

The little man turned away.

"Ye're all agin me!" he said in small, quaking voice [an]d bent over Red Wull, who lay at his feet like a dead [th]ing.

At the touch of his master's hands, the puppy opened

his eyes, and glared with devilish hate at the grey dog and group with him.

The little man lifted him tenderly and turned on to the bridge. Half-way across he stopped. The plank shivered feverishly beneath him, for he still trembled like one palsied.

"Man, Moore!" he called, striving to quell the agitation in his voice, "I wad shoot yon dog."

Across the bridge he turned again; his face grey, dead lights smouldering; the blood about his jaw; and the dank red devil cub nursed in his arms.

"Man, Moore!" he called and paused. . . . "Ye'll no' forget this day!"

Part II

The Little Man

Chapter VI

A MAN'S SON

THE storm having burst, M'Adam allowed loose rein to his implacable hostility for James [M]ore.

[T]he two often encountered. For the little man was [wo]nt to return home by the footpath across Kenmuir. [It] took him out of his course, indeed; but he preferred [it] for the opportunities it offered of harrying his enemy. [N]ow he haunted Kenmuir like some evil familiar. [Wh]en clumsy Sam'l slashed a valuable ewe in the [she]aring and was repairing the damage with tow and [tar], a yellow mask, wreathed into the semblance of [sy]mpathy, crowned the farm wall.

"Oh dear! Oh dear!" came a mocking voice, all [sol]icitous. "Send for oor Bob! Fetch auld Bobbums. [He]'ll kiss it and mak' it"— A flash; a crash; a grey [fig]ure skimming the wall; and the little man was fleeing [down] the public path and his life, amidst a tempest of [cu]rs. And that was the not infrequent climax of his [jee]rings.

There were two attempts to patch up the feud. Jim Mason, who went about the world seeking to do good, tried in his shy way to mend matters. But M'Adam and his Red Wull soon put him and Betsy to rout.

"You mind yer letters and yer wires, Mr. Poacher—postman. Ay, I saw 'em baith: th'ane doon by the Haughs, t'ither in the Bottom. . . .'And "—a tender smile breaking over his face—"there's Wullie, the humoursome chiel, takin' a feel at Betsy's throat." There, indeed, lay the faithful Betsy, suppliant on her back; while Red Wull, now a great-grown puppy, stood athwart her with wrinkled muzzle and savage wheeze, awaiting a movement as pretext to pin. "Wullie, let the leddy be. Ye've had yer dinner."

Parson Leggy, by right of his office, was the other would-be mediator. First he tackled James Moore on the subject; but that laconic person cut him short with, "I've nowt agin t' little man," and would say no more. And in truth the quarrel was none of his making.

When the Parson approached M'Adam on the matter, the little man stood sucking his eternal twig and listening with an ominous calm upon his face.

"There's no ca' for the interference o' the Church in this business, and thank ye, Mr. Hornbut," he said at length sourly. Whereat the Parson, had he been wise as well meaning, would have desisted; but did not.

Of the wrangle that ensued; the heat of the one; the cynical indifference of the other, changing as it did to sudden, impassioned earnestness; of the calm succeeding; of the intervention of Cyril Gilbraith to hinder the angry old minister from assaulting his adversary; of the little man's parting shot—"Wullie, let the gentleman's legs their lane, and come ben. Corbies and clergy are but shot right kittle!" there is no need to tell. But thereafter the vendetta must pursue its own sinister course.

David was now the only link between the two farms.
the flagrant face of his father's interdict the boy
ing to his intimacy with the Moores with a doggedness
at no thrashing could overcome. Not a minute of
e day when out of school, holidays and Sundays
cluded, but was passed at Kenmuir. It was not till
te at night that he would sneak back to the Grange,
id creep up to his tiny, bare room in the roof—not
pperless, indeed; motherly Mrs. Moore had seen to
at. And there he would lie awake and listen with a
rce contempt as his father, hours later, lurched into
e kitchen below, lilting liquorishly—

> " 'We are na fou, we're nae that fou,
> But just a drappie in our e'e;
> The cock may craw, the day may daw',
> And aye we'll taste the barley bree!' "

nd in the morning the boy would slip quietly out of
e house while his father still slept; only Red Wull
ould thrust out his savage head as the lad passed and
arl hungrily.

Sometimes weeks would pass thus and no word
)oken between father and son, no glance passed. And
at was David's aim—to obliterate himself. It was his
inning at this game of evasion that saved him many a
rashing; though still during his father's relapses into
)berness a reign of terror was wont to intervene.

The little man seemed devoid of all natural affection
r his son. He lavished the whole fondness of which
is small nature appeared capable on the Tailless Tyke:
r so the Dalesmen called Red Wull. And the dog
e treated with a careful tenderness that made David
nile, the Parson fume, the villagers sarcastic, and their
ives indignant.

The little man and his dog were as alike in moral
ttributes as they were contrasted physically. Each

owed a grudge against the world, and was determined to pay it. Each was an Ishmael amongst his kind. Each was alone save for the other; and their desolateness wrapped them the closer. The ill-humour of the one found expression in his tongue, of the other in his teeth. The dog was the incarnation of brute strength, the man of human weakness.

Soon the two earned an evil notoriety in the countryside. For they shoved through the world together with sour looks and surly actions, utterly regardless of any save the other. You saw them thus, or standing apart, leper-like, in the turmoil of life, and it came as a revelation to happen upon them on the hill below the house of sober summer evenings, playing together, each wrapped in the game, innocent, tender, forgetful of the hostile world.

The two were never apart except only when M'Adam came home across Kenmuir. After that first misadventure he never allowed his twin-soul to accompany him on the journey through the enemy's country: for well he knew that sheep-dogs have long memories.

To the stile on the lane Red Wull would escort his master. There he would halt and stand, his villain mask grinning through the gate, and watch his master out of sight; then he would turn and trot, self-reliant and defiant, sturdy and surly, down the very centre of the road through the village—no playing, no enticing away, and woe to that man or dog who tried to stay him in his course! past Mother Ross's shop, past the Sylvester Arms, to the right by Kirby's smithy, over the Wastrel by the Haughs, to await his master at the brink of the Stony Bottom.

The little man, when thus crossing Kenmuir, often encountered Owd Bob. But on these occasions he passed discreetly by; for though he was no coward, yet it is bad, single-handed, to tackle a Grey Dog of Kenmuir. While the dog trotted soberly on his way, only a steely glint in the snowcloud eyes betraying his knowledge of a foe. As surely, however, as the little man in his desire to spy out the nakedness of the land strayed off the public path, so surely a grey figure, seeming to spring from out the blue, would come fiercely, silently, hurling down on him; and he would turn and run for his life, amidst the loud-voiced contumely of any who were witness to the meeting.

On these occasions David vied with Tammas in facetiousness at his father's expense.

"Wheer away, little 'un!" he roared from behind a wall, after one such incident.

"Ma sarty, but he can scut and run!" yelled Tammas, not to be outdone. "Hoo fends-ta', M'Adam? —gaily, eh?"

"Look to his knees a-wamblin'!" from the undutiful son in ecstasy. "If I'd knees the marrer o' them, I'd wear petticoats."

As he spoke, a swinging box on the ear brought the young reprobate to his knees. Turning, he found James Moore behind him, his heavy eyebrows lowering over his eyes.

"Tak' shame to thysel', David M'Adam. Does ta think God gave thee a dad for thee to fleer at? Ye should be 'shamed. Serve thee reet if he does thrash thee when ye get home."

Luckily M'Adam had not distinguished his son's voice. But the little man had an unwitting revenge; for on the following morning he said to his son—

"David, ye'll come hame after school to-day."

"Will I?" said David pertly.

"Ye will."

"What for?"

"Because I tell ye to, ma lad." And that was all the reason he would assign. Had he told the simple fact: that he needed help to drench a "husking" ewe, things might have gone differently. As it was, David, stung into defiance, turned down the hill.

The afternoon wore on; schooltime was long over; and still there was no David.

The little man waited at the door of the Grange, fuming, hopping from one leg to the other, talking to Red Wull, who lay at his feet, his head on his paws, like a tiger waiting for his prey.

At length the little man could hold himself no longer. He started running down the hill, his heart red-hot with indignation.

"Wait till we lay hands on ye, ma lad," he muttered "We'll warm ye, we'll teach ye."

At the edge of the Stony Bottom he left Red Wull. Crossing it himself, and rounding Langholm How, he soon espied James Moore, David, and Owd Bob walking away from him in the direction of Kenmuir. The grey dog and David were playing together, wrestling, racing, and rolling. The boy had never a thought for his father.

The little man ran up behind, unseen and unheard, his feet softly pattering on the grass. His hand had fallen on David's shoulder before the boy had guessed his approach.

"Did I bid ye come hame after school, David?" he asked, concealing his heat beneath a suspicious suavity.

"Mebbe. Did I say I wud come?"

The pertness of tone and words alike fanned the little man's resentment into a blaze. In a burst of passion he lunged at the boy with his stout ash-plant. But as he smote, a grey whirlwind struck him fair on the chest, and he fell like a snapped stake, and lay half-stunned, with a dark muzzle hovering at his throat

"Hod back, Bob!" shouted James Moore, running up. "Hod away, I tell thee!" He bent over the prostrate figure, propping it up anxiously. "Art' hurt, M'Adam? Eh, but I am vexed. He thowt ye were for strikin' t' lad."

David had now run up, and he, too, bent over his father with a very scared face.

"Art' hurt, dad?" he asked, his voice trembling.

The little man rose unsteadily to his feet and shook off his supporters. His face was twitching, and he stood all dust-begrimed looking at his son.

"Ye're content, aiblins, noo ye've seen yer father's grey head bowed in the dust," he said.

"'Twas a mishap," pleaded James Moore; "but I *am* sorry. He thowt ye were goin' for to bang the lad."

"So I was; so I will."

"If ony's beat it should be ma Bob here, though he bobbut thought he was actin' reet.... An' ye were aff path."

The little man regarded his enemy, a sneer mantling his lips.

"Ye canna thrash him for doin' what ye bid him, James Moore. Set yer dog on me if ye will, but dinna beat him when he does yer biddin'!"

"I didna set him on thee, and well thoo kens it!" the Master replied warmly.

M'Adam shrugged his shoulders.

"I'll no' argie wi' ye, James Moore," he replied. "I'll leave you and what ye call yer conscience to settle that. My business is not wi' you.... David!" turning to his son.

A stranger might well have been lost to distinguish of these two men the boy's father. For the lad stood now holding the Master's hand; while a few paces above them was M'Adam, pale but resolute, his expression betraying his consciousness of the irony of the situation.

"Will ye come hame wi' me and have it noo, or stop wi' him and wait till ye get it?" he asked his son.

"M'Adam, I'd like thee to"—

"None o' that, James Moore. David, what d'ye say?"

David looked up into his protector's face.

"Gang wi' thy father, lad," said the Master at last thickly. The boy hesitated and clung tighter to the shielding arm; then he walked slowly over to his father.

A bitter smile spread over the little man's face, as he marked this new test of his son's obedience to the other.

"To obey his frien' he foregoes the pleasure o' disobeyin' his father," he muttered.

Then he turned homewards and the boy followed.

James Moore and the grey dog stood looking after them.

"I know ye willna pay aff yer spite agin me on t' lad's head, M'Adam!" the Master called, almost appealingly.

"I'll do ma duty, niver fear, James Moore, wi'oot respect o' persons," the little man cried back, never turning.

So father and son walked away, one behind the other like a man and his dog, and there was no word said between them. Across the Stony Bottom, Red Wull, scowling with bared teeth at David, joined them. Together the three went up the hill to the Grange.

In the kitchen M'Adam turned.

"Noo, I'm gaein' to gie ye the gran'est thrashin' ye iver dreamed of. Tak' aff yer coat."

The boy obeyed and stood up in his thin shirt, his face white and set as a statue's. Red Wull seated himself hard by on his haunches, ears pricked, licking his lips, all attention.

The little man suppled the ash-plant in his hands

nd raised it. The expression on the boy's face
rrested his arm.

"Say ye're sorry and I'll let ye aff easy."

"I'll not."

"One mair chance—yer last! Say ye're 'shamed o' ersel'."

"I'm not."

The little man brandished his cruel weapon, and Red Bull shifted to obtain a better view.

"Git on wi' it!" ordered David angrily.

The little man raised his stick again and—threw it into the farthest corner of the room. It fell with a rattle on the floor, and M'Adam turned away.

"Ye're the pitifullest son iver a man had!" he cried brokenly. "And gin a man's son dinna haud to him, wha can he expect to?—no one. . . . Ye're ondootiful, ye're disrespectfu', ye're maist ilka thing ye shouldna be; there's but ae thing I thocht ye werena—a coward. And as to that, ye've no' the pluck to say ye're sorry when God kens ye might be. . . . I canna thrash ye the day. But ye shall gang nae mair to school! I send ye there to learn. Ye'll no' learn—ye've learnt naethin' except disobedience to me—ye shall stop at hame and work."

His father's rare emotion, his broken voice and working face, moved the boy as all the stripes and jeers failed to do. His conscience smote him. It dimly dawned on him that maybe his father, too, had some ground for complaint; that perhaps he was not a faultless son.

He half turned.

"Father"—

"Git oot o' ma sight!" M'Adam cried.

The boy turned and went; and another swelled the huge sad host of Lost Opportunities.

CHAPTER VII

A LAD'S FATHER

THENCEFORWARD David buckled to work at home. And in one point only father and son resembled—industry. A drunkard M'Adam was, but a drone, no.

The boy worked at the Grange with tireless, indomitable energy; yet he could never satisfy his father. The little man would stand, a sneer on his face, his thin lips contemptuously curled, and flout the lad's brave labours.

"Is he no' a gran' worker, Wullie? 'Tis a pleasure to watch him, his hands in his pockets, his eyes turned heavenwards!" as the boy snatched a hard-earned moment's rest. "You and I, Wullie, we'll brak' oorsel's slavin' for him while he looks on and laffs."

And so on, the whole day through, week in, week out; till the lad sickened with weariness of it all.

In his darkest hours David thought sometimes to run away. He was miserably alone on the cold bosom of the world. The very fact that he was the son of his father isolated him in the Dale-land. Naturally of a reserved disposition, he had no single friend outside Kenmuir. And it was only the thought of his friends there that withheld him. He could not bring himself to part from them; they were all he had in the world, and he cherished them accordingly.

A LAD'S FATHER 63

So he worked on at the Grange, miserably, doggedly, [tak]ing blows and abuse alike in burning silence. But [eve]ry evening, his work over, he stepped off to his [oth]er home beyond the Stony Bottom. And on [Sun]days and holidays — for of these latter he took, [a]sking, what he knew to be his due — all day long, [fro]m cock-crowing to the going down of the sun, he [wou]ld pass at Kenmuir. In this one matter the boy [was] invincibly stubborn. Words or blows, tongue or [whi]p, alike proved impotent to wean him from this [end.] He endured it all with white-lipped silent forti[tud]e, and held on his course.

Once past the Stony Bottom he threw his troubles [beh]ind him with a courage that honoured him. Too [pro]ud to voice his woes, of all the people at Kenmuir [Bob] only ever dreamed the whole depth of his unhappi[nes]s. James Moore suspected something of it all; for [he] knew more of M'Adam than did the rest. While [Ol]d Bob knew it all as did no other. He could tell [f]rom the touch of the boy's hand on his head; for [the] story was writ bold in each caress for a dog to [rea]d. And he would follow the lad about, compassion [in] his sad grey eyes; giving him all of that most [ten]der comfort—a dog's dumb sympathy.

David might well compare his grey friend at Ken[mu]ir with that other at the Grange.

The Tailless Tyke had now grown into a huge [Cer]berus. Deep-chested as a barrel; legs like Gothic [arc]hes; great bull-head; lower jaw reaching per[pet]ually forward as if for prey; eyes scowling always [ask]ance; cropped ears perking mouse-like on a round [har]d skull; a coat like coir; and back running up [fro]m shoulder to loins, abruptly terminated by the [kn]ob-like tail; and when he regarded you his eyes rolled round and his head moved not at all. In all, he looked like the Satan of a dog's Hell.

And he looked only less wicked than he was. He feared neither man nor dog nor devil. He never attacked unprovoked; but a challenge was never ignored, and he loved insults and sought for them. Already he had nigh killed Rob Saunderson's Shep; Long Kirby glanced round uneasily at the muffled slop-slop of his coming; ay, he had even fought a round with that redoubtable trio, the Wexer, Wenus, and Wan Tromp; and not been worsted.

More than once he and Owd Bob had essayed to wipe out mutual memories, Red Wull in this case always the aggressor. As yet, however, while they fenced for that deathly throat-grip, the value of which each knew so well, James Moore had always intervened.

"That's right; hide him ahint yer petticoats," sneered M'Adam, on one such occasion.

"Hide? 'Twillna be him I'll hide, I's uphod thee, M'Adam!" the Master answered grimly, as he twirled his good oak-staff between the would-be duellists. Whereat was a derisive laugh at the little man's expense.

It seemed there were to be other points of enmity between the two than memories. For in the matter of his business—the marshalling of sheep—Red Wull bid fair to be second only throughout the Dale-land to the Grey Dog of Kenmuir. Their styles, indeed, were all antithesis: the one quiet, persuasive, a woman in tact, a Solomon in wisdom, a very Bayard in action; the other terrific in his truculence, strong as Samson, violent as Saul.

And M'Adam was patient and painstaking in the

aining of his Wullie in a manner to astonish David.
would have been touching, had it not been so un-
tural in view of his treatment of his own blood, to
atch the fond discretion with which the little man
oulded the dog beneath his hands.

After a promising display he would stand, twig in
outh, hands clasped, dreaming of the rosy future
near content as man may be.

"Weel done, Wullie!" he would murmur. "Bide a
hile, and we'll show 'em a thing or two, you and I,
'ullie.

'The warld's wrack we share o't,
The warstle and the care o't.'"

And the dog would lift himself, place his fore-paws
the other's shoulders, and stand thus, ears back,
ull round against the sky, grinning love into his
aster's face.

From the first David and Red Wull had been open
emies. Under the circumstances, indeed, there could
no alternative. The two were never at peace.
ometimes the great dog would slink at the lad's
els with surly, greedy eyes, never quitting him from
nrise to sundown, till David could hardly hold his
nd.

So matters continued for a never-ending year. Then
e inevitable climax came.

On a day throughout which Red Wull had dogged
m thus hungrily, David, his work over, went to pick
his coat, preparatory to wending Kenmuirwards.
ying upon it he found Red Wull.

"Git off ma coat!" the boy ordered angrily.

The great dog made no move. The curtain of his
p hovered and disclosed a wall of woman-white; that
uel under-jaw reached for its prey; and he sunk low

and lower in the ground, his head on his paws, his eyes burning beneath his brows.

Now, what between master and dog, David had endured to his utmost that day.

"What! ye willna, girt brute!" he shouted, snatched a corner of the coat, and attempted to jerk it away.

At that, Red Wull rose, shivering, and with a gurgle sprang at the boy.

David, quick as a flash, dodged; bent; and picked up an ugly stake lying at his feet. Swinging round all in a crack, he dealt his antagonist a mighty buffet on the head.

Dazed with the blow, the great dog fell; then recovering, with a terrible deep roar he came again. Then it must have gone hard with the boy, fine-grown young Titan though he was: for Red Wull was now in the first bloom of that great strength which earned him afterwards an undying notoriety in the land.

As it chanced, however, M'Adam had watched the scene from the kitchen. And now out he plunged headlong, shrieking commands and curses at the combatants. As Red Wull sprang, he interposed between the two, head back, eyes flashing. His small person received the full shock of the charge. He staggered but recovered, and in an imperative voice ordered the log to heel.

Then he turned on David, seized the stake from his hand, and began furiously to belabour the boy.

"I'll—teach—ye—to—strike—a puir—dumb—harmless—creetur, ye—cruel—cruel—lad!" he cried. "Hoo daur ye strike—ma—Wull? yer—father's—Wull? Adam—M'Adam's—Red—Wull?" He was panting from his exertions, and his eyes blazing. "I pit up as best I can wi' all manner o' disrespect to masel', but when it comes to 'tackin' ma puir Wullie, I canna thole

t. . . . Ha' ye no heart?" he asked, unconscious of the
rony of the question.

"As mickle as some, I reck'n," David growled, his
ace white.

" Eh, what's that? what d'ye say?"

" Ye thrash me till ye're blind, and it's nobbut yer duty,
)ut if ony dares so mickle as to look at yer Wullie, ye're
nad," the boy answered bitterly. And with that he
urned away defiantly and openly in the direction of
Kenmuir.

M'Adam made a step forward; then stopped.

"I'll see ye again, ma lad, this evenin'," he cried, with
:ruel significance.

" I doot ye'll be far ower fou to see owt—except,
lappen, your bottle," the boy shouted back, and
waggered down the hill.

At Kenmuir that night the marked and particular
:indness of Elizabeth Moore filled to overflowing the
)oy's cup. Overwhelmed by the contrast of her sweet
notherliness, he burst into a rare storm of invective
gainst his father, his home, his life, the universe.

" Dunnot, Davie; dunnot, dearie!" cried Mrs. Moore,
nuch distressed. "Dunnot take on that gate. He'll
nend, I warrant he will." And taking him to her, she
oothed the great, sobbing boy as though he were a child.

At length he lifted his face and looked up; and
eeing the white wan countenance of his dear comforter,
vas stricken with fond remorse that he had given way
nd pained her whom he knew so frail herself.

Mastering himself with an effort, for the rest of the
:vening he was his usual cheery self. He teased Maggie,
haffed stolid little Andrew, and bantered Sam'l Todd
intil that generally impassive man threatened to bash
iis snout for him.

Yet it was with a great swallowing at the throat that later he turned down the slope for home.

James Moore and Parson Leggy accompanied him to the bridge, and stood a while looking after him as he disappeared into the summer night.

"Yon's a good lad," said the Master, half to himself.

"Yes," the Parson replied, "I'm sure of it. Look at the affection between him and Owd Bob; and I'd take a wise dog's estimate of anyone before many a man's. Certainly there's none of the old Adam about the boy. . . . Ah, I wish his father 'd give the lad a chance. As it is, he's paving the way for a nasty business at the Grange in the future."

"If it com' to murder one o' these days," answered the Master quietly, "I'd hardly blame t' lad."

David slipped up into his room and into bed, unseen. Alone with the darkness, he allowed himself the rare relief of tears. And soon pitiful sleep folded him in her arms.

He woke to find his father at his bedside. The little man held a dip-candle in his hand, which limned his sallow face in crude black and yellow. In the doorway, dimly outlined, was the great figure of Red Wull.

"Where ha' ye been the day?" the little man asked; then looking down on the stained face beneath him, added quickly, "If ye like to lee, I'll believe ye."

David was out of bed and standing up in his night-shirt. He looked at his father contemptuously.

"I's bin at Kenmuir. I'll not lee for you or your likes."

The little man shrugged his shoulders.

"'Tell a lee and stick to it,' is my rule, and a good one, too, in honest England. I for one 'll no' think ony the woise o' ye should yer memory play yer false."

A LAD'S FATHER

"Doesta' think I care a kick what you think o' me?" the boy asked brutally. "Nay; there's 'nough leears in this fam'ly wi'oot me."

The candle trembled and was still again.

"A lickin' or a lee: tak' yer choice!"

The boy looked scornfully down on his father. Standing on his naked feet, he already towered half a head above the other and was twice the man.

"Doesta' reck'n I'm fear'd o' a thrashin' fra' thee? Lord o' me!" he sneered, "why I'd as lief let a wench lick me for all I care."

A reference to his physical insufficiencies fired the little man as surely as a lighted match powder.

"Ye maun be cauld, standin' there so. Rin ye doon and fetch oor little frien'. I'll see if I can warm ye."

David turned and stumbled down the unlit, narrow stairs. The stone-cold boards struck like death against his naked feet; while at his heels followed Red Wull, his hot breath fanning the boy's legs.

So into the kitchen and back up the stairs, and Red Wull always following.

"I'll no' despair yet o' teachin' ye—tho' I kill masel' in doin' it—to honour yer father!" cried the little man, and seized the strap from the boy's numb grasp.

When it was over, M'Adam turned away breathless. At the threshold of the room he paused and looked round: a little, dim-lit, devilish figure framed in the door; while from the blackness behind Red Wull's eyes gleamed molten.

Glancing back, the little man caught such an expression on his son's face, that for once he was fairly afraid. Banging the door, he hobbled actively down the stairs.

CHAPTER VIII

THE WHITE WINTER

M'ADAM, in his sober moments, at least, never touched David again. Instead, he applied himself to the more congenial exercise of the whip-lash of his tongue. And he was wise; for David could, if he would, have taken his father in the hollow of his hand and crumpled him. Moreover with the subtler weapon the little man could always wring a wince. And so the war was carried on none the less vindictively

Meanwhile another summer was passing. It proved a brazen, merciless season; the whole land from Thames to Tweed was brown with thirst, its lips cracked and crying out in pain; and Sexton Ross so bitterly bemoaned the hardness of his labour that Sam'l turned on him one night in the Arms and offered to relieve him of his job for good and all. Whereafter the old Sexton never missed an opportunity of laying a gnarled hand on the big man's knee and remarking—

"A do reck'n as A've twenty year o' hole-hoickin afoor me yet, Sam'l."

To which the other as invariably replied—

"Niver no tellin', Mr. Ross. Thoo's niver bin the same man to ma thinkin' since thoo'd that there noo-moanin' in yer innards two winters gone."

That year Roderick Dhu, splendid Highland gentleman, carried away the Shepherds' Trophy into

THE WHITE WINTER

the far North. James Moore still refused to run the grey dog, and that though Owd Bob o' Kenmuir was now amongst the faculty a name to conjure with. Parson, Squire, and even Lady Eleanour essayed to shake the Master's decision; but he proved quite immutable. He had failed so often, he said, that he wished to make sure of victory; and to his mind, waiting was winning; for, as he explained, no sheep-dog is at his best till his brain is at its best; and the brain, as in the human, is a long while maturing.

Of all the dwellers in the Dale-land the Master's determination gratified only one — Adam M'Adam. And at the news that little man winked and rubbed and chuckled, "Next year, Wullie—he! he! We twa, lad, we twa."

. . . .

Meanwhile the summer ended abruptly. Hard on the heels of a sweltering autumn the winter came down. In that year the Dale-land assumed very early its white cloak. The Silver Mere was soon ice-veiled; the Wastrel rolled sullenly down below Kenmuir, its creeks and quiet places tented with jagged sheets of ice; while the Scaur and Muir Pike raised hoary heads against the blue.

It was the season still remembered in the North as the White Winter; the worst, they say, since the famous 1808.

For days together Jim Mason was stuck with his bags in the Dalesman's Daughter; and there was no communication between the two Dales. The lean hill-foxes assumed an almost wolfish ferocity, hunting in packs, pulling down great-grown sheep at the very gates of the folds On the moors the only break in the eternal white would be a carrion crow flapping along, coal-black against the snow; a grouse, sentinel at a burrow's mouth· and the dark screens of night-capped wood,

On the Mere Marches the snow massed deep and impassable in thick, billowy drifts. In the Devil's Bowl men said it lay piled some score feet deep. And sheep, seeking shelter in the ghylls and protected spots, were buried and lost in their hundreds.

That is the time to test the hearts of shepherds and sheep-dogs, when the wind runs ice-cold across the waste of white, and the low woods on the upland walks shiver black through a veil of snow, and sheep must be found and folded or lost: a trial of head as well as heart, of resource as well as resolution.

In that winter more than one man and many a dog lost his life in the quiet performance of his duty, gliding to death over the slippery snowshelves, or overwhelmed beneath an avalanche of the warm suffocating white: "smoored," as they call it. Many a deed was done, many a death died, recorded only in that Book which holds the names of those—men or animals, souls or no souls—who Tried.

They found old Wrottesley, the Squire's head-shepherd, lying one morning at Gill's Foot like a statue in its white bed, the snow gently blowing about the venerable face, calm and beautiful in death. And stretched upon his bosom, her master's hands, blue and stiff, still clasped about her neck, his old dog, Jess. She had huddled there as a last hope to keep the dear, dead master warm, her great heart riven, hoping where there was no hope. That night she followed him to herd sheep in a better land. Death from exposure, Dingley, the vet., gave it; but as little M'Adam, his eyes dimmer than their wont, declared huskily, "We ken better, Wullie."

Cyril Gilbraith, a young man not overburdened with emotions, told with a sob in his voice how, at the terrible Rowan Crags, Jim Mason had stood, impotent, dumb, big-eyed, watching Betsy—Betsy, the friend and partner

THE WHITE WINTER

of the last ten years—slipping over the ice-cold surface, silently appealing to the hand that had never failed her before—sliding to Eternity.

In the Dale-land that winter the endurance of many a shepherd and his dog was strained past breaking-point. From the frozen Black Water to the white-peaked Grammoch Pike two men only, each always with his shaggy adjutant, never owned defeat, never turned back, never failed in a thing attempted.

In the following spring Mr. Tinkerton, the Squire's agent, declared that James Moore and Adam M'Adam —Owd Bob, rather, and Red Wull—had lost between them fewer sheep than any single farmer on the whole March Mere estate—a proud record.

Of the two many a tale was told that winter at wayside inn and lonely cottage. They were invincible, incomparable: worthy antagonists.

It was Owd Bob who, when he could not *drive* the band of Black-faces over the narrow Razor-back which led to safety, induced them to *follow* him across that ten-inch death-track, one by one, like children behind their mistress. It was Red Wull who was seen coming down the precipitous Saddler's How shouldering up that grand old gentleman, King o' the Dale, whose leg was broken.

The grey dog it was who found Cyril Gilbraith by the White Stones with a cigarette and sprained ankle, on the night the whole village was out with lanterns searching for that well-loved young scapegrace. It was the Tailless Tyke and his master who one bitter evening came upon Mrs. Burton lying in a huddle beneath the lea of the fast-whitening Druid's Pillar with her latest baby on her breast. It was little M'Adam who took off his coat and wrapped the child in it; little M'Adam who unwound his plaid, threw it like a breast-band across the dog's mighty chest, and tied the ends round the clemm'd woman's waist. Red Wull it was who dragged her back to the Sylvester Arms and life, straining like a giant through the snow; while his master staggered behind with the babe in his arms. When they reached the inn it was M'Adam who, with a smile on his face, twig in his mouth, told the landlord with wry dry stinging bonhomie what he thought of him for sending his wife across the Marches on such a day and on *his* errand. To which—"I'd a cauld," pleaded honest Jem.

For days together David could not cross the Stony Bottom to Kenmuir. His enforced confinement to the Grange led, however, to no more frequent collisions than usual with his father. For M'Adam and Red Wull were out at all hours in all weathers, night and day, toiling at their work of salvation.

At last, one afternoon, the boy managed to cross the Bottom at a point where a fallen thorn-tree gave him a bridge over the soft snow. He stayed but little while at Kenmuir, yet when he started for home it was snowing again.

By the time he had crossed the ice-draped bridge over the Wastrel, a blizzard was raging. The wind roared past him, smiting him so that he could barely stand. The snow leaped and whirled and flashed and blinded him. But he held on doggedly, slipping, sliding, tripping, down and up again, with one arm shielding his face; on, on, into the white darkness, blindly on, sobbing, stumbling, dazed.

At length, nigh dead, he reached the brink of the Stony Bottom. He looked up and he looked down, but nowhere in the suffocating mist could he see the fallen thorn-tree. He took a step forward into the white morass, and sank up to his thigh. He struggled

THE WHITE WINTER

feebly to free himself, and sank deeper. The snow wreathed twisting round him like a white flame, and he collapsed, softly crying, on that soft bed.

"I canna, I canna," he moaned.

Mrs. Moore, her face whiter and frailer than ever, stood at the window looking out into the storm.

"I canna rest for thinkin' o' t' lad," she said; then turning, saw her husband, his fur cap down over his ears, buttoning his pilot-coat about the throat, while Owd Bob stood at his feet, waiting.

"Ye're not goin', James?" she asked, anxiously.

"But I am, lass," he answered. And she knew him too well to say more.

So those two went quietly out to save life or lose it, nor counted the cost.

Down a wind-shattered slope, over a spar of ice, up an eternal hill—a forlorn hope.

In a whirlwind chaos of snow, the tempest storming at them, the white earth lashing them, they fought a good fight. In front, the dog, snow clogging his long coat, hair cutting like lashes of steel across his eyes, his head lowered as he followed the finger of God; close behind, the man, his back stern against the storm, stalwart still, yet swaying like a tree before the wind.

So they battled through to the brink of the Stony Bottom, only to arrive too late.

For just as the Master, peering about him, had sighted a shapeless hump lying motionless in front, there loomed across the snow-choked gulf, through the white riot of the storm, a gigantic lion-like figure forging doggedly forward, his great head down to meet the hurricane, his giant chest iron-bound, coat dripping black icicles. And at his heels, buffeted and bruised, stiff and staggering, a little dauntless figure holding stubbornly on, clutching with one hand at the gale, and a shrill voice, whirled away on the trumpet tones of the wind, crying—

"Noo, Wullie, wi' me—

> 'Scots, wha hae wi' Wallace bled!
> Scots, wham Bruce has aften led!
> Welcome to '—

Here he is, Wullie—

> 'Or to victorie.'"

The brave little voice died away. The quest was over; the lost sheep found. And the last James Moore saw of the couple was the same small gallant form dragging the rescued boy out of the Valley of the Shadow and away.

David was none the worse for his adventure. On reaching home, M'Adam produced a familiar bottle.

"Here's something to warm yer inside, and"— making a feint at the strap on the wall—"here's something to do the same by yer— But, Wullie, oot again!"

And out they went—unwritten heroes.

It was but a week later, in the very heart of the bitter time, that there came a day when from grey dawn to greyer eve neither James Moore nor Owd Bob stirred out into the wintry white. And the Master's face was hard and set, as it always was in time of trouble.

Outside, the wind screamed down the Dale; while the snow fell relentlessly, softly fingering the windows, blocking the doors, and piling deep against the walls. Inside the house there was a strange quiet; no sound save for hushed voices, and upstairs the shuffling of muffled feet.

Below, all day long, Owd Bob patrolled the passage like some silent grey spectre.

Once there came a low knocking at the door; and David, his face and hair and cap smothered in the all-pervading white, entered in with an eddy of snow. He patted Owd Bob, and moved on tiptoe into the kitchen

THE WHITE WINTER

To him came Maggie, shoes in hand, big-eyed, white-faced. The two whispered anxiously awhile like brother and sister as they were ; then the boy crept softly away, only a little pool of water on the floor, and wet treacherous foot-dabs towards the door testifying to his visit.

Towards evening the wind died down, but the mourning flakes still fell.

With the darkening of night Owd Bob retreated to the porch and lay down on his blanket. The light from the lamp at the head of the stairs shone through the crack of open door on his dark head and the eyes that never slept.

The hours passed ; and still the grey knight kept his vigil. Alone in the darkness, alone, it almost seemed, in the house, he watched. His head lay motionless along his paws ; but the steady, grey eyes never flinched or drooped.

Time tramped on on leaden foot, and still he waited ; and ever the pain of hovering anxiety was stamped deeper in the grey eyes.

At length it grew past bearing. The hollow stillness of the house overcame him. He rose, pushed open the door, and softly pattered across the passage.

At the foot of the stairs he halted, his fore-paws on the first step, his grave face and pleading eyes uplifted, as though he were praying The dim light fell on the raised head ; and the white escutcheon on his breast shone out like the snow on Salmon.

At length, with a sound like a sob, he dropped to the ground, and stood listening, his tail drooping and head raised. Then he turned, and began softly pacing up and down like some velvet-footed sentinel at the gate of Death.

Up and down, up and down, softly as the falling snow, for a weary, weary while.

Again he stopped and stood listening intently at the foot of the stairs; and his grey coat quivered as though there were a draught.

Of a sudden, the deathly stillness of the house was broken. Upstairs, feet were running hurriedly. There was a cry and again silence.

A life was coming in ; a life was going out.

The minutes passed; hours passed; and, at the sunless dawn, a life passed.

And all through that night of age-long agony the grey figure stood, still as a statue, at the foot of the stairs. Only when, with the first chill breath of the morning, a dry quick-quenched sob of a strong man sorrowing for the help-meet of a score of years, and a tiny cry of a new-born child wailing because its mother was not, came down to his ears, the Grey Watchman dropped his head upon his bosom, and with a little whimpering note crept back to his blanket.

A little later, the door above opened and James Moore tramped down the stairs. He looked taller and gaunter than his wont, but there was no trace of emotion on his face.

At the foot of the stairs Owd Bob stole out to meet him. He came crouching up, as though guilty of the deadly sin, head and tail down, in a manner no man ever saw before or since. At his master's feet he stopped and whined pitifully.

Then, for one short moment, James Moore's whole face quivered.

"Weel, lad," he said, quite low, and his voice broke—"she's awa'."

That was all: for they were an undemonstrative couple.

Then they turned and went out together into the bleak morning.

CHAPTER IX

M'ADAM AND HIS COAT

TO David M'Adam the loss of gentle Elizabeth Moore was as real a grief as to her children. Yet the boy manfully smothered his own aching heart and gave himself to comforting the mourners at Kenmuir.

In the days succeeding Mrs. Moore's death, the lad recklessly neglected his duties at the Grange. But M'Adam forbore to rebuke him. At times, indeed, he essayed to be passively kind. David, however, was too deeply sunk in his great sorrow to note the change.

The day of the funeral came. The earth was throwing off its ice-fetters; and the Dale was lost in a mourning mist.

In the afternoon, M'Adam was standing at the window of the kitchen, contemplating the infinite weariness of the scene, when the door of the house opened and shut. Red Wull raised himself on to the sill and growled; and David hurried past the window, making for Kenmuir. M'Adam watched the passing figure indifferently; then with an angry oath sprang to the window.

"Bring me back that coat, ye thief!" he cried, tapping fiercely on the pane. "Tak' it aff at onst, ye muckle gowk, or I'll come and tear it aff ye. D'ye see him, Wullie? the great coof has ma coat—ma black coat, noo last Michaelmas; and it rainin' fit to melt it!"

He threw the window up with a bang and leaned out. "Bring it back, I tell ye, ondootiful, or I'll summons ye! Tho' ye've no respect for me ye might have for ma claithes. D'ye think I had it cut for a elephant? it's burstin', I tell ye. Tak' it aff! Fetch it here! or I'll e'en send Wullie to bring it."

For answer, David set to running down the hill. The coat was stretched in wrinkled agony across his back; his big red wrists protruded like shank-bones from the sleeves; and the little tails flapped wearily in vain attempts to reach the wearer's legs.

M'Adam, bubbling over with indignation, scrambled half-through the window. But a sense of humour is many a man's salvation; and tickled at the amazing impudence of the thing, he paused, smiled, dropped to the ground again, and watched the uncouth retreating figure with chuckling amusement.

"Did ye ever see the like o' that, Wullie?" he muttered. "Ma puir coat—puir wee coatie! it gars me greet to see her in her pain. . . . A man's coat, Wullie, is aften unco' sma' for his son's back; and David, there, is strainin' and stretchin' her, nigh to brakin', for a' the world as he does ma forbearance. And what's he care aboot th' ain or t'ither?—not a finger-flip."

As he stood watching the disappearing figure, there began the slow tolling of the minute bell. Now near now far, now loud now low, its dull chant rang out through the mist, like the slow-dropping tears of a mourning world.

M'Adam listened almost reverently as the bell tolled on, the only sound in the quiet Dale. Outside a drizzling rain was falling; the snow dribbled down the hill in muddy tricklets; and trees and roofs and windows dripped, dripped.

And still the bell tolled on, calling up relentlessly sad memories of the long ago.

It was on just such another dreary day, in just such another December, and not so many years gone by, that the light had gone for ever out of his life.

The whole picture rose as instant to his eyes as if it had been yesterday. That dead insistent bell brought the scene surging back to him: the dismal day; the drizzle; the few mourners; little David decked out in black, his fair hair contrasting with his gloomy clothes, his face swollen with weeping; the Dale hushed, it seemed, in Death, save for the tolling of the bell—and his love had left him and gone to the happy land the hymn-books talked of.

Red Wull, who had been watching him uneasily, now approached and shoved his muzzle into his master's hand. The cold touch brought the little man back to earth. He shook himself, turned wearily away from the window, and went to the door of the house.

He stood there, looking out; and all round him was the eternal drip-drip of the thaw. The wind lulled, and again the minute bell tolled out clear and inexorable, resolute to recall what was and what had been.

With a choking gasp, the little man turned into the house and ran up the stairs and into his room. Beside the great chest in the corner he dropped on his knees and unlocked the bottom drawer.

In it he searched with feverish fingers, and produced at length a little paper packet wrapped about with a stained yellow ribbon. It was the ribbon she had used to weave on Sundays into her soft hair.

Inside the packet was a cheap, heart-shaped frame, and in the frame a daguerreotyped photograph.

Up there it was too dark to see. The little man ran down the stairs, Red Wull jostling him as he went, and hurried to the window in the kitchen.

It was a sweet, laughing face that looked up at him, demure yet arch, shy yet roguish; a face to look at and a face to love.

As he looked, a wintry smile, half tears, all tenderness, stole over the little man's face.

"Lassie," he whispered, and his voice was infinitely fond, "it's lang sin' I've daur'd look at ye. But it's no' that ye're forgotten, dearie."

Then he covered his eyes with his hand as though he were blinded.

"Dinna look at me sae, lass!" he cried and fell on his knees, kissing the picture, hugging it to him, and sobbing passionately.

Red Wull came up and pushed his face compassionately into his master's; but the little man shoved him roughly away, and the dog retreated into a corner, abashed and reproachful.

Memories swarmed back on the little man.

He recalled the days when he had worked at old M'Leod's, up in the heather-hills he often longed for; and his courtship of Flora M'Leod. How she would tease him and he would leave her, swearing never to see her again; for then as always he was quick to anger. And next day she would come to him, tripping through the heather, her skirts kilted to show the slenderest ankles in the countryside, demureness on her lips, the mischief dancing in her eyes, and he would love her more than ever.

How at last he had asked her, humbly and fearfully,

to be his wife, and she, the acknowledged queen of all the lasses round, had accepted him—miserable, sour-tempered Adam M'Adam, when she might have had the pick of the countryside.

Yet of them all he had been her choice, and he never ceased to wonder at it.

The little man, down on his knees, held the photograph from him, and looked at the face in the frame through tear-bleared eyes. "But ye took me, lass— God bless ye for 't!"

From that he fell to thinking of the leaving of Scotland; the coming to the Grange; the advent of David, and his wife's insatiable pride in the great boy she had born, until he had fairly raged with jealousy.

"Is he no' a buirdly callan'?" she would ask, fondly dandling the child's big limbs.

"Ay, he'll no' tak' after his father," he would answer bitterly; and then she must coax him back into good-humour.

Those were the best days of his life, when his wife, himself, and son had lived together in sober happiness in the little house on the hill.

But the end soon came.

It was more than a decade ago now, and yet he dared barely think of that last evening when she had lain so white and still in the little room above.

"Pit the bairn on the bed, Adam, man," she had said in low tones; "I'll be gaein' in a wee while noo... It's the lang good-bye to you—and him."

He had done her bidding and lifted David up. The tiny boy lay still a moment, looking at this white-faced mother whom he hardly recognised.

"Minnie!" he called piteously; then, thrusting a

mall, dirty hand into his pocket, pulled out a grubby weet.

"Minnie, ha' a sweetie—ain o' Davie's sweeties!" He ield it out anxiously in his warm, plump palm, thinking t a certain cure for any ill.

"Eat it for mither," she said, smiling tenderly; and hen—"Davie, ma heart, I'm leavin' ye."

The boy ceased sucking the sweet and looked at her, he corners of his mouth drooping pitifully.

"Ye're no' gaein' awa', mither?" he asked, his face .ll working. "Ye'll no' leave yer wee laddie?"

"Ay, laddie, awa'—reet awa'. He's callin' me."

She tried to smile; but her mother's heart was near o bursting.

"Ye'll tak' yer wee Davie wi' ye, mither?" the child)leaded, crawling up towards her face. The great tears olled down her cheeks, and M'Adam, at the head of he bed, was sobbing openly.

"Eh, ma bairn, ma bairn, I'm sair to leave ye!" she ried, brokenly. "Lift him for me, Adam."

He placed the child in her arms; but she could not 1old him. So he laid him on his mother's pillows, and he boy wreathed his soft arms about her neck and obbed tempestuously.

Thus the two lay together.

Just before the end she had turned her head and vhispered,

"Adam, ma man, ye'll ha' to be mither and father)aith to him the noo," and had looked at him with ender confidence in her dying eyes.

"I wull! afore God, as I stan' here, I wull!" he 1ad cried passionately. Then she had died at peace.

. . . . . .

"Mither and father baith!"

The little man rose to his feet, and flung the photograph from him. Red Wull pounced on it; but M'Adam leaped at him as he mouthed it.

"Git awa', ye devil!" he screamed, and picking it up, stroked it lovingly with trembling fingers.

"Mither and father baith!"

How had he fulfilled his love's last wish?

"O God!" and he fell upon his knees at the table-side, hugging the picture, in a tempest of tears.

Red Wull cowered in the far corner of the room, and then crept whining up to where his master knelt. But M'Adam ignored him and the great dog slunk away again.

There the little man knelt in the gloom of the winter's afternoon, a miserable penitent. His grey-flecked head was bowed upon his arms; his hands clutched the miniature; and he prayed aloud in gasping, halting tones.

"Gie me grace, O God! 'Father and mither baith, ye said, Flora—and I haena done it. But 'tis no' too late—say it's no', lass. Tell me there's time yet; and say ye forgie me. I've tried to bear wi' him mony and mony a time. But he's vexed me, and set himself agin me, and stiffened my back, and ye ken hoo I was aye quick to tak' offence. But I'll mak' it up to him—mak' it up to him and mair. I'll humble masel' afore him, and that'll be bitter enough. And I'll be father and mither baith to him. But there's bin none to help me; and it's bin sair wi'oot ye. And—but, 'eh, lassie, I'm wearyin' for ye."

. . . .

It was a dismal procession that wound in the drizzle from Kenmuir to the little Dale church. At its head stalked James Moore, and close behind, David in his meagre coat; while last of all, as if to guide the stragglers in the weary road, came Owd Bob.

There was a full congregation in the tiny church now. In the Squire's pew were Cyril Gilbraith, Muriel Sylvester, and, most conspicuous, Lady Eleanour. Her slender figure was simply draped in grey, with grey fur about the neck, and grey fur edging sleeves and jacket; her veil was lifted, and you could see the soft hair about her temples, and her eyes big with tender sympathy as she glanced towards the pew upon her right.

For there were the mourners from Kenmuir: the Master, tall, grim, and gaunt; and beside him Maggie, striving to be calm, and little Andrew, the miniature of his father.

Alone in the pew behind was David M'Adam in his father's coat.

The back of the church was packed with farmers from the whole March Mere estate, friends from Silverdale and Grammoch-town, and nearly every soul in Wastrel-dale, come to show their sympathy for the living and reverence for the dead.

Tammas was there, grave for once; Sam'l Todd, blubbering ponderously; Job Maddox, 'Enry Farewether, and the other workers from Kenmuir. Behind them, Mother Ross, Melia Ross and Liz Burton, side by side, and little Mrs. Burton, sobbing audibly for the best woman friend she had known. Even old Ross's battered countenance was less grimly complacent than usual as he pottered about his business.

At the bottom of the church were Londesley of the Home Farm, Teddy Bolstock, Rob Saunderson, Jim Mason, Tupper of Swinsthwaite, Long Kirby, John Swan, of the Border Ram, Big Bell, and as many more as the

M'ADAM AND HIS COAT 87

little church would hold: all grave-faced, stern, affected, and determined to disguise it.

And outside, lying patiently in the yellow-puddled snow, a host of dogs: Saunderson's Shep, Tupper's big blue Rasper, Londesley's Lassie, and apart from the rest, their grotesque Maori-wrinkled masks strangely inter-writhed, the three fair sisters, the Vexer, Venus, and Van Tromp. While in the door throughout the service stood Owd Bob, like some esquire keeping his vigil on the eve of knighthood.

. . . .

Parson Leggy, his tanned face contrasting with the whiteness of his surplice, read on in his steady, earnest voice. The harmonium, fingered lovingly by the Squire's eldest daughter, groaned out its part. But the voices which joined in were few and fewer: the sniffling of Mrs Burton, the shuffling of old Ross: for the rest almost a silent congregation.

James Moore stood with his lips tight and head up, only an occasional surging at his throat betraying his emotion. David's lips moved, indeed, but there issued no sound. And Maggie was crying quietly.

And when it came to that most heartening of all our hymns—

"A few more years shall roll,
A few more seasons come,"

Lady Eleanour's sweet voice rang out alone, clear and calm and inspiring, like some herald angel singing as he bears a soul to Paradise.

. . . .

At last the end came in the wet dreariness of the little churchyard. Slowly the mourners departed. At length were left only the Parson, the Master, and Owd Bob.

The Parson was speaking in rough, short accents,

digging nervously at the sopping ground. The other
tall and gaunt, his face drawn and half-averted, stood
listening. By his side was Owd Bob, scanning his
master's countenance, his sad grey eyes clouded with
the dark pain of pity—compassionate with that deep
sympathy of silence which only a dog can rightly
tender; while close by, one of the Parson's terriers was
nosing in the grass.

Of a sudden James Moore, his face still turned away,
stretched out a hand. The Parson broke off abruptly
and grasped it. Then the two men strode away in
opposite directions, the terrier hopping on three legs
and shaking the rain off his hard coat.

So another was added to the long list of Moores
already sleeping in the quiet God's acre beneath the
Pike.

A plain stone tablet tells the simple tale:

ELIZABETH MOORE,
Dearly loved wife of James Moore of Kenmuir.
December 2nd, 18—.

.   .   .   .

David's steps sounded outside. M'Adam rose from
his knees. The door of the house opened, and the boy's
feet shuffled in the passage.

"David!" the little man called in tremulous voice.

He stood in the half-light, one hand on the table, the
other clasping the picture. His eyes were bleared, his
thin hair tossed, and he was trembling.

"David," he called again; "I've somethin' I wush to
say to ye."

The boy burst into the room. His face was stained
with tears and rain; and the new black coat was mud-
slimed down the front, and on the elbows were green-

brown blots. For, on his way home, he had flung himself down in the Stony Bottom just as he was, heedless of the wet earth and his father's coat, and lying on his face, thinking of that second mother lost to him, had wept his heart out in a passion of tears.

Now he stood defiantly, hand upon the door.

"What?"

The little man looked from him to the picture in his hand.

"Help me, Flora—he'll no'," he prayed. Then, raising his eyes—"I'd like to say . . . I've bin thinkin' . . . think I should tell ye . . . It's no' an easy thing for a man to say"—

He broke off short. The self-imposed task was almost more than he could accomplish.

He looked appealingly at David. There was no glimmer of understanding in that white, set countenance.

"O God, its 'maist mair than I can do!" the father muttered; and the perspiration stood upon his forehead. Again he began—"David, after I saw ye this afternoon steppin' doon the hill"—

Again he paused. His glance rested unconsciously upon the coat. David mistook the look; mistook the dimness in his father's eyes; mistook the tremor in his voice.

"Here 'tis! tak' yer coat!" he cried passionately; and tearing it off, flung it down at his father's feet. 'Tak' it—and—and—curse ye."

He banged out of the room, and ran upstairs; and turning the key, threw himself on to his bed, and sobbed.

Red Wull made a movement to fly at the retreating figure; then turned to his master, his stump-tail vibrating: now again things were as they should be.

But M'Adam was looking at the coat which lay in a limp bundle at his feet.

"'Curse ye!'" he repeated softly. "'Curse ye'—ye heard him, Wullie."

A bitter smile crept across his face. He looked again at the picture, now crushed within his hand.

"Ye canna say I didna try; ye canna ask me to agin," he muttered, and slipped it into his pocket. "Niver agin, Wullie—not if the Queen were to ask it!"

Then he went out into the gloom and drizzle, still smiling the same bitter smile.

. . . .

That night, when it came to closing time at the Sylvester Arms, Jem Burton found a little grey-haired figure lying on the floor in the tap-room. At the little man's head lay a great dog.

"Thoo parfet beast!" exclaimed the righteous publican, regarding the figure of his best customer with fine scorn. Then catching sight of a photograph in the little man's hand,

'"Eh, one o' that mak' are ye, Foxy?" he leered. "Gie us a peep at 'er!" and he tried to disengage the picture from the other's grasp. At that the great dog rose, bared his teeth, and assumed such a diabolical expression, rolling his eyes dreadfully upward, that the big landlord retreated hurriedly behind the bar.

"Two on ye," he shouted viciously, rattling his heels, " beasts baith!

Part III

The Shepherds' Trophy

CHAPTER X

RIVALS

M'ADAM never forgave his son. After the scene on the evening of the funeral there could be no alternative but war for all time. The little man had attempted to humble himself and been rejected; and the bitterness of defeat, when he had deserved victory, rankled like a poisoned barb in his bosom.

Yet the heat of his indignation was directed not against David but against the Master of Kenmuir. To the influence and agency of James Moore he attributed his discomfiture, and bore himself accordingly. In public or in private, in tap-room or market, he never wearied of his villain invective.

"Feel the loss o' his wife, d'ye say? Ay, as muckle as I feel the loss o' my hair. James Moore can feel naethin', I tell ye, except, aiblins, a mischance to his meeserable dog."

When the two met, as they often must, it was always M'Adam's endeavour to vex his enemy into an unworthy self-betrayal. But James Moore, man of iron self-restraint, never gave way. He met the little man's sneers with a quelling silence, looking down on his asp-tongued antagonist with such a contempt flashing from his steel-blue eyes as hurt his adversary more than words.

Only once was he spurred into reply. It was in the tap-room of the Dalesman's Daughter when there was a goodly gathering of farmers and their dogs in the room. M'Adam was standing at the fireplace, Red Wull at his side.

"It's a noble pairt ye play, James Moore," he cried loudly, "settin' son against father, and dividin' hoose against hoose. It is worthy o' ye wi' yer church-goin', and yer psalm-singin', and yer godliness."

The Master looked up from the farther end of the room.

"Happen, ye're not aware, M'Adam," he said sternly, "that if it had not bin for me David 'd ha' left you lang syne—and 'twould nobbut ha' served ye reet, I'm thinkin'."

The little man hitched his trousers, smirked, and changed front.

"Dinna shout so, man: I have ears to hear. Forbye, ye irritate Wullie."

The Tailless Tyke, indeed, had advanced from the fireplace, and now stood, huge and hideous, in the very centre of the room. There was distant thunder in his throat, a threat upon his face, a challenge in every wrinkle. And the grey dog stole gladly out from behind his master to take up the gage of battle.

Straightway there was silence: tongues ceased to wag, tankards to clink. Every man and every dog was quietly gathering about those two. Not one of them all but had his score to wipe off against the Tailless Tyke;

RIVALS

ot one of them but was burning to join in, the battle
ice begun. And the two gladiators stood staring
assily past one another, muzzle to muzzle, each with
 tiny flash of teeth glinting between his lips: the one
rpe of scarred criminal, the other of the high-bred
entleman.

But the fight was not to be. For the twentieth time
ie Master intervened.

"Bob, lad, coom in!" he called, and grasped his
ivourite.

M'Adam laughed softly.

"Wullie, Wullie, to me!" he cried. "The look o'
ou's enough for yon braw callant."

"If they get fightin' it wunna be Bob here I'll whang,
warn thee, M'Adam," said the Master grimly.

"Gin ye sae muckle as fingered Wullie, d'ye ken what
'd do, James Moore?" asked the little man very
moothly.

"Ay: sweer," the other answered, and strode out of
he room amidst a roar of derisive laughter at M'Adam's
xpense.

In James Moore the little man found no easy target
or his attacks; but with David it was different. Insults
irected at himself the boy bore with a stolidity born of
ong use. But a poisonous dart aimed at Kenmuir
ever failed of its purpose. And the little man evinced
n amazing talent for the concoction of deft lies respect-
ng his enemy.

"I'm hearin'," said he one evening, sitting in he
itchen, twig in mouth; "I'm hearin' James Moore is
aein' to git married agin."

"Ye're hearin' lies—or mair like tellin' 'em," David
nswered carelessly.

"Seven months sin' his wife died," the other continued

musing. "Aweel, I'm only 'stonished he's waited sae lang. . . . Ain buried anither come on, that's James Moore." And he was left chuckling to Wullie as the boy burst angrily out of the room.

David had now a new interest at Kenmuir. In Maggie he found an endless source of wonderment. It seemed to him that the girl had sprung up in a night from a winsome child into a woman. And very soon he discovered that Maggie, Mistress of Kenmuir, was wholly changed from his erstwhile comrade and slave. They were on different footing now. She was queen where he had been king; hers was to command, his to obey; and consequently there was perpetual war, as he battled vainly to regain his lost sovereignty. Yet, blinded though he was by prejudice, the boy could not but allow that Maggie performed her new part, young though she was, with a sweet, wholly surprising discretion; whether in the sterner matters of household work, or in tenderly mothering the baby, Wee Anne.

This latter labour of love she only shared with Owd Bob; and, sure, no nurse ever had trustier assistant. There he would lie at the cradle-side, watching his charge, fond, wise, careful, the mute eyes softly sad, as he dreamed on this last tender trust bequeathed him by the dear dead mistress; while the child would bubble and bounce and bathe fat hands in his silver deeps, or scream in petulant delight as the dark muzzle stole over the side of the cot and thrust her back, softly remorseless, into security.

. . . . .

Owd Bob had now attained well-nigh the perfection of his art. Parson Leggy declared roundly that his like had not been seen since the glorious days of Rex, son of Rally. Amongst the Dalesmen he was an heroic favourite. The Grey Dogs of Kenmuir have ever been worshipped in the land; their prowess and gentle ways winning them friends on every hand; and now the Dalesmen's confidence in the latest of the line was immutable. Sometimes on market-days he would execute some unaccountable manœuvre, and a stranger drover would inquire—

" What's the grey dog at?"

To which the nearest Dalesman—

"Nay, I canna tell thee. But he's reet enough. Yon's Owd Bob o' Kenmuir." Whereat the stranger would cock his ears and watch attentively; for at that time there were few in the profession but had heard of the new star risen in the North. And never in such case did the grey dog betray the confidence reposed in him.

They loved him, one and all, for his own sake; loved him for his sweet manner, his shy courtesy; loved him for his loud-clanging deeds; loved him for his noble rage when roused, his continence fine as his master's; and most of all they loved him, for that he was the antithesis, antagonist to the death, of the Tailless Tyke.

Barely a man in the countryside but owed a grudge against that ferocious savage; not a man of them all who dared pay it. Once, indeed, Long Kirby, full of beer and valour, had tried to settle his account. Coming on M'Adam and Red Wull between Grammoch-town and the Dalesman's Daughter, he leant over and with his thong dealt the dog a terrible sword-like slash that raised a ridge of red from hip to shoulder; and was settled to his gallop ere the little man's shrill yells struck his ear, whelmed in a dreadful bellow.

Standing up, he lashed the colt. But glancing over his shoulder he saw a hounding form behind, catching him as though he walked. His face blenched chalky hue; he screamed, flogged, looked back. Right beneath the tail-board was the red devil in the dust; while racing a furlong behind on the turnpike road the mad figure of M'Adam.

The smith struck back and flogged forward. In vain. With a bound the avenger flung on to the flying trap. At the impact the colt was thrown violently on his side; Kirby tossed over the hedge; and Red Wull pinned beneath the débris.

M'Adam rushed up in time to save a tragedy.

"I've a mind to knife ye, Kirby," he panted, as he bandaged the smith's broken head.

After that the Dalesmen preferred to swallow insults offered rather than risk their lives; and you may be sure their impotence only served to fan their animosity to white glow.

Yet, however the heat of their hate might prejudice their judgment, they were compelled to confess that in the matter of his own work Red Wull owned but one superior in the land—Owd Bob o' Kenmuir. And those two, conspicuous a head and shoulders above the ruck were thrown of necessity into eternal antagonism. The admiration for the one was only increased by the challenging ability of the other. The known feud between their masters added point to the rivalry, and competition by comparison—deadliest of jealous strifes —waxed more vehement day by day.

The working methods of the antagonists were as contrasted as their appearances. In a word, the one compelled; the other coaxed. His enemies said the Tailless Tyke was rough, not even Tammas denied he was ready. His brain was as big as his body, and he used them both to some purpose. "As quick as a cat, with the heart of a lion, the strength of Anak,

nd the temper of Nick's self," was Parson Leggy's
pecification.

What determination could effect that could Red
Vull; but achievement by inaction—supremest of all
trategies—the art of performance by suggestion was
ot for him. Self-suppression might be for amiable
ncompetents; for the Tailless Tyke, Action, always
Action. In matters of the subtlest handling, where to
ct anything except indifference was to lose; with
heep restless, fearful forebodings hymned to them by
he wind, panic hovering unseen above them, when an
l-considered movement spelt Catastrophe—then was
)wd Bob o' Kenmuir incomparable.

Men still tell how, when the Squire's new thrashing
nachine ran amuck in Grammoch-town, and for some
ninutes the market-square was a turbulent sea of
laspheming men, yelping dogs, and stampeding sheep,
nly one flock stood calm as a mill-pond by the bull-
ing, watching the riot with almost indifference. For in
heir full face, lying conspicuous at his ease, was a quiet
;rey dog, his mouth stretched in a capacious yawn: to
'awn was to win, and he won.

When the worst of the uproar was over, many a
;lance of triumph was shot first at that one still pack
.nd then at M'Adam, as he waded through the disorder
)f huddling sheep.

"And wheer's Wullie noo?" asked Tupper scornfully.

"Weel," the little man answered with his inscrutable
mile, "at this minit' he's killin' your Rasper doon by
he pump." Which proved indeed the case; for big
)lue Rasper had interfered with the great dog in the
erformance of his duty and had suffered accordingly.

That tale is but one amongst a multitude. There
vere others with a different hero. Jim Mason told

how, once, Red Wull's flock, frightened by a galloping cart, bolted down the steep Swine's Slope which ends abruptly in the new railway cutting. To gallop in front was to split, not stop them. The one chance was to turn them together. And the great dog, racing alongside the leaders, shouldering, shoving, snarling, bore them round by sheer bodily strength; and the whole swept to the left, still at the gallop, ten yards from the brink of death.

So things went on: Owd Bob backed by the many, Red Wull by the one. And the near coming of the Dale Trials, when the two great rivals would wrestle foot to foot in the fight for the Shepherds' Trophy, set the match to the long-smouldering powder-train.

CHAPTER XI

IN THE PASS

THE Dale Trials had their source a hundred years ago in a local competition. The meeting became annual. It grew in worth and dignity, until very soon the battle for the Shepherds' Trophy became the head and chief event of the pastoral year. And ever since its supremacy has been maintained unchallenged.

It is good to be hailed victor of the Cambrian Stakes at Llangollen; it is better to carry off in roaring triumph the famous Ram's Head of the Highland meeting; but to have your dog's name and your own engraved on the fair white sides of the mighty Cup is to win an envied immortality. Ay, in the North we fix the year as " Jock's," " the black cur betch's," " Rex, son o' Rally's," and the like.

It was nigh fifty years since that illustrious scion of the line had won his final victory; fifty years since the Cup had been brought back to the land that gave it birth. And now two aspirants to highest honours had risen—a Grey Dog and another.

Proud is that countryside which for the year reflects the burning lustre of the Cup; high-stomached he who hails from the winner's neighbourhood; yet rather than see this upstart interloper usurp his laurels from their grey champion, rather than hear ten thousand shepherd folk acclaim the Tailless Tyke triumphant on thunder's voice, no Dalesman but affirmed with emphatic fist that he preferred to see it borne back to the Highland North.

As the summer sweltered away and the day drew nigh the ferment surpassed power of pen. Wholehearted animosity for the one rival and fervent loyalty to the other shook hands at every corner, and excitement as to the event reached such a pitch as Parson Leggy hardly could recall.

Down in the Sylvester Arms there was nightly a long-drawn bout of words between M'Adam and Tammas Thornton, the spokesman of the Dalesmen. From these duels Tammas was wont to emerge second best. His temper would get the better of his tongue ; the cynical debater was lost in the hot-mouthed partisan. Only, when their champion was suffering shameful rout all along the line, and it was time for strength of lung to vanquish strength of logic, Rob Saunderson and the rest joined in right lustily and roared the little man down with Babel voice, for all the world like the gentlemen who rule the empire at Westminster.

"Aweel, I ken James Moore'd liefer ha' lost his wife nor his grey dog."

"His dog is his dog and his wife is his wife," from Tammas, stubborn as a tup.

"Ay, ay, and a man shouldna treat his wife as a dog, and his dog as a wife, as they say our friend"—

Then they arose as one and would have murdered him, but that the Tailless Tyke lay as always at his master's feet, in hideous one-eyed watchfulness, praying aloud for blood.

In Tammas and David, M'Adam found gratifying targets for his tongue. But with the Master it was altogether other. The fortress of the strong man's

IN THE PASS

self-restraint seemed impregnable. The little man's undying animosity was now fresh-fired by the unanimous hostility evinced towards him in the big matter of the Cup, and no less unanimous advocacy of his enemy. He waged against his foe a petty perpetual war. He tried him with aggravation, insult, calumny—all in vain. The man of iron was as proof against his venomous darts as an armour-hided battleship against an adder's onslaught. It was only when presuming on the other's long-enduringness, M'Adam trespassed by an inch upon his just due that he found the Master took his stand immovable upon the rock of his rights.

Then, indeed, the two clashed; and then M'Adam tasted of defeat. For spite in the wrong is but a poor weapon with which to oppose might in the right.

It was this immutable resolve on the Master's part not to cede one tittle of his rightful claims, that led to a collision the issue of which was to send M'Adam on his way in a tremble of exultation; and that though smarting under the sting of a repulse.

It happened thus. The Murk Muir Pass, before debouching into the Devil's Bowl, narrows a space. This strait and perilous part is known as the Neck. There three men linked arm-in-arm may walk abreast; one treading eternity, the other rubbing the rock-face. Were two flocks to encounter here, disaster might well ensue. And so expediency has made her rule: that the flock descending gives the road to the flock upon the upward grade. It thus becomes the business of the down-going shepherd to assure himself that no up-climbing pack holds the way. Such is the acknowledged, all-inviolable rule.

Now on a day in that late summer James Moore had already entered the Neck, his pack solid before him, when over the brink of the Bowl a host of slow, black, horn-crowned faces loomed on the skyline and began the descent. The Master holloaed, gesticulated—in vain.

A little wizened figure shot up against the sky, a lion form slouching at his side; paused, gazed, and then held on his downward course.

"The blame is his," the Master muttered, and pursued his upward way.

Slowly the two came together, closing in to inevitable collision like the march of opposing fates.

Within a hand's cast the leading sheep checked, stared, greeted timorously, and advanced.

Face to face they halted, shy, gauche, ill at ease; then tried to turn. But the ruthless compulsion from behind whelmed them forward; and they pressed and huddled, whimpering still, like slaves placed in the fore-front of the battle.

Across the yellow, ma-a-ing huddle, the two men regarded one another; the Master grim, M'Adam sardonic.

"I'm grieved ye should ha' to turn, James Moore," the little man called civilly.

"Nay; that's for thee to do, M'Adam," the other answered, herding his sheep on.

"Aweel," said the other leisurely, "aweel. We must wait till the clouds roll by, Wullie," and he leaned against the rock-face and began to suck his twig.

The Master pressed his line on. Two tups in front dropped their heads and butted doggedly. The Master waved a wordless command. The grey dog stole like a cloud over the backs of his flock. Red Wull marked his enemy, his eyes flamed red, and he rumbled hugely. The two sheep butted, butted. A crack opened in the yellow crush. Like a fairy the grey dog dropped into it. Gentle, slow, persistent, he shoved along the rock-face, cleaving a hard way between wall and sheep, looking back to see if his children followed.

"Canniely, lad! canniely!" urged the Master, herding the flock into the opening wedge; apprehensive all the while lest Red Wull should contest the advance.

But no. A sheep-dog's duty—his first duty and always his first—is to his sheep. Private wrongs, personal vendettas, all yield to the inexorable call of the profession. And now Red Wull, shivering with the hate-lust though he was, assumed his rightful position at the danger-point, poised on the grim brink of the abyss; a firm and formidable bannister between his dependants and the deathly blank.

It was at best a precarious manœuvre, and not facilitated by the bristling antipathy of Red Wull, and his master's ill-hidden rancour. Still, men and dogs, at the acme of alertness, achieved the thing at length.

As the convoys formed afresh and the two men passed, each bending instinctively to grip his dog, M'Adam shot a sneer at the other: for even in the trifles of the world to be bested by his foe mortified him.

" I see what ye're at, James Moore," he cried, in ugly, tremulous voice. " Better luck next time."

"What?" asked the other, uncomprehending.

"Why, just a bit of a tip to Wullie while he hung on the cliff—and the way's clear for yon grey devil for the Cup."

The Master looked at the sinister-smiling malignant, amazement at the man's ill-imagining lost in his scorn for the matter of it.

He passed on, paused, and turned.

" As to that, M'Adam," he answered, " I'm not runnin' ma Bob," and turned on his way.

M'Adam drew an abrupt breath.

" You lee!" he gasped, as one in shock of sudden breathlessness.

The Master swung about, thunder in his face; and then again passed on.

M'Adam watched him. He was trembling in his agitation. The flame of suppressed excitement burned in his eyes.

"Hie, man!" he called, following. "I'll withdraw that. I'll pit it at, I *think* that you lee!"

His concession of grace failed to move. The other still strode away at the tail of his sheep.

M'Adam watched him; marked the stern tall form clothed in its sombre garb, marked the mourning band upon his arm, and in a flash bethought himself.

An ugly smile puckered his lips. In any other man such evidence of tender reverence for a late-dead wife would have touched him; in the Master of Kenmuir it seemed merely self-seeking hypocrisy.

"Noo I see," he sneered. "He thinks to get a reduction o' rent by sic a display o' proper feelin'."

Then James Moore turned, and in such a white blaze of wrath that M'Adam was aghast.

"Thank God, M'Adam, on your bended knees this neet," he cried, his voice thrilling, "that He's seen good to fashion ye as He has. It's bin yer salvation this day." And he turned again.

A moment's pause; then a small, set voice came echoing after him.

"James Moore! James Moore! . . . I'm sorry I spoke that last bit."

The Master held on, still too deeply moved to trust himself.

"And noo"—after a second's respite—"I'm sorrier still I ever said I was."

And his act of grace done and undone, the little man darted after his pack, his heart a whirl of emotions.

CHAPTER XII

WE TWA

OWD BOB was not to run for the Cup. The announcement fell like a thunderbolt, scattering dismay broadcast. Yet no remonstrance could be attempted. Indeed there could be no word but of commendation for the Master's motive. And such a self-denying ordinance speaks more for the reality of a man's love for a lost one than many a lordly cenotaph.

Still to the people of the Dale-land from the Muir Pike to the market-cross in Grammoch-town, the draught was none the less bitter. They had set their hearts on the grey dog's success; had thought to have the Cup amongst them after fifty long years. That, indeed, might yet be. But to have the trophy brought home by other than a Grey Dog of Kenmuir revolted their Tory senses. Under no circumstances could it be seemly; but the thought that the Tailless Tyke—this infernal, saturnine parvenu—might well wear the laurels that should have been their favourite's, set even the children in the streets a-swearing.

And M'Adam's bearing embittered the blow three-fold. He was plunged into a very frenzy of delight by that news which was death to them. Their misery was his delight, and he told them so and revelled in the telling. For to win the Shepherds' Trophy was now the goal of his ambition. David was less than nothing to the lonely little man, Red Wull his all-in-all. And to have that name immortalised, emblazoned in the ranks of the world's most famous sheep-dogs, was his soul's desire.

As Cup Day drew near, the little man, his fine-strung temperament attuned to the highest pitch of nervous anticipation, was tossed on a sea of dread and doubt. His hopes and fears ebbed and flowed on the tide of the moment. His moods were various as the winds in March. At one minute he paced the barren kitchen, his face already flushed with the glow of victory, chanting his battle-song. At the next he was down at the table, his head in his hands, his whole figure convulsed, as he cried in choking voice, "Eh, Wullie, Wullie! they're all agin us."

. . . .

All things end save eternity. And when at length the little man found himself in the presence of the reality, he was calm, confident, palely resolute to achieve his Wullie's glory.

Cup Day is always a general holiday in the North. Shops are shut; every soul crowds to Silver-dale; and soon the paddock below the Dalesman's Daughter teems with the crowd of sportsmen and spectators come from far and near to see the battle for the Shepherds' Trophy.

There stood the great Kenmuir wain. Many an eye was directed on the young couple therein: Maggie looking in her simple print frock as sweet and fresh as any flower; while David's fair face was all overcast. In front of the waggon was a cluster of Dalesmen discussing M'Adam's chance. In the centre stood Tammas, declaiming vehemently.

"A man, Mr. Saunderson?—a h'ape, I calls 'im!

A dog?—more like an 'og, I tell thee!" About the old orator were Rob Saunderson, Kirby, Burton, Jim Mason, and others; while on the outskirts stood Sam'l prophesying rain and M'Adam's victory.

All about was a mass of seething heads; to right and left a long array of carriages and carts; behind, bookmakers' stools, booths, Aunt Sallies, and all the tawdry panoply of such a meeting; while on the far bank of the stream, beneath the shadow of the Scaur, was a bevy of men and dogs, observed of all.

The Juvenile Stakes had been run and won; Londesley's Lassie had beaten Rob's Shep for the Local Cup; and the fight for the Shepherds' Trophy began.

When at length Red Wull came out to run his course, he worked with the savage fury that always characterised him. His method was his own; but the result was beyond cavil.

"Keeps right on the backs of his sheep," said Parson Leggy, watching intent. "Strange they don't break!" But they didn't.

There was no waiting; no coaxing: it was drive and devilry all through. The dog brought his sheep along at a terrific rate, never missing a turn, never faltering, never running out. And the crowd applauded, for the crowd loves novelty. While little M'Adam, hopping agilely about, his face ablaze with excitement, handled dog and sheep with a masterly precision that compelled the admiration even of his enemies.[1]

---

[1] For the Dale Trials are a test less of the dog than of the shepherding machine—of the two, man and dog, who together make the perfect one. And if you tell a Dalesman that in the silly South, the shepherd at such meetings must be tethered to a stake lest he aid his dog over much, he will smile slow scorn, and maybe remark, "Parfet sumphs, to be sure, them Londoners!"

"M'Adam wins!" roared a bookmaker. "Twelve to one agin the field!"

"He wins, dang him!" muttered David.

"Wull wins!" said the Parson, clenching his lips.

"And deserves to," said James Moore.

"Wull wins!" hummed the crowd.

"We don't," said Sam'l gloomily.

And in the end there were none save Tammas the bigot, and Long Kirby, who had lost a great deal of his wife's money and a little of his own, to challenge the justice of the verdict. Only Sam'l evinced a tempered joy.

"'Course, I niver knows nowt, Tammas Thornton. The wery worms in the h'earth know more'n Sam'l Todd!"

The win had but an icy reception. At first was faint cheering; but it sounded like the echo of an echo, and soon died of inanition. To get up an ovation there must be money at the back, or a few roaring fanatics to lead the dance. Here was neither: ugly stories; disparaging remarks. And the thousands who did not know caught the contagion and took their tone as always from the one who said he did.

M'Adam could but remark the absence of enthusiasm as he pushed through the throng to the committee tent. No single voice applauded him; no friendly hand smote its congratulations. Broad backs spurned him; contemptuous eyes impaled him; spiteful tongues scalded him. Only the foreign element looked curiously at the little bent figure with the glowing face, and shrank back at the size and savagery of the great dog at his heels.

But what cared he? His Wullie was crowned King —the best sheep-dog of the year; and the little man was happy. They could turn their backs on him, but they could not alter that; and he laughed to himself.

"They dinna like it, lad,—he! he! But they'll e'en ha' to thole it. We've won it, Wullie, won it fair."

In the ring he took his stand with Red Wull; doffing his hat with almost courtly deference to Lady Eleanour.

Chill silence held the multitude in thrall. Lady Eleanour for once seemed ill at ease. The thing was uncannie, unprecedented, ominous. She glanced up at the ring of lowering faces hemming them all around. There was no reponse to her dumb appeal; and her gentle heart bled for the forlorn, little man before her.

Then David from the rear flouted his father; Tammas shot a jeer; uproar followed; and the storm broke.

The mob went mad. They howled, hissed, hooted, surging dangerously about the ring. They clamoured, cursed, every passion let loose; then a stentorian voice called above the din for cheers for Owd Bob, and they gave them thrice and thrice again; and the strangers, though they did not understand, caught the madness, and roared too. And all the while the little man stood in the vortex of the tempest, sourly smiling; while Red Wull fronted defiantly that black-deep tempestuous wall, shivering with desire of war.

It needed Lady Eleanour at last, standing in the narrow circle, the flush on her cheeks, the flame in her eyes, like a Queen at bay, to scorn them into shame, lash them to order.

In the end it was in a sullen silence that she presented the Cup. The flash was yet in her eyes, and her bosom heaving; but she so smiled on the little man and spoke to him such words as more than compensated him for the outrage he had endured.

Cap in hand, he smiled, blushed, bowed, and took the Cup tenderly.

"It shall no' leave the estate, or ma hoose, yer Leddyship, gin Wullie and I can help it," he said emphatically

Lady Eleanour retreated. The crowd swarmed over the ropes and round the little man. Long Kirby laid irreverent hands upon the Cup.

"Dinna finger it."

"Shall."

"Shan't. Wullie, keep him aff." And the big man's sudden rout evoked laughter, and served to restore the mob's self-respect.

Amongst the last, James Moore was borne past the victor. At sight of him M'Adam's face assumed an expression of intense concern.

"Man, Moore!" he cried, all solicitous—"man, Moore! ye're green—positeevely verdant. Are ye in pain?" Then catching sight of Owd Bob, he started back in horror. "And ma certes! so's yer dog! Yer dog as was grey is green." Then in bantering tones, "Ah, James Moore, godly man, ye shouldna covet"—

"He wunna need to covet lang, I's uphod!" interposed Tammas's shrill accents.

"And why for no?"

"Becos next year he'll win. Oor Bob'll win it fra' thee, lil man. Why? that's why."

The retort was greeted with a yell of applause from the Dalesmen in the crowd.

But M'Adam swaggered away into the tent, head high, the Cup beneath his arm, Red Wull guarding his rear.

"First of a' ye'll ha' to beat Adam M'Adam and his Red Wull!" he cried back proudly.

CHAPTER XIII

THE FIGHT IN THE FLOOD

M'ADAM'S pride in the Cup that now graced his kitchen was more than motherly. It stood conspicuously alone in the very centre of the mantelpiece beneath the bell-mouthed blunderbuss upon the wall; the only ornament in the room, it shone out in silvery chastity like the moon in a bleak night.

So long as the little man could gaze upon it, the desire of his eyes was more than sated.

"Adam M'Adam's Red Wull! Adam M'Adam's Red Wull! Champion—Challenge—Dale—Cup!" he would repeat and linger on the words lover-like; then in a whisper—"Should we win it agin, Wullie, once, twice, 'twill be oors for iver. Think o't, Wullie, think o't!" And that was the haven of his hopes.

M'Adam indeed was now an altered man. Since his mother's death, David had never known such peace. It was not that his father became kind; rather that he omitted to be unkind. Almost the little man forgot his animosity against James Moore and the grey devil. And he was a seldom visitor at the Sylvester Arms.

"Soaks at home instead," suggested Tammas.

"Far ower fou to get so far," said Long Kirby, kindly man.

"I reck'n the Cup is kind o' company to him," said Jim Mason. "Happen it's lonesomeness drives him here so often." And happen you were right, charitable Jim.

In fact, the little man spent all his empty hours with the Cup between his knees; burnishing, polishing, crooning of the glorious future to Wullie.

He was very jealous of his treasure. David might not so much as handle it, and if he approached too near was ordered harshly off.

So it was that M'Adam, on entering the kitchen on a day, was consumed with hot resentment to find the boy desecrating the forbidden object; and the manner of his doing it added a thousand-fold to the offence.

He was lolling indolently against the mantelpiece; his fair head was hard against the Cup, his breath dimming its lustre; while his big raw hands revolved it before his eyes.

Bursting with indignation, the little man crept up behind. David was reading down the Cup's glory-scroll.

"'Theer's the first on 'em!" he muttered, his tongue as indicator. "'Andrew Moore's Rough, 178-.' And theer agin—'James Moore's Pinch, 179-.' And agin—'Beck, 182-.' Ah, and theer's 'im Tammas tells on—'Rex, 183-, and Rex 183-.' Eh, but he mun ha' bin a rare 'un, by all accounts!" He broke off abrupt. His eye had fallen on the latest added name. "M'Adam's Wull!" he read with blighting contempt, and deleted the words with large blasphemous thumb. "M'Adam's Wull! Lord o'me!"

But a little shoulder was into his side; two small fists were hammering him; a shrill voice was yelling—"Devil! devil! stan' awa'!" and he was tumbled precipitately against the side-wall.

The precious Cup swayed on its ebony stand. Yet,

THE FIGHT IN THE FLOOD

beside himself as he was, the little man's first instinctive impulse was to steady it with hurried hands.

Then he turned on the boy, clutched him by the collar, and rattled him to and fro.

"M'Adam's Wull! I wish he was here to teach ye, ye ox-limbed, snod-faced profleegit!" he screamed, tossing to and fro, as a man who thinks to shake an oak. "So ye're hopin' that James Moore will win ma Cup awa' from me—yer ain dad. I wonder ye're no' shamed. Ye live on us; ye suck oor blood; Wullie and me, we brak' oorsel's to keep ye in hoose and hame —and what's yer gratitude? ye plot to rob us of our rights."

He dropped the boy's coat and stood back.

"No reets about it," said David, calm still.

"If I win is it no' ma right as muckle as ony Englishman's?"

Red Wull now entered, scowled at David, and took his stand beside his master.

"Ay, *if* you win," said David, edging towards the door.

"And wha's to beat us?"

David affected large surprise.

"Owd Bob's rinnin'," he said blankly.

"And what if he is?"

The sneer on the boy's face was eloquent in reply.

His father could not fail to comprehend.

"So that's it," he cried; then in a scream, with one finger pointing to the great dog—"And what o' him? What'll ma Wullie be doin' the while?"

David edged on towards the door. He little liked the aspect of affairs; for the Tailless Tyke was bristling on tiptoe of battle alertness.

"What'll Wullie be doin', ye chicken-hearted brock?"

"'Im?" said the boy, now close upon the door.

"'Im?" he cried, with a slow contempt that stiffened the red bristles on the dog's neck. " Ho, lookin' on, I should reck'n, lookin' on. What else is he fit for? I tell thee oor Bob "—

"'Oor' Bob!" screamed the father, darting forward "'Oor' Bob! I'll 'oor'—Wullie! Wullie!"—

But the Tailless Tyke needed no spur. With a roar he launched to the engage, only to crash against the thwarting door.

In another second a mocking finger tapped at the window.

" Better luck to the two on ye next time!" laughed a scornful voice; and the boy shot down the hill for Kenmuir.

. . . . . .

From that hour the fire of M'Adam's jealousy raged.

At home David might hardly enter the room sanctified by the presence of the Trophy.

"I'll no' ha' ye nigh ma Cup, ye ill-begotten wastrel! Wullie and me won it—you'd naught to do wi' it. Go you to James Moore and his dog."

"Ay, and shall I tak' Cup along o' me? or wilta' bide till it's took fra' thee?" And so the two went on.

In the Dale the little man endured a thousand-fold the things he had inflicted a year before. The hearts of the Dalesmen were adamant against him. To a man they were for the grey dog and his master. And utterly alone, bereft of any sympathy, distraught with day-and-night long agony of jealous fear, the little man became the Adam M'Adam of his later years. Every man was his enemy, not one but was hell-deep in a black conspiracy to rob him and his Wullie of their rights. Whereas once at the Sylvester Arms his shrill ill tongue had shot its venom tireless; now he maintained uncannie silence. Crouched away, hag-like, in a corner, with his huge familiar blinking red eyes, impassable bulwark between him and the world, the little man sat dumbly, dreadfully glowering as the Dalesmen talked of the grey dog's coming victory.

Sometimes he could endure it no longer. Then he would spring to his feet, a little swaying figure, and denounce them passionately in almost pathetic eloquence. And always these appeals concluded in set fashion.

"Ye're all agin us!" the little man would cry.

"We are that," from the complacent Tammas.

Then a long sobbing silence; and at length a cry touching in heart-whole bitterness.

"Eh, Wullie, Wullie, they're all agin us!"

The little man became full of ill-imaginings. At his enemy he glared stealthy murder. No action of the Master's but in it he discerned some dark intrigue; some hideous plot to best him. And his deadly earnestness to proceed to any length in the guarding of his treasure was well displayed by an incident in the late spring of the year.

The winter had tarried long, but of late there had been heavy rain; and the tardy snow, dribbling from the hills, had swollen the Wastrel into flood.

M'Adam and Red Wull were down at the red-swinging water's edge. In the churchyard, across the flood, were Parson Leggy and Cyril Gilbraith.

As the three watched the stream, wondering at its strange violence, there came tumbling down the hill towards them a truant fairy.

"Wee Anne!" said the Parson.

"Babbles!" cried Cyril.

"'Lassie wi' the lint-white locks,'" quoted M'Adam.

As the fairy staggered on, a grey galloping figure spun over the crest in pursuit. The fairy looked back, screamed delight, toddled faster, looked back again, stumbled, caught at the air, screamed a child's terror scream; and the greedy water had clutched her and swirled her away.

Cyril yelled and plunged in. The Parson followed.

M'Adam heard, looked up, and saw the wreck-waif in the flood.

"The wean's in, Wullie. . . . After her!" There was no need: Red Wull was already on his way.

Simultaneously the grey dog hurtled through the air and crashed far into the flood.

It proved a race between the rivals. The bull-like mask of red and the dark head of grey were closing in from either side upon their prize. Each kept one eye on the other, one on the bundle in front; each left an eddy in his trail from the fury of his swimming.

For M'Adam this chance race for a life typified the struggle soon to be. In the outcome he saw the issue of the great event.

"Yours, Wullie, mind!" he ordered, hopping along the bank, thrilled and thrilling. "Weel done, Wullie! On wi' ye! Ye're leavin' him! Weel done, laddie!"

The Tailless Tyke first reached the prize, swung about, and struck for the bank.

"Come on, Wullie!" cheered his master. "Weel done for you. Ye've left him agin."

The stream was running like a tide-race, and the child was all dead-weight. But the great dog fought through the flood, striking out like a horse trotting; his cropped ears back, teeth clenched on his burden, and nostrils wrinkled from the effort. While hard on his trail swam the grey pursuer, tail broad-cast on the water

A huge log came lumbering down upon the leader.

"Ha' a care, Wullie! on yer right!" screamed M'Adam.

The dog saw but could not avoid. He turned his head to save the child, and took the blow full on the shoulder. At the thud of the impact, the little man gasped.

"Eh, puir, puir laddie! A sair knock! . . . But haud to it, Wullie! Wullie never says die! Scots wha hae! we've whipped him agin."

He waded into the stream, took the child from its rescuer, and splashed back to the bank.

At the moment, David, issuing from the house, marked the commotion and came blundering down the hill.

"What's oop? Whativer is t' fuss?" he cried; then catching a glimpse of the flower-like face in his father's arms, "What the blazes art' doin' wi' oor Anne?" he roared.

"Droonin' her, of course," his father replied. "Fetch us a brick and a bit o' string, will ye, lad? She winna sink, deil tak' the hissie!"

Two score paces lower down Owd Bob had landed. Wee Anne, his Anne, had been wrested from him by the Tailless Tyke. He beheld her now in M'Adam's arms, and that little man making for the Grange. Splashing through the shallow water, he came like a thunder-bolt; coat dripping, eyes lurid, with the silent bloody fury of the Grey Dogs of Kenmuir.

M'Adam turned to meet him. His face was deathly; but he stood his ground like a hero.

"Wullie! Wullie! to me!"

The great dog's shoulder had been nigh to smashed; yet at the call, at the sight of his master's distress, and the onslaught of his blood-foe, he came limping terrific through the water like some dread Leviathan, every bristle aghast, mad for fighting.

He would have been too late. M'Adam must have gone down before that hurricane attack, had not David interposed.

"Back, Bob!" he called. wrestling madly with the grey dog. " Mr. Gilbraith! gie me a hand, wilta'?"

"Keep him aff, or tak' the consequences!" cried M'Adam, breast heaving. Then as Red Wull lurched furiously up—"Wullie, heel! heel, I say!"

Then he turned and trotted up the hill, his burden in his arms. After him panted Parson Leggy, dripping

"Well done, M'Adam! Well done you and Red Wull! I—I'd "—

"Not too close, Mr. Hornbut; Wullie's a wee vexed."

"I'd never have—I mean—you of all men "—

"Tho' I am a heathen, I may ha' a heart."

"But d'you know whose child "—

The little man looked up.

"I dinna war wi' weans, Mr. Hornbut," he said, with quiet quenching scorn.

It was M'Adam who stripped her icy garments off the child; M'Adam who wrapped her in hot blankets; M'Adam on whom the wee thing smiled when first she found her stolen senses.

In the end—

"Can I do anything to help?" asked the Parson humbly.

"Ye can shift oot o' this," the little man replied.

Wee Anne was soon recovered, and passed a pleasant hour, her plump fist in Red Wull's mouth pumping his tongue vigorously to and fro, while she compared him and her Bob to her new friend's disadvantage.

That evening David carried the child back to
Kenmuir.

. . . .

Early next morning, James Moore with Owd Bob
crossed the Stony Bottom for the first time for years.
M'Adam was at work at the top of the hill. At the
sound of the other's coming he looked up.

Straightway his eyes started. He turned, darted
into the house, his face ghastly over his shoulder, as
though at last in face of some long-anticipated fear.

The door slammed; a bolt rang home; feet clattered;
an upper window slashed wide. Then a shirt-sleeved
figure leant out; there was the flash and glint of a
gun-barrel sweeping round: and the whole in a crack.

"Bob! ahint me!"

The grey dog leapt; the gun-barrel swept; the click
of flint in a pan; and there towered, stern, cold, imperturbable, a bulwark of six-foot flesh between death
and its object.

So for a while; then the white face along the barrel
lifted a little, grinning horribly.

"Weel, James Moore?"

The other answered calm as though this was the
reception he had looked for.

"I com', M'Adam, to thank you"—

"Man! man! d'ye think I dinna ken what ye're
pyin' after? Na, na; ye'll e'en ha' to bide a while
yet. Ye've to win it first; ye've to beat Adam M'Adam
and his Red Wull—he! **he!**"

.

CHAPTER XIV

RED WULL HOLDS THE BRIDGE

AND always the rivals, red and grey, went about seeking their opportunity. But the Master was ever too quick for them.

Towards the end M'Adam, silent and secret, would urge on the red dog to battle; until, on a day in Grammoch-town, James Moore turned on him, eyes flashing steel.

"Does ta' think, thoo lil fule!" he cried, in his hard voice, "that onst they gat set we should iver git owder of them aff alive?"

The words pierced right home; for thereafter the little man was ever foremost to oppose his small form, buffer-like, between the would-be combatants. Indeed, it was no unmoving sight to see M'Adam, when the great dog's lust for war had overstepped right bounds, chastening him with a straw and crying reproachfully, "Wullie, Wullie, wad ye?" While the Tailless Tyke, who knew not what fear was, cowered into the ground as the fairy blows descended; scut hard down, eyes rolling upwards, craving grace less for the sin committed than for the master offended.

. . . .

Curse as M'Adam might, threaten as he might, when the time came Owd Bob won.

The styles of the rivals were well contrasted: the

patience, the insinuating eloquence, the splendid dash of the one; and the infernal bully fury of the other.

The issue was never in doubt. It may have been that the temper of the Tailless Tyke gave in the time of trial; it may have been that his sheep were wild, as M'Adam declared; assuredly not, as the little man alleged in choking voice, that they had been set aside of deliberate intent to ruin his chance. Certain it is that the great dog's tactics scared them into panic madness; and he never got them together again.

As for Owd Bob, his dropping, his driving, his penning, aroused the loud-tongued admiration of crowd and competitors alike. Patient yet persistent, quiet yet resolute, he allured his charges in the way with all his own inimitable tact.

When at length the verdict went forth, and it was known that, at long-last, after an interval of half a century, the Shepherds' Trophy was won again by a Grey Dog of Kenmuir, there was such a scene as has' been rarely witnessed on the slope behind the Dalesman's Daughter.

Great fists were slapped on mighty backs; great feet were stamped on the sun-dried banks of the Lea; stalwart lungs were strained to their uttermost capacity; and roars of "Moore!" "Owd Bob o' Kenmuir!" "The Grey Dogs!" thundered up the fell-sides and were flung thundering back.

Even James Moore was visibly moved as he worked through the cheering multitude; and Owd Bob, trotting by his side in quiet dignity, seemed to wave his silvery brush in acknowledgment.

Lady Eleanour, her cheeks flushed, waved her parasol. Parson Leggy danced an unclerical jig and shook hands with the Squire till both those fine old gentlemen were purple in the face. Long Kirby selected a small man in the crowd and bonneted him. While Tammas, Rob Saunderson, Tupper, Hoppin, Londesley, and the rest joined hands and went raving round like so many giddy girls.

But of them all, none was so uproarious in the mad heat of his enthusiasm as David M'Adam. Standing in the Kenmuir waggon beside Maggie, a conspicuous figure above the crowd, he roared in hoarse ecstasy, " Weel done, oor Bob! Weel done, Mr. Moore! Thoo's knocked him! Knock him agin! Owd Bob o' Kenmuir! Moore! Moore o' Kenmuir! Hip! hip!" until the noisy young giant attracted such attention in his boisterous delight, that Maggie must needs restrain him.

Alone on the far bank stood the vanquished pair.

The little man was trembling; his face was still wet from his exertions ; and as he hearkened to the ovation accorded to his conqueror, there was a piteous grin upon his face. In front stood the defeated dog, lips wrinkling, hackles rising, gazing across the stream like Satan cast from Paradise, as he, too, saw, heard, and understood.

"It's a gran' thing to ha' a dutiful son, Wullie!" the little man whispered, watching David's tossing figure. " He's happy—and so are they a'—not sae muckle that James Moore has won as that Adam M'Adam and his Red Wull are beat."

Then, breaking down for a moment—

" Eh, Wullie, Wullie! they're all agin us. It's you and I alane, lad."

Again, seeing the Squire followed by Parson Leggy, Viscount Birdsaye, and others of the gentry, forcing their way through the press to acclaim the victor, he continued—

" It's good to be in wi' the quality, Wullie. Niver

mak' a friend of a man beneath ye in rank, nor an enemy of a man aboon ye; that's a soond principle, gin ye'd thrive in honest England."

He stood there, alone with his dog, watching the crowd on the far slope as it surged around the committee tent. Only when the mass had packed in forest-thick phalanges about that ring, wherein, just a year ago, he had stood in very different circumstances, and was at length still, a wintry smile played for a moment on his lips. He laughed a mirthless laugh—

"Bide a wee, Wullie—he! he! bide a wee:

'The best laid schemes o' mice and men
Gang aft aglee.'"

As he spoke, there came down to him, above the noise of the many, a cry of wrathful dismay. The cheering ceased abruptly. A moment of blank silence, then there burst on the stillness such a tornado of indignation as rocked the air.

The crowd surged forward, then turned. Every eye was directed across the stream. A hundred damning fingers pointed at the lone figure there. Hoarse yells were raised, "Theer he be! Yon's him! What's he done wi' it! Thief! Throttle him!"

The mob came lumbering down the slope like one, thundering their imprecations on a thousand throats. They looked dangerous, and their wrath was stimulated by the knot of angry Dalesmen in the van. There was more than one white face amongst the women at the back, as they watched the crowd blundering blindly down the hill to the overwhelming of that small solitary. There were others besides Parson Leggy, the Squire, James Moore, and the police, in the thick of it all, striving frantically with voice and gesture, ay, and stick too, to stem the advance.

In vain. The dark wave rolled on, irresistible.

On the far bank stood the little man, motionless; awaiting them with a grin upon his face. And a little farther in front was the Tailless Tyke, his jagged underjaw shot forward in horrid invitation, his back and neck like a new-shorn wheat-field, as he rumbled a vast challenge.

"Come on, gentlemen!" the little man cried. "Come on! I'll bide for ye, never fear. Ye're a thousand to one and a dog. It's the odds ye like, Englishmen a'."

And the mob with murder in its throat, accepted the invitation and came on.

Then from the slope above, clear above the tramp of the multitude, a great voice bellowed, "Way! Way! Way for Mr. Trotter!"

The advancing host checked and opened out to let the Secretary of the meeting bundle through.

A small fat man, fussy at any time, and perpetually perspiring, he was now crimson with rage and running. He gesticulated wildly; vague words bubbled forth; and his short legs twinkled down the slope.

The crowd paused to admire. Someone shouted a witticism, and the crowd laughed. For the moment the situation was saved.

The fat Secretary hurried on, unheeding of any insult but the one. He bounced across the plank-bridge, and as he came closer M'Adam saw that in either hand he brandished a brick.

"What's this? What's this?" gasped the Secretary, puffing up, pudding-wise.

"Bricks, 'twad seem," the other answered.

"Where's the Cup? Champion, Challenge, etc.," the Secretary jerked out. "Mind, Sir, you're responsible! wholly responsible! Dents damages, delays! What's it

mean, Sir? these—these monstrous creations wrapped, I live, in straw, Sir, in the Cup case, Sir! the Cup case!) Cup! Infamous! Disgraceful! Insult—me—meet-;—committee—everyone. What's it mean, Sir?"
He paused to pant.

M'Adam approached him with one eye on the)wd which was heaving forward again, ominously ent now.

"I pit 'em there!" he whispered, and drew back to .tch the effect of his disclosure.

The Secretary gasped.

"You—you not only do this—amazing thing—these)nstrosities "— he hurled the bricks furiously down— ut you dare to tell me so!"

The little man smirked.

"'Do wrang and conceal it, do right and confess it,' it's Englishmen's motto and mine, as a rule. But this 1e I had ma reasons."

"Reasons, Sir! No reasons can justify such an extra- Jinary breach of all the—the decencies. Reasons? ε reasons of a maniac—a melodramatic maniac. Not say worse, Sir. Fraudulent detention—indictable ence, I say, Sir! . . . What were your precious 1sons?"

The mob, with Tammas and Long Kirby at their ad, had now attained the plank-bridge. For the)st part dangerously dumb, there were still isolated es of—

"Duck him!"

"Chuck him in!"

"An' the dorg!"

"There are my reasons!" said M'Adam, pointing at e forest of menacing faces. "Ye see I'm not beloved 1ang yonder gentlemen, and "— in a stage whisper in the other's ear—" I thocht maybe I'd be 'tacked on the road."

Tammas, foremost of the crowd, had now his foot upon the bridge.

"Robber! thief! Bide till we set hands on thee!" he yelled.

M'Adam turned.

"Wullie," he murmured, "keep the bridge!"

At the order, the Tailless Tyke shot gladly forward, and the leaders on the bridge as hastily back. The dog galloped on to the rattling plank, took his post fair and square in the centre of the narrow way, and stood facing the hostile crew like Cerberus guarding the gates of hell: his bull-head was thrust forward, hackles up, teeth glinting, and an earth-shaking rumble in his throat.

"Thoo first, ole lad!" urged Tammas, hopping agilely behind Long Kirby.

"Nay; t' old' 'uns lead," cried the big smith, his face grey-white. And wrenching round, he pinned the veteran by the arms, and held him forcibly before him as a covering shield. There ensued an unseemly struggle between the two valiants; Tammas bellowing in the throes of mortal fear and Long Kirby.

"Jim Mason 'll show us," he panted, at last.

"Nay," said honest Jim, "I'm none of a brave man."

Then Jem Burton 'd go first?

Nay; Jem had a lovin' wife and dear little kids at 'ome.

Rob Saunderson, happen?

Rob thowt not.

Then a tall figure came forcing through the crowd, a formidable knob-kerry in his hand.

"I's goin'!" said David.

'But thoo's not," answered burly Sam'l, gripping the y with arms like the roots of an oak. And the sense the Dalesmen was with the big man, for, as Rob underson put it, " I reck'n he'd liefer claw on to thy oat, lad, nor ony o' oors."

As there was no one forthcoming to claim the nour of the lead, Tammas came forward with ning counsel.

The strangers in the crowd were to be allowed the nour of the lead. Once on the bridge, the Dalesmen re to follow up, and keep a-shovin' and a-bovin on 1 forr'ad. "Then comes oor turn, sista'."

The wisdom of the serpent prevailed. Those who ew the Tailless Tyke were to wait on those who ln't. But these were in no hurry for the job. The sly aspect of the gaunt wolf-warrior of the bridge ore than sated them. Besides, there were ugly tales road.

By now there was a little naked space of green round : bridge-head. Round this the mob hedged; the Dales-:n in front striving knavishly back and bawling to)se behind to let be that shovin' ; and these latter ying valorously forward, yelling jeers and contumely their coward leaders.

And as they wedged and jostled thus, there stole out m their midst as gallant a champion as ever trod the 1ss.

He trotted out into the ring, the observed of all, d paused to gaze at the holder of the bridge. The n lit the sprinkling of snow on his head ; one fore-w was uplifted ; and he stood there, royally alert, th his airy grace, gallant insouciance, scanning his tagonist.

"Th' Owd 'Un!" went up in a roar fit to split the

air as the hero of the day was recognised. And the Dalesmen gave a pace forward spontaneously, as the grey knight-errant stole across the green.

"Oor Bob 'll fetch him!" they roared, their blood leaping to fever-heat, and gripped their sticks, determined in stern reality to follow now.

The gentleman in grey trotted up and on to the bridge, and paused. The silver standard of his line was waving high, his majestic frill clouding his neck like a Herdwick's ruff. And the holder of the bridge never moved.

Red and grey stood thus, face to face, the one gay yet resolute, the other petrified, his grim head slowly sinking between his fore-legs.

There was no shouting now: it was time for deeds, not words. Only, above the stillness, came a sound from the bridge like the snore of a giant in his sleep, and, blending with it, a low, deep, purring thunder like some monster cat well pleased.

"Wullie," came a solitary voice from the far side, "keep the bridge!"

One ear went back, one ear was still forward; the great head low and lower, that under-jaw clamorous for its prey, the molten eyes rolling upwards so that the watchers could see the murderous white.

The gentleman in grey advanced.

Then for the second time that afternoon, a voice, stern and hard, came ringing down from the slope above.

"Bob, lad, coom back."

"He! he! I thocht that was comin'," came the answering sneer from over the stream.

The grey dog heard, and checked.

Again the Master called.

"Bob, lad, coom in, I say."

At that the dog swung round, and marched slowly back, gallant as he had come, dignified still in his mortification.

And Red Wull threw back his head and bellowed a pæan of victory: challenge, triumph, scorn, all blended in that bull-like, earth-shaking blare.

.   .   .   .

In the meantime M'Adam and the Secretary had concluded their business. It had been settled that the Cup was to be delivered over to James Moore not later than the following Saturday.

"Saturday, see, at the latest!" the Secretary cried, as he turned and trotted off.

"Mr. Trotter," M'Adam called after him, "I'm sorry, but ye maun bide this side the Lea till I've reached the foot o' the Pass. Gin they gentlemen should set hands on me, why—Wullie has little sense o' humour!" and he shrugged his shoulders significantly. "Forbye, he's keepin' the bridge."

With that the little man strolled off leisurely; now dallying to pick a flower, now to wave a mocking hand at the thwarted mob; and so slowly on to the foot of the Pass.

Then he turned and whistled his shrill, peculiar call—

"Wullie, Wullie, to me!"

At that, with one last threat thrown at the thousand he had held at bay, the Tailless Tyke swung about and galloped heavily after his lord.

CHAPTER XV

THE PASSING OF THE CUP

ALL Friday M'Adam never left the kitchen. He sat opposite the Cup, hands on knees, staring with dim eyes: so a fond husband may sit for the last time beside the comrade of his life. And Red Wull watched with him.

Saturday came, and still the two kept their vigil. Towards night the little man rose all in a tremble, took the Cup tenderly in his arms, and sat down again.

Rocking like a mother with a dying child, he hugged it to him, crying silently. And Red Wull sat upon his haunches and weaved from side to side in mute sympathy.

As the dark was falling, David looked in. At the sound of the door the little man swung round, the Cup nursed in his arms, and glared sullen, noiseless, suspicious, yet seemed to recognise the boy no wit. In the half-light David could see the tears coursing down the wizened cheeks.

"'Pon ma life, he's gaein' daft," was his comment, as he turned away for Kenmuir. And the mourners were left to mourn.

"A few hours noo, Wullie," the little man wailed, "and she'll be gone. We won her, Wullie—won her fair. She's lit the hoose for us, she's saftened a' for us —and God kens we needed it; she was the ae thing e had to look to and love, and now they're takin' her wa', and 'twill be night agin."

He rose to his feet, and the great dog rose with him. His voice shrilled to a scream, and he swayed with the up in his arms till it seemed he must fall.

"Did they win her fair, Wullie? Na; they plotted, they conspired, they worked ilka man o' them agin us; and they beat us. But they shallna ha' her. Oor's or naebody's, Wullie! oor's or naebody's!"

He banged the Cup down and darted madly out. In a moment he was back again, brandishing an axe.

"Come on, Wullie! Noo's the day, and noo's the our!"

On the table before him shone the Trophy, serene and beautiful. The little man fell upon it, swinging his weapon like a flail.

"Oor's or naebody's, Wullie! Come on! Lay the proud usurpers low!" He aimed a deadly buffet; and the Shepherds' Trophy—the Shepherds' Trophy which had won through the hardships of a hundred years—was almost gone. It trembled as the blow descended. But the cruel steel missed, and sunk into the wood, clean and deep as a spade in snow.

Red Wull had leapt on to the table, and in cavernous voice was grumbling a chorus to his master's yells.

The little man danced up and down, tugging at the axe-shaft. "You and I, Wullie! you and I!

'Tyrants fall in every foe!
Liberty's in every blow!'"

The axe-head was immovable as the Pike.

"'Let us do or die.'"

The shaft snapped, and the little man tottered back. Red Wull jumped from the table, and in the act overthrew the Cup It toppled on to the floor, and rolled tinkling away. And the little man fled out of the house still screaming his war-song.

．．．．．．．

When late that night he returned home, the Cup was gone.

Down on his hands and knees, he traced its plain path in the dust, and marked the spot where it had rocked to sleep. Beyond that there was no sign.

At first his loss stunned him. Then he caught himself up and swung about the room like a derelict ship in a storm. He cursed; he screamed and beat the walls with fevered hands; he invoked a dreadful doom on James Moore, the grey dog, and his persecutors; he called on the hosts of heaven and hell to avenge him on his enemies, to damn them eternally, and in a breath implored Christ to right his wrong.

At length, wholly spent, he collapsed into a corner.

"It's David, Wullie, ye may depend; David that's robbed his father's hoose. Oh, it's a gran' thing to ha' a dutiful son!" And he bowed his grey head.

．．．．．．．

David it was. He had returned to the Grange during his father's absence, and taking the Cup from its grimy bed, had marched it away to its rightful home. For that evening at Kenmuir James Moore had said to him—

"David, your father's not sent t' Cup. I shall coom fetch it the morn." And David knew he meant it. Therefore, in order to save a collision between his father and his friend—a collision, the issue of which he dared hardly contemplate, knowing, as he did, the unalterable determination of the one and the lunatic passion of the other—the boy had resolved to fetch the Cup himself,

THE PASSING OF THE CUP 133

en and there, in the teeth, if needs be, of his father
nd the Tailless Tyke. And he had done it.

When he reached home that night, contrary to his
ont he marched straight into the kitchen.

There sat his father facing the door, awaiting him,
ands on knees. For once the little man was alone;
nd David, brave though he was, thanked Heaven
evoutly that Red Wull was elsewhere.

For a while father and son kept silence, watching one
nother like two fencers.

"'Twas you as took ma Cup?" asked the little man
t last, leaning forward in his chair.

"'Twas me as took Mr. Moore's Cup," the boy replied.

"You took it—pit up to it, nae doot, by James Moore!"
David made a gesture of dissent.

"Ay, by James Moore!" his father continued. "He
aurna come hissel' for his ill-gotten spoils, so he sent
he son to rob the father—the coward!" his whole
rame shook with passion. "I'd ha' thocht James
Moore 'd bin man enough to come hissel' for what he
anted. I see noo I did him a wrang—I misjudged
im. I kent him a heepocrite, ain o' yer unco gudes;
man as looks ae thing, says anither, and does a third;
nd noo I ken he's a coward. He's feared o' me, sic as
am." He rose from his chair and drew himself up to
is full meagre height.

"Mr. Moore had nowt to do wid it," David persisted.

"Ye're lyin'—James Moore pit ye to it. Ye'd ha' bin
villin' enough wi'oot him, if ye'd thocht o't, I grant ye.
But ye've no' the wits. All there is o' ye has gane to
nak' yer muckle body. Hooiver, that's no matter. I'll
ettle wi' James Moore anither time. I'll settle wi' you
oo David M'Adam!"

He paused and looked the boy over from head to foot.

"So ye're not only an idler! a wastrel! a liar!"—he spat the words out—"ye're—God help ye!—a thief!"

"I'm none of a thief!" the boy returned hotly; "I nobbut gave to a man what ma father—shame on him!—kept from him."

"Shame?" cried the little man, advancing with burning face.

"'Twas honourably done, keepin' what wasna thine to keep, holdin' back his reets from a man! Ay, if ony one's the thief it's not me, it's thee, I say, thee!" and he looked his father in the face with flashing eyes.

"I'm the thief, am I?" cried the other. "Tho' ye're three times ma size I'll teach ma son to speak so to me."

The old strap, now long disused, hung in the chimney corner. As he spoke the little man sprang back, ripped it from the wall, and, almost before David realised what he was at, had brought it down with a savage slash across his shoulders, and as he smote he whistled his shrill, imperative note—

"Wullie, Wullie, to me!"

David felt the blow through his coat, like a bar of hot iron across his back. His passion seethed within him. In a minute he would wipe out, once and for all, the score of years; for the moment, however, there was urgent business on hand; for outside he could hear the quick patter of feet hard-galloping, and the scurry of a huge creature racing madly to a call.

With a bound he sprang at the open door; and again the strap came lashing down, and a wild voice—

"Quick, Wullie! for God's sake, quick!"

David slammed the door. It shut with a rasping snap. At the same moment a great body from without thundered against it with terrific violence, and a deep voice roared like the sea thwarted of its prey.

"Too late, agin!" said David, breathing hard; and shut the bolt home with a clang. Then he turned on his father.

"Noo," said he; "man to man!"

"Ay," cried the other; "father to son!"

The little man half turned and leaped at the old musketoon hanging on the wall. He missed it, turned again, and struck with the strap full at his son's face. David caught the falling arm at the wrist, hitting it aside. Then he smote his father upon the chest, and the little man staggered back, gasping, while the strap dropped from his numbed fingers.

Outside, Red Wull whined and scratched, but the two men ignored him.

David strode forward: there was death in his face. The little man saw it: his time was come; but his bitterest foe never impugned Adam M'Adam's courage.

He stood huddled in the corner, all dishevelled, nursing one arm with the other, entirely unafraid.

"Mind, David," he said, quite calm, "murder 'twill be."

"Murder 'twill be!" the boy answered in thick voice, and was across the room.

Outside, Red Wull banged and clawed high up on the door with impotent pats.

Of a sudden the little man slipped his hand into his pocket, pulled out something, and flung it. The missile pattered on David's face like a raindrop on a charging bull, and he smiled as he came on. It dropped softly on the table at his side; he looked down and—it was the face of his mother which gazed up at him.

"Mother," he sobbed, stopping short—"Mother! ma God, ye saved him—and me!"

He stood there, utterly unhinged, whimpering.

It was a while before he had pulled himself together; then he walked to the wall, took down a pair of shears and seated himself at the table, still trembling. Near him lay the miniature, all torn and crumpled, and beside it the deep-buried axe-head.

Picking up the strap, he began to snip it into little pieces.

"Theer! and theer! and theer!" he said, with each snip; "if ye hit me agin there may be no mother to save ye."

Red and Grey

RED AND GREY

TIME has rolled on.
In the kitchen of Kenmuir the firelight rollicks on red-tiled floor, on dark shutters, and great oak press. Before the blaze sits James Moore, unchanged despite the whirligig of time. On his knee dances Wee Anne, the ruddy firelight in her hair, battering at the lean cheek above her. The Master's grim mouth is relaxed; love mellows the austere face. It is only at such moments that you see James Moore as he is: a stern, cold man, with a very tender nature deep hid beneath a veil of ice.

From the back of the room Maggie, a woman now in face and figure, looks up to laughingly remonstrate with her father for spoiling the child; while beneath the table, young Andrew whittles at a bludgeon.

Above the mantelpiece hangs a bright-barrelled musket, with flask and powder-horn. Beneath again, a painting of a grey dog's head. Crude it is, unsatisfactory, yet the painter has caught a little that wistful languor of the sad-clouded eyes that only appertains, and always, to a Grey Dog of Kenmuir—Rex, son of Rally. And worthily placed beneath the old hero's portrait, challenging the eye in that homely kitchen as a diamond strung on a necklace of pearls, in large chaste majesty, is the Shepherds' Trophy. On its glory-scroll the last three names—

    A. M'Adam's . . . . . Wull
    J. Moore's . . . . . Bob
    J. Moore's . . . . . Bob

And there beneath his master's chair, his dark head peering out, his two soul-lights now softly shuttered now shining out again like beacon-fires, lies Owd Bob o' Kenmuir—the best sheep-dog in the North.

One more tremendous victory on the banks of the Silver Lea, one last, and the Dale Cup, which for a hundred years had wandered homeless from North to South, from South to North again, would find a final resting-place in the hoar farmhouse beneath the Pike.

It was on the occasion of his second victory that old Lochrae, most critical of captious Scots, declared roundly in a lull in the cheering—

"The best sheep-dog in the North, as I live!" Whereat the uproar was renewed ten-fold.

"And why not the best in the world, my lord?" asked Parson Leggy, as soon as he could make himself heard.

"An' why not that, owd Cod-fish?" asked a shrill, fierce voice from the crowd. (It was Tammas—alack-the-day!—Tammas Thornton, drunk with victory and other things.)

The old lord had his answer pat.

"Aren't the sheep-dogs of the North the best in the world?" he cried, and straightway found himself the best-loved man among ten thousand. It was after the presentation of the Cup that Lochrae, cannie man, offered James Moore one hundred pounds down for the grey dog; and when that was refused handed him a blank cheque, remarking resignedly, "Do what you like with 't."

"Then, my lord;" said the Master drily, "I'll do this!" and tore the paper into little pieces. Whereat there were roars of—"Faithfu' as the Moores and their tykes!" —"Mak' him eat it!"—"Stuff it down t'owd lad's gizzern!" and more to the same effect. It was then that James Moore had said, "We've never parted wid oor dogs and I'd be the last to part wid the best."

Since that day the one burning question discussed in every tap-room from the Black Water to Grammoch Pike had been: Would oor Bob—"Th' Owd 'Un," as they loved to call him—win again—win outright? Could he, owd as he was in truth now, beat but once again that other? of whom after the last battle Teddy Bolstock had heard one judge to another, "But for the turn at the ghyll Red had won."

. . . . . .

Owd Bob o' Kenmuir.

Mention that name to any man within a score mile radius of the Muir Pike; ask him if he has ever known or heard tell of a name to be paired with that. At first he will look you up and down in that slow, critical way these Dalesmen have, as if to gauge your earnestness. Satisfied on that point, he will laugh you to scorn; and finally, if he thinks to have a ready listener will yarn for hours about the doings of the "best sheepdog as ever was or will be."

And many are the stories of him: some heavy with the solemn interest of life and death, some light as laughter; some dealing with his own profession—shepherding; some touching on wider and graver issues. Only, in hearing them, you must ever be prepared for that inevitable corollary, "An' I mind me hoo, as it med be just then, Adam M'Adam and his Red Wull"—

The old dog's feats were the one subject on which

James Moore waxed sometimes almost voluble. "Get him on about Th' Owd 'Un, and, 'pon my life, he's quite the orator, eh, eh!" said Squire Sylvester.

"Yes," agreed Parson Leggy; "the two of them are more like a man and his familiar friend than master and dog. Only yesterday he said to me, 'I've had a mort of the Grey Dogs in ma time and yet none has bin the same to me as t' owd lad here.' And I believe him."

Yet a stranger, seeing the two together, might never have guessed the bond between them, so undemonstrative were they. Of that silent, subtle sympathy there could be no doubt, however, did you watch them at work; quiet, resolute, swift to action, slow to anger.

And the Dalesmen were bursting with pride in that dog whose reputation had spread through half two kingdoms.

"There's no' the marrer of him in t' land," they would affirm; and were fierily jealous for his claim as peerless.

In those days it was bad to depreciate the best sheep-dog in the North anywhere between the Scaur and the White Stones. Jim Mason, a man of peace, chased a scoffing stranger all down the High, ran him to ground in the blind Butcher's Alley, and there instilled the truth into his bosom as he sat upon it. Tupper banged and danged a huge Yorkshireman in the market-place for mentioning Owd Bob and spitting on the ground in the same breath. The Tyke had no insolent intent, at least so he afterwards declared, but—well, he sinned and he suffered, and what would you more? Whilst even Sam'l Todd, a hard man to rouse, but, once roused, harder still to stop, offered at the Border Ram to flatten any man's snout who dared to impugn the grey dog's supremacy—a standing challenge which was

RED AND GREY

never taken up—except, indeed, by little M'Adam; and him Sam'l met with, "Iss, but thoo goes for nowt, thoo does: I said a man—not a maggot." Whereat M'Adam smote him in the face—which is not this tale.

. . . .

On some defeat has an inspiring effect, on some the reverse. In the case of Adam M'Adam and his Red Wull, it seemed to bring out the best and the worst that was in them.

Amongst the Dalesmen, fear, intense yet never intense enough, hate, bubbling daily to the boiling-point, and jealousy of this little man they said was mad, and the great dog they alleged was bent on murder, were tinged with an unwilling spice of admiration for the pair who would not own defeat, whose deeds were only second to one other couple's.

And the little man, day by day more dangerous, hourly arousing bitterer resentment, cursing them all and James Moore in particular as agin him and his Wullie, would many a time have been handled to his hurt but that the Tailless Tyke was always there, praying aloud for blood.

As a sheep-dog, the Dalesmen to this day have nothing but abuse for Th' Owd 'Un's rival, so bitter is the old antipathy, so jealous their loyalty to that other name. But as the "Terror o' th' Border," the most terrific punisher who ever slew his foe, many a man still cherishes a sneaking pride in the Tailless Tyke.

You may yet hear in the land of lakes how he dealt with that terrible trio, the Wexer, Wenus, and Wan Tromp; those three fair sisters of whom John Swan declared, tears in his eyes, as he looked upon their ruin, "I did reck'n my three could tackle any livin' thing as showed teeth."

Yet with that ferocity which won him an infernal notoriety through three countries, men who would then have murdered him for a song will now confess that he combined a certain rude chivalry, a savage nobility that scorned to take advantage of an adversary. Not even Long Kirby could call him bully; not even Tammas Thornton could deny him courage. Never — with always one exception — was he the aggressor.

Like his master's, his personality invited antipathy. He was outlawed amongst his kind as M'Adam amongst his. Barely a dog in the countryside, barring only the little draggle-tailed lady of the Border Ram, but had at some time bowed before his teeth, and was nursing his revenge till a day should bring his chance. Yet—always with the one exception—he never attacked. One by one they sought him in battle, and he pinned them, shook them, and let them go; and they never came again. Now, when he followed his master into a tap-room, where M'Adam established himself there did he; and the other dogs, ousted if necessary from their place, gathered together, scowled, bristled, and yet dared nothing: for they knew their lord, and, wise in their generation, waited.

It was all on behalf of the little lady of the Border Ram that he fought the bloodiest battle of them all— his great fight with the Lion Dogs of Wood's travelling circus: Wilhelm and Bismarck, that truculent pair, who nightly walked the stage in charge of Great Cæsar of the mighty mane.

"On to him, Bissy! Eat him, Wilhelm! Mince the poker for his insolence—ha! ha!" laughed young Wood as the fray began.

And "He! he!" giggled M'Adam, biting his nails; but his face was dead-white.

"Separate 'em!" cried a stranger in the fast-hurrying crowd.

"Oh, ay," said M'Adam, leaping aside as the fighting three nigh swung him off his legs; "the sand from the sea!" And his face was wet as the grass in the morning.

Down the High-street they fought; up the market-place; past the clock-tower; to the Hangman's Field without the town. Silent, murderous, lurching, swinging, heedless of the dumb mob hemming them all around.

It was the only time, they say, but once, the Terror fought in earnest, fought to kill.[1] It was the only time, but once, Red Wull was ever really roused, fighting it to a finish, exerting his whole gigantic strength in the bloody silence of that struggle. Certainly the only time he had every Dalesman present at his back.

And all through, from the noisy grapple to the noiseless end, a little white-faced figure pattered round and round betwixt the combatants and crowd.

"Here! that'll do: he'll be hurt!" blustered Wood, five minutes from the onset.

"Oh, ay," said M'Adam, like a man in a trance; "he will." And the perspiration rained off his face as he held on his revolving way.

Another five minutes and—

"Call him off!" roared the showman.

([1] Bellerophon, indeed, he killed because it was his duty. The slaying of the Mammoth was, I still believe, a mere mischance; for he meant that truculent mastiff no real harm—only to quell his braggadocio. While the Texer and Van Tromp, great-hearted Amazons, would allow him no alternative, preferring death rather than defeat; and you may be sure that the Venus, fairest of the brindled three, would never have survived her sisters had she not been "outed" at the onset with cracked jaw and broken skull.)

"Oh, ay," muttered M'Adam, never pausing in his run; "Wullie, come aff."

Another pause and then—

"It's murder!" yelled Wood. "He'll kill 'em!"

"Oh, ay," came the little voice; "he will."

"I'll summons ye, by ——, I will!" screamed the other. "Call him off! Fetch a gun someone! Hi! a quid for a gun!"

"Oh, ay," said M'Adam, dodging round; "Wullie come aff." And they heard him gasp as Wilhelm took a deeper hold.

"They're worth two hundred pounds the pair!" shrieked the showman. "They're my livelihood!"

"Oh, ay," said M'Adam, never taking his eyes off the battle; "Wullie's my life." And they say his white-lipped agony, as Red Wull slithered and almost fell, was pitiful to behold.

Another pause.

Bismarck was down; and Wilhelm going under.

The showman rushed in.

"I'll stop it, by ——!"

"Back, thoo madman!" panted the crowd; and someone jerked him off. "He'll do for thee else when he's done thy dogs."

When at length it was over, and Wilhelm and Bismarck, never again to be admired of emperors, never again to be caressed by queens, were borne slowly off the field, Wood swearing and crying alternately, a little man sat by the roadside, bathing the bloody head between his knees, and whispering, "Wullie, Wullie, bad dog! ye play sae rough."

. . . . . .

So through those years one seems to see that pair—Adam M'Adam and his Red Wull—forcing their way through the hostile crowd, doing great deeds and undoing them, indomitable: the little man, who was a hero and thought he was a martyr, with the face of a fanatic, mad eyes, and twitching fingers, plotting revenge, babbling of conspiracy, shouting his challenge; the great dog, saturnine, sinister, scowling defiance: the two facing their enemies always alone and always together.

And ever and anon a dark sad face comes softly on the scene. A dash; an uproar; a little, darting, heroic figure; a shrill voice, "Call him aff, James Moore!" then a hand uplifted; a straw descending; a huge cowering form; and again that voice, "Wullie, Wullie, wad ye?"

In season, out of season, they were always at it, those two. Often and oftener that straw was in request. Again and again the fight that must some day be was staved off by a miracle. At length M'Adam only saved it by turning on Jem Burton and assaulting him. "Wullie! Wullie, to me!" he cried, in voice of last extremity—"They're on me! Murder!" At the cry the great dog turned; the fight was again postponed; and Jem Burton, with a face like the moon and the agility of an athlete, was up the ladder and into the loft.

And so, it seems to me, those two go down the vale— Red and Grey wrestling in mortal rivalry: the one vengeful, vindictive; the other courteous still, gallant as always, ready, ay, and willing; each always outdoing the other; each in his way unapproachable: both awaiting the end.

Part IV

The Black Killer

CHAPTER XVI

A MAD MAN

TAMMAS is on his feet in the tap-room of the Arms, brandishing a pewter.

"Gen'lemen!" he cries, his old face flushed—"I gie ye a toast. Stan' oop!"

The knot of Dalesmen round the fire rise like one. The old man waves his mug before him, reckless of the good ale that drips on to the floor.

"The best sheep-dog i' t' North — Owd Bob o' Kenmuir!" he cries.

In an instant there is uproar: the merry applause of clinking pewters; the stamping of feet; the rattle of sticks. Rob Saunderson and Jim Mason are cheering with the best. Tupper and Ned Hoppin bellow each into the other's ear; Long Kirby and Jem Burton bang one another valorously; even Sam'l Todd and Sexton Ross are roused from their habitual melancholy.

"Here's to Th' Owd 'Un! Here's to oor Bob!" yell stentorian voices; while Rob Saunderson has jumped on to a chair.

"Wid t' best sheep-dog i' t' North I gie ye the Shepherds' Trophy!—won outreet, as will be."

Instantly the clamour redoubles.

"T' Dale Cup and Th' Owd 'Un!—t' Trophy and oor Bob!—'Ip, 'ip for the Grey Dogs!—'Ip, 'ip for t' best sheep-dog as ever was or will be!—'Ooray, 'ooray!"

It is some while before the noise subsides. Slowly the enthusiasts resume their seats.

"Gentlemen a'!"

A little unconsidered man is standing up at the back of the room. His face is aflame, and his hands twitch spasmodically. In front, with hackles drawn and greedy-gleaming jaw, a gaunt red-grizzled dog of war.

"Noo," cries the little man, "I daur ye to repeat that lie!"

"Lie!" screams Tammas; "lie! I'll gie 'im lie! Lemme at 'im, I say!"

The old man in his fury has nigh surmounted the encircling ring of chairs before Jim Mason on the one hand and Rob Saunderson on the other can pull him back.

"Coom, Mr. Thornton!" soothes Rob, "let un' bide. Ye're not angered by the likes o' him, surely?" and he jerks contemptuously towards the solitary figure at his back.

Tammas resumes his seat unwillingly.

The little man behind remains mute, waiting for his challenge to be taken up. In vain. And as he looks at the range of broad, impassive backs turned on him, he smiles bitterly.

"They dursen't, Wullie, not a man of them a'. They're one—two—three—four . . . eleven to one, Wullie, and yet they dursen't. Eleven of them, and every man a coward! Long Kirby — Thornton — Tupper—Todd—Hoppin—Ross—Burton . . . and the

rest, and not one but's a bigger man nor me and yet—
Weel, we might ha' kent it. We should ha' kent
Englishmen by noo. They're aye the same and aye
have bin. They tell lies, black lies"—

Tammas is half out of his chair, and only forcibly
restrained by the men on either hand.

"—And then they haena the courage to stan' by 'em.
Ye're English, ivery man o' ye, to yer marrow."

The little man's voice rises to a sob. He snatches up
a tankard.

"Englishmen!" he cries, waving it before him:
"Here's a health!—The best sheep-dog as iver penned
a flock—Adam M'Adam's Red Wull!" He pauses,
pewter at his lips, and regards his audience with
flashing eyes. There is no response from them.

"Wullie, here's to you!" he cries. "Luck and life to
ye, ma trusty fier'! Death and defeat to yer enemies!

   'The warld's wrack we share o't,
    The warstle and the care o't.'"

He raises the tankard and drains it to the lees.

Then drawing himself up, he addresses his audience
once more.

"An' noo I'll warn ye aince and for a', and ye may
tell James Moore I said it: he may plot agin us,
Wullie and me; he may threaten us; he may win the
Cup outreet for yon grey devil; but there was niver a
man or dog yet as did Adam M'Adam and his Red
Wull a hurt but in the end he wush't his mither hadna
born him."

A little later and he walks out of the inn, his faithful
retainer at his heels.

It is then that Rob Saunderson says—

"The lil man's mad; he'll stop at nothin'," and
Tammas who answers—"Nay; not even murder."

M'Adam had aged much of late. His thin hair was altogether white; his eyes like flames; and his hands were always twittering, as though he were in everlasting pain.

After the grey dog's second victory he had become morose and moody. At home, he would often sit silent for hours, drinking and glaring at the place where the Cup had been. Sometimes he talked in low, eerie voice to Red Wull; and twice David, turning suddenly, had caught his father glowering stealthily at him with such an expression on his face as chilled the boy's blood. The two never spoke now; and David held this sureptitious deadly enmity far worse than the old-time perpetual warfare.

It was the same at the Sylvester Arms. The little man sat alone with Red Wull, exchanging words with no man, drinking steadily, brooding over his wrongs; and ever and anon galvanised into sudden despairing eloquence.

Other people than Tammas Thornton came to the conclusion that M'Adam would stop at nothing in the undoing of James Moore or the grey dog. They said drink and disappointment had turned his head; that he was mad and dangerous. And on New Year's Day matters seemed coming to a crisis; for it was reported that in the gloom of a snowy evening he had drawn a knife on the Master in the High-street, but slipped before he could accomplish his fell design.

Parson Leggy confessed candidly that he should be thankful when the last great struggle was over, and the Trophy won outright or lost for ever. He didn't want a *cause célèbre* in his parish:— Leaded headlines: Murder on the Moors—Dogged by a Dog—The Parson Interviewed—Suspicions! Ugh-h!

Most of them all, David was haunted with an everpresent fear. For he had heard his father when the drink was in him screaming, battering in the deadly silence of the night; calling on God to avenge him on his enemies, to up and smite, to overwhelm them in awful catastrophe—had heard and feared. The boy even went so far as to warn his friend against his father. But the Master only smiled grimly.

"Thank ye, lad, thank ye. But I reck'n we can fend for oorsel's, Bob and I—eh, Owd 'Un?"

Anxious as David in fact was, he was not above presuming on the existing apprehension to take advantage of Maggie's fears. One Sunday night he was escorting her home from church, when, just before the larch-copse,

"Goo' sakes! what's that?" he ejaculated, in horror-laden tones.

"What, Davie?" cried the girl, shrinking to him in a tremble.

"Couldna say for sure. It med be owt, or agin it med be nowt. But grip thoo my arm, I'll grip thy waist."

Maggie demurred.

"Canst see owt?" she asked, still in a flutter.

"Be'ind th' 'edge."

"Wheer?"

"Theer," pointing vaguely.

"I canna see nowt."

"Why, theer! lass. Doestna see? . . . Pit your head along o' mine—so — closer — closer yet!" then in aggrieved tones, "Whativer's gotten to thee, wench? I med be a leprosy, surely."

But the girl was walking away, her head high as the snow-capped Pike.

"So long as I live, David M'Adam, I'll niver go to church wid thee agin."

A retort so obvious could not be passed by.

"Yes, but you will though—onst," he answered low.

Maggie whisked round, superbly indignant.

"What doesta' mean, Sir—r—r?"

"Thoo kens what I mean, lass," he replied, sheepish and shuffling before her queenly anger.

She looked him up and down and down and up again.

"I'll niver speak to thee agin, Mr. M'Adam," she cried, "not if it was ever so. . . . Nay, I'll walk home by myself, thank you. I'll ha' nowt to do wi' thee."

So the two must return to Kenmuir, one behind the other, like a lady and her footman.

David's audacity had many times already been nigh to causing a rupture. The occurrence behind the hedge set the cap on his impertinences. That was past enduring, and Maggie by her bearing let him know it.

David endured the girl's new attitude for twelve minutes by the kitchen clock. Then, "Sulk wi' me, indeed! I'll teach her!" and he marched out of the door, "niver to cross it agin, ma wud!" But afterwards he relented so far as to continue his visits to Kenmuir, always, however, pointedly excluding from his favour the sweet offender, who in her turn would proceed about her business all rosy with chin-tilted disdain.

. . . .

The suspicions that M'Adam cherished dark designs against James Moore were somewhat confirmed in that, on several occasions in the bitter dusks of January afternoons, a little insidious figure was seen lurking amongst the farm-buildings of Kenmuir.

Once Sam'l Todd caught the little man fairly. Sam'l took him up bodily and carried him down the slope to the Wastrel, shaking him gently the while. Across the stream he put him on his feet.

"If I catch thee cadgerin' aroun' the farm agin, lil man," he admonished, with warning finger, "I'll tak' thee and drap thee in t' sheep-wash, sista' noo? I'd ha' done it this time an thoo'd bin a bigger and a younger mon. But theer! thoo's sic an atomy bit. Noo, rin away home." And the little man slunk off.

For a time he appeared there no more. Then, one evening, James Moore, going the round of the outbuildings, felt Owd Bob stiffen against his side.

"What's oop, lad?" he whispered, halting; and, dropping his hand on the old dog's neck, felt a ruff rising beneath it.

"Steady, lad, steady!" he whispered. "What is't?"

Peering forward into the looming night, at length he discerned a little familiar figure huddled away in the crevice between two stacks.

"Thee is't, M'Adam?" he cried, and bending, seized a wisp of Owd Bob's coat in a grip like a vice.

Then in a great voice, moved to rare anger,

"Oot o' this afoor I do thee a hurt, thoo miserable spyin' creetur! Ye mun wait till dark cooms to hide ye, ye coward, afoor ye daur coom crawlin' aboot ma hoose, skearin' t' women-folk, and up to yer devilments. An thoo's owt to say to me, coom like a man in the open day.... Noo pack! afoor I lay ma clutches on thee."

He stood there in the dusk, tall and mighty, a terrible figure, one hand pointing to the gate, the other still grasping the grey dog.

The little man scuttled away in the half-light, and out of the yard.

On the plank-bridge he turned and shook his fist at the darkening house.

"Curse ye, James Moore!" he sobbed. "I'll be even wi' ye yet."

CHAPTER XVII

DEATH ON THE MARCHES

ON the top of this there followed an attempt on Th' Owd 'Un. At least there was no other accounting for the affair.

In the dead of a long-remembered night James Moore was waked by a low moaning beneath his room. He leaped out of bed and ran to the window to see his favourite dragging about the yard, the dark head down, the proud brush for once lowered, the supple limbs, wooden, heavy, unnatural—altogether pitiful.

In a moment he was downstairs and out.

"Whativer's gotten to thee, Owd 'Un?" he cried, in anguish.

At the sound of that dear voice the old dog tried to struggle to him; could not, and fell, whimpering.

In a second the Master was with him, examining him tenderly, and crying for Sam'l, who slept above the stables.

There was every symptom of foul play: the tongue was swollen and almost black; the breathing laboured; the body twitched horribly; and the soft grey eyes were blood-streaked and straining in agony.

With the aid of Sam'l and Maggie, drenching first and stimulants after, the Master pulled him round. And soon Jim Mason and Parson Leggy, hurriedly summoned, came running hot-foot to the rescue.

Prompt and stringent measures saved the victim, but only just. For a time the best sheep-dog in the North was pawing at the Gate of Death. And as they doctored him in the kitchen it almost seemed that the great silver Cup upon the mantelpiece quivered in its anxiety. It was a close thing: Owd Bob o' Kenmuir was nigh gone. In the end, as the grey dawn broke, the danger passed.

The attempt, if attempt it was, aroused passionate indignation in the countryside. It seemed the culminating point of the excitement long seething.

There were no traces of the culprit; not a vestige to lead to incrimination. But as to the perpetrator, if there were no proofs there were yet fewer doubts. Parson Leggy, who was seldom hard upon his fellow-men, declared to the Squire with an emphatic shrug of his shoulders, "You know the motive and you know the man." Whilst amongst the Dalesmen suspicion amounted to certainty.

At the Sylvester Arms, Long Kirby asked M'Adam point blank for his explanation of the matter.

"Hoo do I 'count for it?" the little man cried. "I dinna 'count for it ava."

"Then hoo did it happen?" asked Tammas harshly.

"I dinna believe it did happen," the little man replied. "I haud it's a lee o' James Moore's — a charactereestic lee."

Whereat they chucked him out incontinently; for the Terror for once was elsewhere.

Now that afternoon is to be remembered for threefold causes. Firstly, as has been said, M'Adam was alone. Secondly, a minute after his ejectment, the window of the tap-room was thrown wide and the little man looked in. He spoke no word, but those dim,

Master!" and he set off running towards the dog; while James Moore, himself excited now, followed hard.

Some score yards from the lower edge of the spinney, upon the farther side of the ridge, a tiny beck tinkled in its black bed. The two men, as they topped the rise, noticed a flock of black-faced sheep clustered in the dip twixt wood and stream. They stood marshalled in close array, facing half towards the wood, half towards the new comers; heads up, eyes glaring, handsome as sheep only look when scared.

On the crest of the ridge the two men halted. The postman stood with his head a little forward, listening intently. Then he dropped in the heather like a dead man, pulling the other with him.

"Doon, man!" he whispered, clutching at Gyp with his spare hand.

"What is't?" asked the Master, now thoroughly roused.

"Summat movin' i' t' wood," the other whispered, listening weasel-eared.

So they lay motionless for a while; but there came no sound from the copse.

"Happen 'twas nowt," the postman at length allowed, peering cautiously about. "And yet I thowt—I dunno reetly what I thowt." Then starting to his knees, with a hoarse cry of terror, "Save us! what's yon theer?"

Then the Master raised his head and noticed, lying in the gloom between them and the array of sheep, a still, white huddle.

James Moore was a man of deeds.

"It's past waitin'," he cried, and sprang forward, heart in mouth.

The sheep stamped and shuffled as he came, and yet did not break.

"Ah, thanks be!" he cried, dropping beside the dull-glimmering heap; "it's nobbut a sheep." As he spoke, his hands were wandering deftly over the carcase. "But what's this?" he called. "Stout[1] she was as me. Look at her fleece—crisp, close, strong; feel the flesh—firm as a rock. And ne'er a bone broke, ne'er a scrat on her body a pin could mak'. Healthy as a man—and yet dead as mutton!"

Jim, still all a-shake from the horror of his fear, came up and knelt beside his friend.

"Ah, but theer's bin devilry in this!" he said; "I reck'ned they sheep had bin badly skeared and not so long agone."

"Sheep-murder, sure enough," the other answered. "No fox's doin': a girt-grown two-shear as could 'maist knock a h'ox."

Jim's hands travelled from the body to the dead thing's throat. He screamed.

"Odswinge, Master! See theer!" He held his hand up in the moonlight. It dripped red. "And warm—yet warm!"

"Tear some bracken, Jim," ordered the other; "and set a-light."

The postman did as bid. For a moment the fern smouldered and smoked, then the flame ran crackling along and shot up in the darkness, weirdly lighting the scene: to the right the low wood, a block of solid blackness against the sky; in front the yellow wall of sheep, with spurting breath and eyes shining in the gloom; and as centrepiece that white, ghastly corpse with the kneeling men and lurcher sniffing tentatively round.

The victim was subjected to a critical examination.

[1] Stout—hearty.

smouldering eyes wandered from face to face, resting for a second on each as if to burn them on his memory.

"I'll remember ye, gentlemen," he said at length, shut the window and was gone.

Thirdly, for a reason now to be told.

On this day, James Moore, leaving the old dog behind to rest and resume his outraged vitality, had crossed to Grammoch-town. On his way home he met Jim Mason with Gyp, the faithful Betsy's unworthy successor. Together they started for the long tramp home. And that journey is marked with a red stone in this story.

All day long the hills had been lost in mist. Throughout there had been an accompanying drizzle; and in the distance the wind had moaned a storm-menace. To the darkness of the day was added the sombreness of falling night as the three began the ascent of the Pass. As they emerged into the Devil's Bowl, it was altogether black and blind. But the threat of wind had passed, leaving utter stillness; and the splash of an otter on the far side of the Tarn clanged in the silence as they skirted that darkling water. When at length the last steep rise on to the Marches had been topped, a breath of soft air smote them lightly, and the curtain of fog began drifting away, leaving behind luminous night.

The two men swung steadily through the heather with that reaching stride the birthright of moor-men and Highlanders. They talked but little: a word or two on sheep and the approaching lambing-time; thence on to the coming Trials; the Shepherds' Trophy; Owd Bob and the attempt on him; and from that to M'Adam and the Tailless Tyke.

"Doesta' reck'n M'Adam had a hand in't?" the postman was asking.

"There's no proof."

"'Ceptin' he's mad to get shut o' Th' Owd 'Un afoor Cup Day."

"'Im or me; it mak's no differ."

Jim looked up at his companion.

"Doesta' think it'll coom to that?" he asked.

"What?"

"Why; murder."

"Not if I can help it," the other answered grimly.

The fog had quite cleared off by now, and the moon was up. To their right, on the crest of a rise some two hundred yards away, a murk cloud of wood bristled against the sky. As they passed it, a blackbird rose up screaming; and a brace of wood-pigeons winged noisily away.

"Hullo! hark to the yammerin'!" muttered Jim, stopping; "and at this time o' neet too!"

Some rabbits, playing in the moonlight on the outskirts of the wood, sat up, listened, and hopped back into security. At the same moment a big hill-fox slunk out of the covert. He stole a pace forward and halted, listening with one ear back and one paw raised; then cantered silently away in the gloom, passing close to the two men, yet observing them not at all.

"What's oop, I wonder?" mused the postman.

"The fox set 'em clackerin', I reck'n."

"Not he; he was skeared 'maist oot o' his skin," the other answered; then in tones of suppressed excitement, with his hand on the Master's arm, "And sitha'! theer's ma Gyp a-beckonin' on us!"

There, indeed, on the crest of the rise beside the wood stood the little lurcher, now looking back at his master, and then stealing forward.

"Ma wud! theer's summat wrong yonder," cried Jim, and jerked the postbags off his shoulder. "Coom on

CHAPTER XVIII

THE BLACK KILLER

THAT was the first only of a long series of such crimes.

Those who have not lived in a desolate country like that about the Muir Pike, where sheep are paramount and every other man engaged in the profession pastoral, can hardly imagine the sensation aroused. In market-place, tavern, or cottage, the subject of conversation was always the latest sheep-murder and the yet undetected criminal.

Sometimes there would be a lull, and the shepherds would begin to breathe more freely. Then there would come a stormy night, when the heavens were veiled in the cloak of crime and the wind moaned fitfully over mere and marches, and another victim was added to the lengthening list.

It was always such black nights, nights of wind and weather when no man would be abroad, that the murderer chose for his bloody work. And that was how he earned his ominous name—the Black Killer. In the Dale-land they still call a wild, wet night a "Black Killer's neet"; for, say they, " His ghaist'll be oot the neet."

There was hardly a farm in the countryside but was marked with the seal of blood. Kenmuir escaped and the Grange; Rob Saunderson at the Holt, and Tupper at Swinsthwaite; and those four only.

As for Kenmuir, Tammas declared with a certain grim pride, "He knows better'n to coom wheer Th' Owd 'Un be." Whereat M'Adam was seized with a fit of internal spasms, rubbing his knees and cackling insanely for half an hour afterwards. And as for the luck of the Grange—well, there was a reason for that, too, so the Dalesmen affirmed.

Though the area of crime stretched from the Black Water to Grammoch-town, there was never a sign of the perpetrator. The Killer did his bloody work with a thoroughness, a devilish cunning, that defied detection. It was plain that each murder might be set down to the same agency. Each was stamped with the same unmistakable sign-manual: one sheep killed, its throat torn into red rags, and the others untouched.

It was these strange concomitant circumstances, the cold-blooded calculating nature of the crimes, which aroused the general interest. For the matter created a sensation far outside the Dale-land.

In the journals devoted to flock-and-stock interests, each new murder was faithfully catalogued, and its attendant circumstances described in the minutest detail.. There was a lengthy and heated correspondence in the *Fell* on the subject; the general tendency being towards the incredulous. Those who gave themselves out as authorities declared at first that the whole thing must be a hoax. Reluctantly convinced at length that the crimes were, in fact, no myth, these knowing ones were aroused to an ecstasy of ridicule by the assertion — originating in James Moore, upheld by Parson Leggy and every Dalesman—that the Black Killer was a sheep-dog.

In the end Parson Leggy wrote a long letter to the *Fell*, setting forth his reasons for the belief. But the

the throat, and that only, had been hideously mauled; the flesh hung in shreds from gaping wounds; on the ground all about were little pitiful dabs of wool, wrenched off in a struggle; and crawling amongst the torn roots, a snake-like track of red led down to the stream.

"A dog's doin' and no mistakin' that," said Jim, at length.

"Ay," answered the Master, with slow emphasis; "and a sheep-dog's, too, and an old 'un's, sista'? or I'm no shepherd."

"Why that?" the postman asked, puzzled.

"Becos," the Master answered, "'im as did this killed for blood—and for blood only. If it had bin any other dog—greyground, bull, tarrier, or even a young sheep-dog—d'ye think he'd ha' stopped wid the one? Not he; he'd ha' gone through 'em, and be runnin' 'em as like as not yet, nippin' 'em, pullin' 'em down, till he'd mebbe killed the half. But 'im as did this killed for food, I's uphod. He got it—killed just the one, and nary touched t' others, sista', Jim?"

The postman whistled long and low.

"It's what owd Wrottesley'd tell on," he said; "I never nobbut half-believed him then—I do noo, though. D'ye mind what t' owd lad 'd tell, Master?"

James Moore nodded.

"That's it. I've never seen the like afoor myself, but I've heard ma grand-dad speak o't gay often. An owd dog 'll get the cravin' for sheep's blood on him, just the same as a man does for t' drink; he creeps oot o' neets, gallops afar, hunts his sheep, doons 'er, and satisfies the cravin'. And he nary kills but the one, they say, for he kens the valie o' sheep same as you and me. He has his gallop, quenches the thirst, and then he's for home, mebbe a score mile away, and no one the wiser i' t' morn. And so on, till he comes to a bloody death, the murderin' traitor."

"If he does," said Jim.

"And he does, they say, nigh always. For he gets bolder and bolder wi' not bein' caught, until one gay neet a bullet lets leet intil him; and some man gets knocked nigh endways when they bring his best tyke home i' t' morn, dead, wi' t' sheep's woo' yet stickin' in his gab."

The postman whistled.

"It's what owd Wrottesley 'd tell on to a tick. And he'd say, if ye mind, Master, as hoo the dog 'd niver kill his master's sheep—kind o' conscience like."

"Ay, I've heard that," allowed the Master.

Jim Mason rose from his knees.

"Ma wud!" he said, "I wish Th' Owd 'Un was here. He'd haply show us summat."

"I nobbut wish he was," said the master.

As he spoke there was a crash in the wood above them; a sound as of some big body bursting furiously through brushwood.

The two men rushed to the top of the rise. In the darkness nothing could be seen; only, standing motionless and holding their breaths, they could hear the faint sound, ever growing fainter, of some creature splashing in a hasty gallop over the wet moors.

"Yon's him! Yon's no fox, I'll lay! And a parlish big 'un, too; heark to him!" cried Jim. Then to Gyp, who had rushed off in hot pursuit, "Coom away back, chuckle-'ead! what's use o' you agin a gallopin' 'potamus?"

The sounds died away and away, and were no more.

"That's 'im, the devil!" said the Master.

"Nay; the devil has a tail, they do say," replied Jim thoughtfully. For already the light of suspicion was focusing its red glare.

the tap-room starts from deep-seeming slumber.
pper's big bob-tail rises to his feet and scowls fear-
y; the Venus stands four-square, petrified, grinning
hope; old Shep, Lassie, and the rest cluster round
se two, moving slow, stiff, wooden, eyes rolling
ance to watch the door.

The shuffling steps draw nigh; the slow-cadenced
sh-hush-hush of those ghostly whispering feet thrills
silence.

The dogs stand now motionless; heads shot far
ward, lips lifting, teeth that grin in deadly tiers, and
:s glassy—picture of cowed rage; and there swells
i sinks and swells again a noise as of the far sea,
ffled, tremendous, booming, such as to shake the room.
A hand rattles the lock; a stringy voice quavers,
quats he—he in Wallace's bed!" Tammas's nut-face
ns round the door; and the dogs resume their former
itudes — scowling, suspicious, sulky at being thus
ped.

. . . .

Meanwhile over M'Adam, all unsuspicious of these
picions, a change had come. Whether it was that
the nonce he heard less of the best sheep-dog in
North, or for some more occult reason, certain it is
it he became his old self. His tongue wagged as
ly and bitterly as ever; and hardly a night passed
t he infuriated Tammas to blows with his insidious
casms. Asked by Long Kirby if he had any
planation of the Black Killer mystery, "Why *black*?"
Adam asked earnestly; "why *black* mair than *white*,
grey, we'll say?" It was not the only time he put
: identical question in that identical form; and in the
i Tammas and the more far-seeing ones opined there
ist be something behind it, though they knew not what.

David, too, marked the difference in the little man. For his father nagged at him now with all the old spirit. At first he rejoiced in the change, preferring this outward and open warfare to that aforetime stealthy enmity. But soon he almost wished the other back; for the older he grew the more difficult did he find it to endure these everlasting bickerings.

For one reason he was truly glad of the altered condition of affairs; he believed that for the nonce, at least, his father had abandoned his ill-designs against James Moore; those sneaking night-visits to Kenmuir were, he hoped, discontinued.

Yet Maggie Moore, had she been on speaking terms with him, could have undeceived him. For one night when alone in the kitchen, on looking up she saw to her horror a dim, moon-like face glued against the window-pane. In the first mad panic of the moment she almost screamed and dropped her work; then—a true Moore—controlled herself, and sat feigning to work, yet watching all the while.

It was M'Adam—she recognised that: the face pale in its framework of black; the hair lying dank upon his forehead; the white eyelids blinking, slow, regular horrible. She thought of the stories she had heard of his sworn vengeance on her father. Her heart stood still, and yet she made no move. Then with a gasp of relief she discerned that the eyes were not directed upon her. Secretly following their gaze, she saw they rested on the Shepherds' Trophy; and on the Cup they remained fixed immovable, while she sat motionless and watched.

An hour, it seemed to her, elapsed before they shifted their gaze and wandered round the room. For a second they dwelt on her; then the face withdrew into the night

or was not to be convinced. In a footnote he
ked the Parson for his "romantic and interesting"
r; but dismissed the explanation as preposterous;
said he, " We have never heard of such a case."

t was at the instigation of Parson Leggy that the
ire imported a bloodhound to track the Killer to
doom. Set on at a fresh-killed carcase at the One-
e Knowe, he carried the line a distance in the
ction of the Muir Pike; then was thrown out by a
e bustling beck, and never acknowledged the scent
in: afterwards he became unmanageable. The
ster of the Border Hunt lent a couple of foxhounds,
) effected nothing. Jim Mason set a cunning trap or
, and caught his own bob-tailed tortoiseshell, and a
ible wigging from his missus; Ned Hoppin sat up
 a gun over a new-slain victim; and Londesley of
Home Farm poisoned a carcase. But the Killer
er returned to the kill and went about in the midst
hem all, carrying on his infamous traffic, and laugh-
up his sleeve.

Teanwhile the Dalesmen raged and swore vengeance;
r impotence, their unsuccess, and losses, heating
r wrath to madness. And the bitterest sting of it
lay in this: that though they could not detect him,
y were nigh to positive as to the culprit.

Many a time was the Black Killer named in low-
:ed conclave; many a time did Long Kirby, as he
)d in the Border Ram and watched M'Adam and
 Terror walking down the High, nudge Jim Mason
 l whisper—

Theer's t' Killer, oneasy be his grave!" To which
ctical Jim always made the same retort—

Ay, theer's t' Killer, but wheer's t' proof?"

And therein lay the crux. There was scarcely a

man in the countryside who doubted the guilt of the Tailless Tyke, but, as Jim said, where was the proof? They could but point to his well-won nickname; declare that he was a byword throughout the land for his ferocity; tell how he slew the Vexer and Van Tromp, and like tales; say that magnificent sheep-dog as he was, he was notorious even in his work as a rough-handler of stock; and last, remark significantly, that the Grange was one of the few farms that had escaped unscathed—not evidence enough, as Parson Leggy declared, on which to drown a flea, much less impeach a sheep-dog on such a charge.

The judgment of the Dalesmen may, indeed, have been distorted by prejudice; for no one of them but bore on his own person or his dog's the mark of that huge savage.

'Look here!" cries Saunderson, and discovers a ragged wound on Shep's throat; "that's t' Terror—black be his fa'!"

"And, see, thiccy—his work!" continues Tupper, and shows the yet raw scars on Rasper's neck.

"And he near killed ma Lassie!" cries Londesley.

"And he did kill the Wexer!"

"And Wan Tromp!"

"But old Wenus 'll pay 'im yet, I's uphod!" says John Swan with bitter confidence, and pulls out that fair smiling Amazon, battered past recognition, yet dreaming always and still dreaming of her revenge.

"Ah," says Tammas, "tykes love him nigh as mickle as we do. Watch noo!"

The old man rises and trots out of the inn. A minute's pause, and then from down the road comes the tap of a stick, the shuffling of uncertain steps, and blending with these the heavy velvet pad-pad of huge hushed feet. Straightway every dog

"If you know sec a mighty heap," he shouted, 'happen you'll tell me what ye do know."

M'Adam looked up.

"Tell ye? Ay, wha should I tell if not ma dear David? Tell? Ay, I'll tell ye this,"—with sudden, snarling bitterness,—"that you'd be the vairy last person I wad tell."

CHAPTER XIX

IN THE FOG

THE Black Killer pursued his bloody way. The public, always greedy of a new sensation, took up the matter. In all the great Dailies, articles on the Agrarian Outrages appeared. Controversy raged high; each correspondent had his own theory and his own solution of the problem; and each waxed indignant as his were discarded for another's.

Locally, strenuous were the efforts made to effect a capture or conviction. The magistrates held meetings; watchers, armed, were posted in likely spots with orders to shoot on sight; John Swan's famous trail-hound, Reiver, was twice tried and twice failed; while the police were energetic to perspiration, and effected, in accordance with the most sacred traditions of that force, nothing.

With immunity, the criminal's audacity grew. He attempted and achieved amazing darings. On the Windy Brant he killed and gutted his sheep not a gat-lowp from the shepherd's hut. Ned Hoppin's carrier-dog, who must have come upon him in the act and forthwith fallen on him—little great-heart!—he slew and meagrely buried at his master's fold-gate.

Still, despite it all, there was no clue. He seemed invulnerable; clothed upon with invisibility. Jake Burton, indeed, vowed he had fought an Homeric battle with the creature in the **Devil's Bowl**, and des-

Maggie told no one what she had seen. Knowing how terrible her father was in anger, she deemed it wiser to keep silence. And as for Mr. David M'Adam, she should never speak to him again!

Nor for a moment did that young man surmise whence his father came, when, on the night in question, M'Adam returned to the Grange, chuckling. David of late was growing accustomed to these fits of silent, causeless merriment; and when his father began to giggle and mutter to Red Wull, at first he paid no heed.

"He! he! Wullie, aiblins we'll beat him yet. There's many a slip 'twixt Cup and lip — eh, Wullie, he! he!" and he made allusions to the flourishing of the wicked and their fall; ending always with the same refrain—"He! he! Wullie, aiblins we'll beat him yet."

So he continued, until David, his patience exhausted, asked roughly—

"What is't, ye're mumblin' aboot? Who is it ye'll beat, you and yer Wullie?"

The lad's tone was as contemptuous as his words. Long ago he had discarded any semblance of respect for his father.

M'Adam rubbed his knees and giggled.

"Heark to the dear lad, Wullie! Listen hoo pleasantly he addresses his auld dad." Then turning on his son and leering; "Wha is it, ye ask? Wha should it be but the Black Killer? Wha else is there I'd be wushin' to hurt?"

"The Black Killer?" echoed the boy, and looked at his father in amazement; for well he knew what rumour said.

"T' Black Killer! What do you know o' t' Killer?"

"Why *black*, I wad ken? Why *black*?" the little man asked, leaning forward.

"What would ye have him then?" the boy asked—"Red—yaller—muck—dirt colour?" and he stared significantly at the Tailless Tyke.

The little man ceased his rubbing and eyed the boy David shifted uneasily.

"Well?" he said at length, gruffly.

The little man giggled, and his two thin hands took up their task.

"Aiblins his puir, auld, doited fool of a dad kens mair than the dear lad thinks for, ay, or wushes. Eh, Wullie—he! he!"

"Then what is it ye do know, or think ye know?" David asked irritably.

The little man nodded and chuckled.

"Naethin' ava, laddie, naethin' worth the mention. Only aiblins the Killer 'll be caught afore sae lang."

David wagged his head in offensive scepticism.

"Ye'll catch him yersel', I s'pose, you and yer Wullie?—tak' a chair on to t' Marches, whistle a while, and when t' Killer cooms, why! pit a pinch a salt upon his tail—*if he has one.*"

At the last words, heavily punctuated, the little man stopped his rubbing as though shot.

"What wad ye mean by that?" very softly.

"What wud I?"

A long silence.

"I dinna ken for sure; and it's aiblins just as well for you, dear lad,"—in fawning accents,—"that I dinna." He began to rub and giggle afresh. "And yet, despite oor facetious lad there, aiblins we will ha' a hand in the Killer's catchin', you and I, Wullie, he! he!" and the great dog wagged his stump-tail in acquiescence.

David rose from his chair and walked across to his father.

IN THE FOG

He tried to still himself, to think. But his mind, quiver like his body, refused reflection. Act—act—ct, he must! if only because he could not stand. Yet ow to strike and where?

He was muffled in the fog as in a blanket. It was his eyes like cataract, hooding him round. There as no sound; nothing to guide him. The murderer ust now be rapt in his red revelry.

He could see nothing, could hear nothing, but still is soul dragged him forward, and his body lagged not ehind. So he plunged into his blind man's night, ow, tapping, tentative; lifting his feet to clear the eather. Once he paused to hearken. The moorland as wrapped still in awful silence; no sound save the ealthy curlew, and the blood buzzing in his fingertips; id on he went again, tapping, tentative. Then there se before him a low, living wall, horn-tipped; and he new it for the rallied sheep; knew he had lost himself; id, turning, plunged again into the white.

The strong man was gasping, his impotence racking im. The wet was bowling down his face; his hands ill as the fog. The minutes were slipping away: on the Killer would be gone.

Then his heart shocked to a halt. Away at his back ere rose a huge, reverberating din; deep raging against eep; terrific thunder-voices like lion-kings in combat; e two clashing, clanging, like warring breakers.

Hope gripped his heart and shouldered it. Some og had chanced upon the murderer; had challenged im. The Killer was at bay. Gorged, he might well fall ictim, and that though he should prove the Terror's self.

Hope rowelled him. The noise of battle lashed his lood. He plunged forward; and stayed.

The sound of roaring had taken on a peculiar rollick-ig savagery, like the roll of musketry along a charging line. Well he knew what that foretold: a running fight was forward. The combatants were striking as they galloped, and drawing ever towards him..

Nigh and nigher flung the battle, raging mad. The fog like some sounding-board tossed and magnified the noise, until it became deafening as heaven and hell's artillery at duel.

The fight swung hard by him, roaring in the fog; then turned and came back upon him; and still he could not see.

Then all around him the battle raged; all around him the tumult rose and swelled and shook in bellowing discord; all around him the fight stormed and wracked; all around him thundered the infernal elements: the whole din and dreadful savagery of the Dogs of War. The firmament swayed; the fog rocked; the ground surged. And he stood there impotent, vortex of it all, like some blind man lost in Niagara; swinging slowly to always face the noise; arms folded, nails biting deep, trembling like a grass-blade in a storm.

Of a sudden, silence: each had at length his everlasting hold.

Still the fight rolled on around, dreadful now by reason of its noiselessness. Still the fog hemmed him about like some white wall. Still he slowly swung to face the dumb battle, like the hub of a silent, revolving wheel—a Samson doomed to hearken while worlds war, nations topple, and he may nothing.

On and on the fight rolled around; noiseless, save for the splash and surge as the fighters heaved through moss-flowes, the crackle of bracken, clank of whinstones, thuds, grunts, gurglings as of two combatant giants; on and on, noiseless still, eternally on; until at length, strong man as he was, the Master knelt down lest he should fall.

bed him with minute particulars—"a monstrous mak' beast, big as a h'elephunk—'orns and all!" And in of of his tale he showed the mud-stains on his eches where, it seems, he had sat down exhausted er the rout of his adversary. But there were found se unkind enough to mimic the sudden staggering lapse of the dreadfully drunk.

It was this recklessness of the Killer's that in the end ed only by a mere mischance of his undoing; and n then it might have served to incriminate but for unhappy coincidence.

In this matter the Master figured principally. He and d Bob were crossing the Marches with a flock: a winds day; the whole vast moorland shrouded in mist.

Slowly the convoy advanced through the still noon. e mist fell thick and thicker. The gaunt Scaur, nal-post in front, was lost to view; the low-lying er brakes melted away and were no more seen.

Then the fog clapped on them like a hood, white, t, impenetrable. The Master called a halt. In vain: sheep surged on, and in a moment were lost to him. For a while the old dog formed a link between him d the flock. A cold, encouraging muzzle thrust into hand would warn him that all was as yet well. eing, however, that it was futile to persevere,

'Keep wid t' sheep, lad," he ordered. The wet nose itted his hand, and he knew himself alone.

He sat down in the heather to wait. A great while, seemed, he lay there, head pillowed in his hands, ising at large: of the coming fight for the Trophy; David and Maggie and their long-time feud; of the ller and Red Wull.

Unseeing and unseen he lay there, the sleepy orland life all round him. Gradually the drone and hargy of it overcame him. The cropping of invisible sheep; the rasping of torn grass; the close bubble of a blackcock; and a far curlew's call, blended into one low lullaby; and soon he fell away into sleep.

He woke with a start, his heart checking in a beat. A sudden hush had fallen on the moor. The sheep had ceased to nibble; the blackcock crooned no more; the curlew was mute; even a tiny tinkling burn he had heard close by was silent. He who had known no fear for two score years experienced afresh the panic of childhood in the night. That dreadful silence; the hollow blank; the impotence of sight, overwhelmed him. Alone in that white gloom, the dumb blindness engulfing him, he felt as one lost in a living tomb.

A curlew hailed, low and stealthy. Ghostly feet brushed softly by. There loomed in the vague a large stealing form; stayed, stared, and faded again.

Then the silence was broken. There came the swish of a large body rushing through the heather; then the scatter of a routed host and all about him in that white night fast shadows flitting past and gone.

The Master looked every way, dismayed. He was toppling on the verge of apprehension.

Then right in his ear there rang of a sudden an agonized m—a—a—ing; followed a scrambling thud; the flap and desperate struggle of a creature fighting death; then a hideous, smothering worry, and silence.

The Master stood quite still. He was quivering like a steel-blade hard tried. The noises in the gloom told their own fell tale. Here was the bloody miscreant at his work within hand's touch; here was this poor victim done to death at his very door; and he impotent utterly!

The man's whole soul rebelled against inaction. His viking veins thundered to be up and doing. The daring, the devilry of it all—here at his very feet!—lashed the cold-continent man to rare fury.

Behind again came Saunderson and Shep—the old dog tattered as a storm-rent sail. Then the crowd closed and cleft once more. This time M'Adam emerged, the Terror at his side in leash of gory rag, his small eyes rolling upwards from beneath a large bandana that swathed his head; bloody, scowling, sinister from his latest victory.

The Master was undone. Any trace of recent duel must be lost inevitably in these fresh scars. And the Dalesmen knew no more than that the three had attacked the Terror in the yard of the Border Ram; that he had fought them round the Croft, through the Butchery, up the market-hill, and finished them beneath the pump. No man could say whether, previous to the onset, the tawny-grizzled coat had shown traces of late war.

. . . .

The Killer had reigned already three months, when, with the advent of lambing-time, matters assumed a yet more fatal aspect. The loss of one sheep had been serious enough, but the harrying of a flock incidental to the slaughter of that one—the scaring of these woolly mothers about-to-be out of their fleeces—spelt for the small farmers something akin to ruin, for the larger ones a loss hardly tolerable.

Many a shepherd during that time patrolled the night through with his dogs only to discover in the dawn that the Killer had slipped him and havocked in some secluded portion of his beat. Such a season had never been known. Loud were the curses; deep the vows of revenge. Of a certainty, M'Adam would have waked one morning to find his Wullie stark in the yard, had it not been that the great dog slept now within the house, as all men knew.

Then in the very height of the lambing-time there

came the seven days, still notorious in the land as the Bloody Week.

On the Sunday the Manor was marked with the red cross. On Monday Ned Hoppin suffered.

On Tuesday—a black night—Tupper came upon the murderer at his work: he fired into the darkness, with no effect; and the Killer escaped with a fright. Next night Londesley lost a shearling ram. Thursday alone was blank; for on the Friday Tupper again was visited and punished heavily, doubtless in revenge for that shot.

On Saturday afternoon a mass meeting was held at the Manor. The Squire presided; gentlemen and magistrates were there in numbers, and every farmer in the countryside. To start the proceedings a windy letter from the Board of Agriculture was read. Afterwards Viscount Birdsaye rose and proposed that a reward more suitable to the gravity of the case than the paltry five pounds of the police should be offered, and backed his proposal with a twenty-five pounds cheque. Several others spoke, and, last of all, Parson Leggy rose.

He briefly summarised the history of the crimes; reiterated his belief that a sheep-dog was the criminal; and concluded by offering what he hoped would prove at least a temporary preventive, simple though it was, he said, to laughableness:—that every man jack of them who owned a sheep-dog should tie him up at night.

The farmers were allowed half an hour to consider the suggestion. They gathered in knots and talked it over. Many an eye was directed on M'Adam; but that little man seemed all unconscious.

"Weel, Mr. Saunderson," his shrill voice could be heard, "and shall ye tie Shep?"

"What doesta' think?" asked Rob, eyeing the man at whom the measure was aimed.

Eyes shut, hands clamping his ears, he tried to gather himself.

For a long while he knelt so; then he unlocked his ears.

There was silence.

He looked up. The fog rent before his gaze. Hard before him lay a huddle of slow-moving flesh, death-locked.

He started up; stole forward, hand tossed to strike; stumbled and crashed into a dream.

. . . .

He woke to find himself beneath the clear-lit night. All about him the moorland rolled away: shadows, black woods, and here the wet glint of moss-hags; and in his nostrils the smell of carrion.

The cause was not to seek. His hand lost itself in a coarse carpet of wool. He turned his head. Beside him lay a lion-maned fell tip in a pond of red; throat gaping, head thrown back, horns glistening, and even the white hoofs dabbled red. It was the murdered sheep had saved his murderer.

The Master closed his eyes. Slowly he recalled it all: the fog; the coming of the Killer; the giddy fight; his agony of impotence; and fall at that last revealing moment.

As he lay thus in thought, a tender finger wetted his brow. He looked up. A sweet, dark face was peering into his; two great grey eyes, distressed, were watching him; and a long grey scarf brushed his cheek.

"Eh, Owd 'Un?" he murmured sleepily, and raised a hand to caress.

Two warm drops splashed upon his fingers.

He looked.

The drops were red.

CHAPTER XX

THE WITCH'S LAP

THE matter was plain. Th' Owd 'Un had come upon the Killer in the fog, had fought him up and down, a terrific battle, and had been rough-handled. Only the old dog's unfathomable ruff had saved him deep hurt, while a brazen-studded collar, which Wee Anne in prankish mood had clasped about his neck, was rung and riven as though by lightning. And of a surety the Killer had not escaped unscathed.

There was grim joy in the Master's heart that morning as he entered Grammoch-town. The criminal was branded now. He wore the proof that should destroy him. Whoever bore upon his person the hallmark, unmistakable, of a Grey Dog of Kenmuir, was damned past all hope of salvation. Not though M'Adam swore to have blood for blood, should Red Wull escape his doom if stamped with that deathly seal.

But fate thwarted the Master. As he turned into the market-square, he noticed a crowd beneath the pump; and as he looked, it opened out. Tupper, black of brow, emerged, bob-tailed Rasper slinking at his heels, his shag coat all ripped and red and dripping. Behind, followed John Swan, the Venus struggling in his arms.

There was blood on the brindled lady's lips; her eyes were red-shot; and she was whimpering to be let down.

cross the Tarn. The Screes was now nothing but a
able flare against the night; yet he could see it as in
clearest day: the seared hillside slanting up from the
atin depths into that sheer curtain of rock, the Reiver's
Lowp; at the summit of the Lowp that darkling
hollow—not twenty yards across—they call the Witch's
Lap; and those two white sheep-trods, the only means
of access to that little dell, crawling dangerously up
between the sheer wall on the one hand and the sheer
fall on the other.

Staring across the Tarn, lost in the vast silence of the
night, he pictured the tale as many a time before: the
grey morning, the grey rock-wall, the seared Screes and
those two dark specks clinging like flies upon a pane.
He thrilled as he thought upon it, and looked down for
the grey head at his knee—scion of the hero of that
day; yet could not see him, so thick hung the pall
of night.

Then he began again the oft-told tale, aloud, for his
unseen comrade's sake: 'Twas in the year 17—, Owd
Un, at the time that the dark is longest. In t' dead o'
neet, old Andra' was wak'd by the Grey Dog's Ca'. He
leaped to the window. Outside there loomed agen t'
snow a lock o' ponies, torchleets in t' fold, and a girt
mak' of a feller on harseback thunderan orders. Than
he kent this was the long-threatened comin' of the
Black—

So far in the tale, when there burst on his ear the
myriad patter of galloping feet. He swung about, half
apprehending a bevy of phantom moss-troopers upon
him; and at the second, a swirl of sheep nigh bore him
down. It was pansy-black, and they fled furiously by;
yet he dimly discerned, driving at their tails, a vague,
hound-like form.

"T' Killer, by thunder!" he yelled, and struck down at that last pursuing shape—only to miss and almost fall.

"Bob, lad!" he hoarsed, "follow on!"

The chase swept on into the night. There was a splash and clatter at the far end of the Tarn, and he knew the sheep were cutting through the shallow water for the Screes. The dark water surged towards him in unwonted waves; it betrayed the fugitives' route in hurrying musketry of sound; a fleeting shower of light splashed up against the black; and in the distance the water flashed and darted like a thousand sword-blades in the night. A last floundering crash: then silence; and again he could hear the rattle of flying feet on the opposing Screes, and tinkle and tiny plunges as dislodged pebbles fell and found a watery grave.

The Master started in pursuit. He prayed that Th' Owd 'Un was on the miscreant's heels; he prayed for the moon. As though in answer the white-faced woman of the night peered round the shoulder of the Scaur, and lit the dour face of the Screes.

The Master looked up as he ran. The sheep had broken and were scattered now over the shimmering steep. In the rout one pair of darting figures caught and held his gaze: the foremost dark, dot-like, speeding upwards; the other hard behind, swift, remorseless as eternity. He looked for a third pursuing form: none could he discern.

"He mun ha' missed him in t' dark," he muttered, the sweat on his brow, his eyes straining across the Tarn, and still with long strides running on.

High and higher sped those two dark specks; up and up; until of a sudden the sheer rock dropped its relentless barrier in the path of the fugitive; away

"Why," the little man replied, "it's this way, I'm hinkin': gin ye haud Shep's the guilty one, I wad by ll manner o' means—or shootin' 'd be aiblins simpler. f not? why"—he shrugged significantly; and, having hown his hand, departed.

James Moore stayed to see the Parson's resolution egatived unanimously; then he, too, left the hall. He ad foreseen the result, and previous to the meeting ad warned the Parson how it would be: for to any)alesman to acquiesce in such an edict would seem a acit confession that his dog might be the culprit—an iference no shepherd for a moment would permit.

"Tie up!" the Master murmured, as the old dog ame to his whistle; "I think I see mysel' chainin' hee, owd lad, like any murderer!"

At the lodge-gate he passed M'Adam, who was for nce without his grisly familiar. The little man was at lay with the lodge-keeper's child; for he loved all hildren but his own, and was beloved of them.

"Weel, Moore," he called, as the other passed, " and re ye gaein' to tie yon grey devil?"

"I will if you will yours," the Master answered grimly.

"Na," the little man replied, tossing the child in ir, "it's Wullie as frichts the Killer aff the Grange. That's why I left him there noo."

"It's t' same wid me," the Master said. "He's not oom to Kenmuir yet, nor he'll not so long as Th' Owd Un's loose o' neets, I's uphod," and he passed on.

"Has he bin fightin' again?" the little man called fter him.

"Nay; not sen his fratch wid t' Killer."

"Ah; weel for the Killer—he! he! he!" and a long iggling laugh pursued him far down the road.

.   .   .   .

The night was clothed in crape when the Master left the Dalesman's Daughter. Crossing the Silver Lea he slung over that arena where, in a few months now, the last great battle for the Trophy would be fought, and began the ascent of the Pass.

His thoughts turned upon M'Adam; he pondered on the little man's hints, his significant manner of late; and could make nothing of them. From that he passed to the Killer and Red Wull; wondering whether, indeed, the two were one. Then he set to musing on David and Maggie: this fool quarrel had endured too long; he would warn the boy it must cease, tell him to play the man and make his amends; for though Maggie affected scornful indifference, her father knew right well that the long-lasting feud was wringing her tender heart.

Thinking thus he entered the Devil's Bowl and began to skirt the Lone Tarn's edge. The night fell black and blacker; the ghostly water lappered at his feet; all about, those dreadful hillocks humped round backs, closing him in; while across the whining deeps the Screes flaunted, a black flame against the night.

Now this Devil's Bowl, awesome to all else, is dear to every Moore with heart-swelling memories. Is it not hallowed to every one of them for ever, from that day on which he first can struggle so far to be shown the spot where his forebear came upon the mother of the Grey Dogs? Does not the Red Screes scowling across the Tarn ring in his ears for ever after by reason of the great daring of Grey Rip's, which then first he hears? Was it not from a never-to-be-forgotten dawn, thrice fifty years ago, that the Reiver's Lowp had had its name?

At a well-known spot by the water's edge, forenenst a hump-backed boulder, the Master paused and stared

"M'Adam!"

And there they were still struggling over the body
a dead sheep.

In a second they had disengaged and rushed to the
ge of the Lowp. In the quiet they could still hear
 scrambling hurry of the fugitive far below; then a
ounding splash reverberated up the hill; and a V-
aped wave of moving light stole death-like across the
tin deeps: the Killer was swimming the Tarn. They
tched the long bars of white converging to the dark
ex; they marked the sudden sparkling shower of light
 he shook on landing; almost they could hear the
companying flappeting of loose skin.

The two men turned and eyed each other: the one
im, the other sardonic; both dishevelled, suspicious.

"Well?"

"Weel?"

A pause; and careful scrutiny.

"There's bluid on your coat."

"And on yours."

Together they walked back into the moonlit hollow
ere lay a hoary-faced old wedder in a crimson pond.
ain it was to see whence the marks on their coats
me.

The two men stood back and eyed one another.

"What art' doin' here?"

"After the Killer. What are you?"

"After t' Killer."

"Hoo did you come?"

"Oop this path. Hoo did you?"

"Up this."

Silence: then again—

"I'd ha' had him but for thee."

"I did have him but ye tore me aff."

A pause again.

"Where's yer grey dog?" This time the challenge was unmistakable.

"After t' Killer. Wheer's your Red Wull?"

"At hame, as I tell't ye at the Manor."

"Ye mean ye left him there?"

M'Adam's fingers twitched.

"He's where I left him."

James Moore shrugged; and the other began—

"When did yer dog leave ye?"

"When t' Killer com' past."

"Ye wad say ye missed him then?"

"I say what I mean."

"Ye say he went after the Killer. Noo the Killer was here," pointing to the dead sheep—"Was your dog here too?"

"If he had been, he'd been here still."

"Gin he didna gang over the Lowp!"

"That was t' Killer, thoo fule."

"Or your dog."

"There was nobbut one beneath me—I felt him."

"Just so," said M'Adam, and laughed.

The other's brow contracted.

"An' that was a banger!" he said.

The little man stopped his cackling.

"There ye lee," he said smoothly. "He was sma'—I swear it."

They fronted one another full.

"It's a matter of opinion," said the Master.

"It's a matter of fact," said the other.

The two stared, silent and stern, each trying to fathom the other's soul; then they turned again to the brink of the Lowp. Beneath them, plain to see, was the splash and furrow in the shingle marking the

dding along the rock-wall; she struck the familiar
ck, and up it, nigh spent.

"He'll doon her in t' Lap!" cried the Master hoarsely,
w rounding the head of the Tarn. "Owd 'Un! Owd
n! wheeriver arta' gotten to?"

As he had foreseen, just as they reached the summit
two black dots were one; and down they rolled
gether into the Lap, out of his ken. At the same
tant the moon, loth to watch the climax of the
ody play, veiled her face.

His long hound-lope had brought him to the Screes'
t. Up the face of it he sped, never pausing, girding
loins for the struggle; on and on in the darkness:
heart thundered against his ribs; he was gasping
infully; the steep slithered away beneath him; yet
held on, running still, until the rock-wall barred
way too.

There he paused and whistled a low call. Could
despatch the old dog up the one path to the Lap
ile himself took the other, the murderer's only road
safety would be blocked. He waited, all expectant;
t no cold muzzle shoved into his hand. Again he
listled. A pebble from above dropped on him, as
the criminal up there had moved to the brink of the
wp to hearken; and he dared no more.

Waiting till all was still again, he crept catlike along
e rock-foot and hit, at length, the track. Up that
gged way he crawled on hands and knees. The
rspiration rolled off his face; one elbow brushed the
ck perpetually; one hand plunged ever and anon
to emptiness.

He prayed that the moon might keep in, that his
t might be saved from falling, where a slip might
ll mean death—certain destruction to his chances of

success. He cursed his luck that Th' Owd 'Un had missed him in the dark; for now he must trust to chance, his own great strength and good oak stick. And as he climbed he laid his plan: to rush in on the Killer as he gorged and grapple with him; if in the darkness he missed—and in that narrow arena that was improbable—the murderer might still in the panic of the moment forget the one path to escape, and leap over the Lowp to his doom.

At length he reached the summit, and paused to draw breath. The black void before him was the Witch's Lap, and in its bosom—not ten yards away—must be lying Killer and killed.

He crouched against the wet rock-face and listened. In that dark silence, poised 'twixt heaven and earth, he seemed a million miles apart from living soul. Above him hung the luminous night: far below the black-glinting water lapped, lapped.

No sound; and yet the murderer must be there. Ay; there was the tinkle of a dislodged stone; and again, the tread of hushed feet.

The Killer was moving; alarmed; was off!

He rose to his full height; gathered himself; and leaped.

Something collided with him as he sprang; something wrestled madly with him; something wrenched from beneath him; and in a clap he heard the thud of a body striking ground far below, and the slither and splattering of some creature speeding down the Screes and away.

"Who the blazes?" roared he.

"What the devil?" screamed a little voice.

The moon shone out.

"Moore!"

of retreat. They looked at one another
each departed the way he had come to
ion of the story.
ed it atween us," said the Master. " If
n had nobbut kept along o' me I should
for sure."

I did have him, but James Moore pulled
nge, too, his dog not bein' wi' him!"

CHAPTER XXI

THREATS OF A STORM

AN immense sensation this affair of the Witch's Lap created. It spurred the Dalesmen into fresh endeavours. James Moore and M'Adam were examined and re-examined as to the minutest details of the encounter—the latter viciously as hostile witness in the law-courts. The whole country was placarded with huge bills offering one hundred pounds reward for the capture of the criminal, dead or alive; while the vigilance of the watchers was such that in a week they bagged a donkey, an old woman, and two amateur detectives.

In Wastrel-dale, the near escape of the Killer, the collision between James Moore and M'Adam, and Owd Bob's unsuccess, who was not wont to fail, aroused a very ferment, with which was mingled a certain anxiety as to their favourite; for when the Master reached home that night he found the old dog already there; and a thorn must have pierced his foot in his blind pursuit, for he was deadly lame. Whereat, when it was reported at the Sylvester Arms, M'Adam winked at Red Wull and burst into such a smothered tempest of giggles that Tammas sharply inquired the cause.

"Naethin', naethin'," the little man replied; "a man may laff."

"Thoo's olas laffin'," snapped the other. "Thoo'll

THREATS OF A STORM

laff t' udder side o' that ugly mug o' thine one o' these days."

The next day, M'Adam called at Kenmuir. As he entered the yard, David was standing outside the kitchen window, as glum and miserable as Adam seeking readmittance at the gate of Eden. On seeing his father, however, the boy leaped to alertness.

"What's ta' want here?" he asked, all suspicion.

"Same as you, dear lad," the other giggled, rubbing his hands. "I come on a visit."

"Yer visits to Kenmuir are mair often paid o' neets, I've hard tell," David sneered.

At the moment the Master came into the yard. Owd Bob was limping behind him, while Wee Anne was tugging at the old dog's brush, bubbling at the humour of her joke. At sight of the visitor, the grey dog's ruff clouded out like a dancer's skirt; involuntarily he stopped and stiffened.

M'Adam was hurrying forward.

"I did but come to ask after the tyke," he said. "Is he gettin' over his lameness?"

James Moore looked surprised; then his stern face relaxed into a smile. Such generous anxiety as to the welfare of Red Wull's rival was a new characteristic in the little man.

"It's gaily kind in thee to coom and ask, M'Adam," he said, almost cordially. "Ay, he's doin' niceish, thank ye."

"Is the thorn oot?" asked the little man, with eager interest, shooting his head forward to stare at the other.

"It com' oot last neet wid t' poulticin'," the Master answered, returning the other's gaze, calm and steady.

"I'm glad o' that," said the other, still staring. But

his yellow grinning mask said as plain as words. "What a liar ye are, James Moore!"

. . . . . .

David and Maggie, meanwhile, were drifting farther and farther apart. James Moore had spoken to the boy, had warned him plainly what the issue of his pride might be; and the lad had heartened himself for his penance. Indeed, he longed for a reconciliation; he longed for that tender sympathy the girl had always extended to him when his troubles with his father were heavy on him. The quarrel had now endured for months; and he was weary of it and utterly ashamed, well knowing that the blame was his and his only. Yet for a while the bitterness of the ordeal—to ask pardon of this slip of a girl—seemed too much for him; and he held on his old miserable way.

Consequently he was seldom at Kenmuir and more often at home, warring with his father. Of late the little man had surpassed himself in that in which he had no peer; his tongue was now never at rest, shooting its glad venom, searching out sores, stinging, piercing. He had torn a leaf from his son's book: David's target had long been Red Wull; his was now Maggie Moore. The very leer and wink with which he soiled the girl's name set the boy's blood seething. And the more effective he saw his shots to be the more persistently he plied them.

"Is't true what they're sayin', that Maggie Moore's nae better nor she should be?" he asked one evening with anxious interest.

"They're not sayin' so, and if they were 'twud be a lee!" the boy answered hotly.

M'Adam nodded.

"Ay, they tell't me gin ony man knew 'twad be David M'Adam."

David strode across the room.

"Noo, nae mair o' that!" he ordered. "Ye sud be hamed, an owd man like you, to speak so o' a lass."

The little man edged up to his son and looked up ito the fair flushed face above him.

"David," he said smoothly, "I'm 'stonished ye dinna :rike yer auld dad." He stood with hands clasped ehind him, daring his giant son to raise a finger against im. "Ye maist might noo. Ye maun be sax inches iller and four stane heavier. Hooiver, aiblins ye're 'ise' to wait. Anither year or twa I'll be an auld man, nd Wullie here 'll be gettin' on, while you'll be in the rime o' yer strength. . . . Then, I think, ye might hit 1e wi' safety to yer person and honour to yerself."

He backed away, smiling.

"Father," David answered huskily, "one day ye'll ush me ower far."

The boy was now no longer a passive target. Ineriting his father's bitter turn of tongue, he gave as ood as he got. The two slashed and parried, utterly nsparing, with no thought except to wound. Day by ay the conflict waxed more bitter. The final crash was oming soon, inevitable.

The little man marked his son's more frequent resence at home, and commented on it in his usual pirit of raillery.

"What's come to ye, David? Yer auld dad's head is iigh turned wi' yer condescension. Is James Moore ear'd ye'll steal the Cup fra' him as ye stole it fra' me, hat he'll no' ha' ye at Kenmuir? or what is it?"

"I thowt I could mebbe keep an eye on t' Killer if I tay't here," David replied, and leered at Red Wull.

The little man stared at him in long silence; then)attered softly across the room, tip-toeing obtrusively.

"I wad not go too far, David!" he whispered in the boy's ear.

David shoved him roughly away.

"I wish you'd gang a gay bit farther," he cried; "shovin' yer girt snout into ma face!"

The little man regarded these everlasting innuendoes as merely the accustomed coin of filial intercourse. That in very truth anyone could be found to think this thing of his Wullie, seemed to him for long incredible. Yet warnings that something was awry were seldom wanting. The sudden stop and silence that ensued upon his entering the Arms, the sullen eyes glowering all together at Red Wull, might well have admonished him that something sinister was forward. Yet for long he refused to be convinced. Long Kirby was at last the means of rousing him.

"And doesta' reck'n t' Killer is a sheep-dog, M'Adam?" the smith asked, after the crime on Oxenby Fells.

"I do," the other replied with conviction.

"And that he'll spare his own sheep?"

"Niver a doubt of it."

"Then," said the smith, cackling nervously; "t' Killer can't help but be"—

M'Adam's eyes had turned on him, glassy.

"Yes, Kirby . . . be"—

The smith stuttered, grinning ghastly.

"Be—be"—

Those dim eyes held him still. The silence appalled him.

"Be-tween, I mean, you and"— He collapsed like a spent bladder. There was no other farm in the countryside but had paid its bloody toll. His daring had landed him in this impasse; and now his imagination refused to rescue him. He could only sit and sweat.

A long staring pause; then at length the little man leant forward and tapped him on the knee.

"Kenmuir, ma friend," he said, "Kenmuir: that's the one ye'd forgotten."

"So it was," guffawed the smith, in noisy relief; "so was—ha! ha!" And all the topers were moved to huge mirth. It was Kenmuir had been forgotten—ha! ha! Th' Owd 'Un the alternative to Red Wull—ho! ho!

It was after this that Long Kirby, who was always for war when someone else was to do the fighting, proposed that David should take an ultimatum to his father. But Jim Mason squashed the proposal, remarking that there was too much bad blood already between father and son; while Tammas suggested with a sneer that the smith should be his own agent in the matter.

Whether it was Tammas's remark which stung the big man into action, or whether it was that the heat of his hate aroused in him rare valour, anyhow, a day later, M'Adam caught the blacksmith lurking in the loft of the Grange. The little man cannot have guessed the intruder's murderous intent, else had it gone hard with him; yet the blacksmith's white-faced terror, as he crouched away in the darkest corner, could hardly have escaped remark.

"Hullo, Kirby!" said M'Adam cordially, "ye'll stay the night?" And the next thing the big man heard was a giggle on the far side the door, and clank of padlock and chain; then, through a crack, "Good-night to ye, Kirby. Hope ye'll be comfie." And there he had to stay—thirty-six hours in all—with swedes for his hunger and the dew off the thatch for his thirst; and thought himself happy to escape thus lightly.

The day after his release, M'Adam met him in the village.

"Kirby, man!" he called softly, and beckoned with crooked, uncannie forefinger.

The smith came to him, his apprehension ill-concealed behind a grin. There was a white gleam about the little man's face that was not encouraging.

"Well?" he asked, stopping over against him.

The little man produced an ill-gleaming sheath-knife. He balanced it on a palm that trembled ever so little. The gleam was on his face, and the glint in his eyes.

"D'ye ken what I'd ha' done gin I'd found this when you were wi' me?" he asked, ever so softly.

"Whey, what?" stammered the smith, essaying hollow mirth.

"Weel," soft and shivering as the west wind in a birch, "I'd ha' locked ye into the parlour wi' Wullie—boarded up the window—and tell't him all about it thro' the crack!"

The smith had done his work, and well. Once lighted, the little man's suspicions flared like dry matchwood. And very shortly the Dalesmen had a lurid glimpse of Adam M'Adam as he might be if wounded through his Wullie.

On a certain market-day in Grammoch-town, about the time when the Killer was working his wickedest, Rob Saunderson was the centre of interest in the Border Ram. For on the previous night Rob had lost a sheep to the Killer; and, far worse, his Herdwicks had been galloped with disastrous consequences.

The old man was telling with tears in his eyes how, on four successive nights, he and Shep had been up to guard against mishap; and on the fifth, worn out with double labour, had fallen asleep at their post. But a very little while he slumbered, yet when in the dawn he woke to hurry on his rounds, he quickly came upon a mangled sheep and the relic of his prized flock. A relic, indeed! for all about were cold wee lambkins, and their mothers dead and dying of exhaustion and their unripe travail—a slaughter of the innocents.

The Dalesmen were clustered round the old shepherd listening with lowering countenances, when a dark grey head peered in at the door and two wistful eyes dwelt for a moment on the speaker.

"Talk o' the devil!" muttered M'Adam; but no man heard him. For Red Wull, too, had seen that sad face, and, rising from his master's feet, had leapt with a roar at his enemy, toppling Jim Mason in the fury of his charge.

In a second every dog in the room—the battered Venus, Tupper's big Rasper, Saunderson's old Shep—was on his feet, bristling to have at the tyrant if the grey dog would but lead the dance.

It was not to be, however; for Long Kirby was standing in the door, a cup of coffee in his hand. Barely had he greeted the grey dog with, " Ullo, Owd Un!" when hoarse yells of "Ware, lad! t' Terror!" mingled with Red Wull's roar.

Half turning, he saw the great dog launching to the assault. Straightway he flung the contents of his cup full in that fiendish mask. The burning liquid swished against the huge bull-head: blinding, bubbling, scalding, it did its fell work well. With a bellow of agony, Red Wull checked in his charge. From without the door was banged to; and again the duel was postponed; while within the tap-room a huddle of men and dogs were left alone with a mad brute and a madder man.

Demented, agonised, the Tailless Tyke thundered

about the room; gnashing, snapping, over-setting; men, tables, chairs, swirled off their legs as though they had been dolls. He spun round like a monstrous teetotum; he banged his tortured head against the wall; he burrowed into the unyielding floor. And all the while M'Adam pattered after him, clasping him only to be flung aside as a terrier flings a rat; now up, now down again, now tossed into a corner, now dragged upon the floor, yet always following on and crying, "Wullie; Wullie, let me to ye! let yer man ease ye!" and then with a scream and a murderous glance, "By ——, Kirby, I'll deal wi' you later!"

The uproar was like hell let loose. You could hear the noise of oaths and blows, as the men fought for the door, a half-mile away. Long Kirby was the first out of that murder-hole. After him the others toppled one by one—men and dogs jostling in the frenzy of their fear: Tupper, Hoppin, Jim Mason, Teddy Bolstock white-faced and trembling, and old Saunderson they pulled out by his heels. Then the door was shut with a clang, and the little man and mad dog were left alone.

In the street was already a big-eyed crowd; while at the door was James Moore, seeking entrance. "Happen I could lend t' lil man a hand," said he; but they withheld him forcibly.

Inside was pandemonium: bangings like the doors of hell; the bellowing of that great voice; the patter of little feet; the slithering of a body on the floor; and always that shrill beseeching prayer, "Wullie, Wullie let me to ye!" and in a scream, "By ——, Kirby, I'll be wi' ye in a crack!"

Jim Mason it was who turned, at length, to the blacksmith and whispered, "Kirby, lad, thoo'd best skip it."

THREATS OF A STORM

The big man obeyed and ran. The stamp, stamp his feet rang on the road above the turmoil. As the big legs vanished round the corner and the sound of the fugitive died away, a panic seized the crowd.

A woman shrieked; a girl fainted; and in two minutes the street was as naked of men as the Strand plague-time: here a white face at a window; there a door ajar; and, peering round a far corner, a frightened boy. One man only refused to run. James Moore walked down the centre of the road, slow and calm, and Bob trotting at his heels.

. . . .

It was a long half-hour before the door of the inn burst open, and M'Adam came out with a run, flinging it behind him.

He rushed into the road; his sleeves were rolled at the wrist like a surgeon's; and in his right hand was a black-handled jack-knife.

"Noo, by —— !" he cried, in a terrible voice, "where is he?"

He looked up and down the street, darting his fiery glances everywhere; and his face was whiter than his hair.

Then he turned and hunted down the whole length of the High, nosing like a weasel in every cranny, stabbing at the air as he went, and crying—

"By ——, Kirby, wait till I lay hands on ye!"

CHAPTER XXII

THE STORM BREAKS

THERE ensued a Saturday long to be remembered by more than David in the Dale.

For that young man the day started sensationally. Rising before cock-crow and going to the window, the first thing he beheld in the misty dawn was a gaunt gigantic figure hounding up the hill from the Stony Bottom. His heart leaped to his throat. Here at last was a substantial something to build upon.

The dog was travelling at a long slouching lope. As he rapidly approached, David marked his flanks splashed with red, tongue out, and the foam flying from his jaws: far he must have come and fast. Slinking up to the house, the great dog leaped on to the sill of the back-kitchen, pushed with his paw at the cranky old hatchment, and in a second the boy, straining far out, heard the rattle of boards as he dropped to the floor.

For the moment, excited as he was, David held his peace. Even the Black Killer took second place in his thoughts that morning. His father's gibes had at last knocked the cap off his pride and forced him up to penance point. All through the week M'Adam had plied his lash with a rare relish of cruelty, as though to pain another eased his own haunting agony, until David could endure no more and had resolved to end the matter one way or the other ere worse came of it. If the girl would receive him back to favour, well—that should only be the prelude to the asking of another boon; if not, he would leave the Grange and all its misery behind and plunge into the world.

All through the week he had been steeling himself to this end; and so when, as he quitted the house on his errand of humiliation, his father turned and said abruptly—

"David, ye'll tak' the Herdwick draft o'er to Grammoch-town at onst," he answered—

"Ye mun tak' 'em yersel' if ye wish 'em to gang to-day."

"Na," the other answered; "Wullie and me we're ower thrang the day."

"If they bide for me they bide till Monday," David replied, and marched out of the house.

"I see what 'tis," his father called; "she's gie ye a tryst.... Oh ye randy, David!"

"You tend yer business, I'll tend mine!" the boy answered hotly.

Now it happened that he carried in his pocket a photograph of Maggie, with intent to return it if the girl would have none of him. As he left the room, it dropped to the floor. The boy passed on, unheeding his loss; but his father pounced.

"He! he! Wullie, what's this? He! he! gin it isna the jade hersel'!" He peered into the picture. "She kens what's what, I'll tak' oath, Wullie. See her eyes—sae saft and languishin'; and her lips—such lips, Wullie!"

He walked out of the room still sniggering, and chucking the face inanely beneath its pasteboard chin.

In the door he collided against David. The boy was hurrying back for his treasure.

"What's ta' gotten theer?" he asked quickly.

"Only the pictur' o' some limmer-leddy," his father answered, absorbed in chuck-chucking.

"Gimme it!" fiercely. "It's mine."

"Na, na; it's ma duty to keep ma douce Davie from sic queans as this."

He turned, still smiling.

"Here, Wullie! Tear her — the Jezebel!" He threw the photograph to the dog.

Red Wull sprang forward, defiled the picture with a dirty pad in the very centre of the face, tore it in half, and gnashed it with unctuous slobbering gluttony.

David dashed forward.

"Touch it if ye daur, ye girt brute!" he yelled, rushing to the attack; but his father withheld him.

"'And the dogs o' the street,'" he quoted.

David turned furiously.

"I've a gay mind to fetch thee seccan a dander onder ' lug as'll knock thee fair endways!"

"Whist, David, whist! 'Twas but for yer ain good yer auld dad did it. 'Twas that he had at heart as he ye has. . . . Rin aff wi' ye noo to Kenmuir. She'll mak' it up till ye; she's leeberal wi' her favours, I hear; ye've but to wheestle and she'll come"—

David seized his father by the shoulders.

"If you gie me mickle mair o' your sauce"—he roared.

"Sauce, Wullie," his father echoed gently.

" —I'll twist yer neck for ye!"

"He'll twist my neck for me."

"I'll gang reet away and leave you and yer Wullie to yer lane, that I will!"

The little man set to whimpering.

"It'll brak' yer auld dad's heart, lad," he protested.

"Nay, ye've gat none. But 'twill ruin ye for good and a', please God."

His father burst into an agony of tears.

"Waesucks, Wullie! d'ye hear him? He's gaein' to

leave us—the son o' my bosom! my Benjamin! my little Davie!"

David turned down the hill. At the Stony Bottom, he turned again.

"I'll gie thee one word o' warnin'!" he shouted back: "Keep a close eye to yer Wullie's gangings on o' neets."

In an instant the little man had ceased his fooling.

"Why that?" he asked, following down the hill.

"Ah," jeered his son, "ye'll likely hear afoor neet."

And with that he crossed the Bottom.

An hour it took him from the Grange to Kenmuir— an hour which had wont to be a quarter. As he dragged across the yard with heavy feet, his father, the Black Killer, Red Wull, were far behind him, and he drove his destiny before him to lay it at the feet of this girl-child.

Maggie was in the kitchen, alone, over against the fireplace, knitting as she stood.

David took his stand in the door. His eyes dwelt lovingly on the slim unconscious figure; the half-averted face; the thatch of pretty brown; and slender ankles peeping modestly from beneath her frock.

"Meg!" he called at length, all low.

She turned, the quick blood in her cheeks, and turned again, stony as a statue.

"Meg!" humbly appealing.

No answer. The steel blades clicked quicker; the steel heart moved not at all; only the human shoulders quivered a little.

A long pause.

"Bairn!" he pleaded, using the old term of fond familiar intercourse.

She knitted on, inexorable. The click-click of the needles in the silence stifled a mute tiny noise that betrayed a brimming soul.

"Wiltna speak to me, lass?" imploringly.

No reply.

The boy's heart hardened. He was hurt; amazed; resentful. This was not the old-time tender Maggie. Anger scorched his cheeks; then a sob rose to his throat and quenched the fire. He had endured so much of late that his whole soul had gone out in longing for a woman's sympathy: a look, a word, a mute caress, such as he had hardly known since his second mother died.

He had hoped so much, and now, reft of all hope, there was nothing before him but the unmotherly world. The end was come; he could no more.

It was a long while ere he could trust himself to speak. The boyish face was grey, there were tears in his voice.

"Fares ta' weel then, lass. I's aff o' Munday. There's nowt to keep me longer. I canna bide at t' Grange a day more. So long as I'd Kenmuir to a home, I could just abide it. Noo there's no place for me anywheres. I's'll pack afoor worse comes on't." He paused, his voice quaking. "I'm behodden to thee, Meg, and a' o' you for yer kindness to me. Kenmuir's bin ma home these ten years ga'en. I'm parlish griev'd it sud ha' coom to this. . . . An' I'd like to say, lass, as I've niver had a happy hour sen—sen this quarrel began. I was in t' wrang o't, I ken weel. I've often wish'd coom say I was sorry and a'—but—but ye ken as I'm a bit—a bit"—

The girl sat down abruptly, buried her face in her apron, and let loose the water-gates of her soul.

David was beside her in a minute, tenderly bending over her.

"Eh, Maggie," he cried, his heart a-flutter, "but I *am* sorry, lass."

"I hate thee!" she wailed, in high-pitched, shaking voice.

"Nay, ye dunnot, lass," he pleaded, and gently removed her hands from before her face. "Say ye forgie me."

"I don't!" she cried, struggling. "I think you's t' hatefulest lad as iver lived."

He drew back slowly, releasing her wrists; then of a sudden he stepped forward, lifted the wet, drooping face, and, holding it between his big hands, kissed it twice.

"Thoo coo'ard!" she cried, her cheeks crimsoning; and she struggled to be free.

"Ye used to let me, Meg," he reminded her.

"I niver did!" she cried, the truth submerged in her indignation.

"Yes, ye did—when we was bits o' things: that is, you was olas for kissin', and I was olas agin it. And oo"—bitterly—"I mayn't so mickle as glime at ye ower stone-wall."

He was gliming at her from closer range now, and in her position—for he held her still—she could not help but glime back. He looked so humble—penitent for once, yet reproachful, his own eyes moist, and, withal, the old, audacious David, that in her own despite her anger waned.

"Say ye forgie me," he pleaded, "and I'll let ye go."

"Niver!" But there was less conviction at heart than in voice; and the boy seemed to recognise the fact.

"Show me then," he pleaded. "There's other things besides words."

"Tak' yer hands away!" she ordered imperiously.

"Nay; not till ye've showed me."

"Hoo daur ye?" she cried through her tears, attempting hollow indignation.

He was remorseless.

"Do'ee, Davie!" changing her tone to pretty supplication, and raising wet eyes.

"Do'ee," he coaxed, and did her bidding now.

The sweet face drooped.

There was an hour-long pause.

"Meg!"

"It's no manner o' use, Davie."

"Yes, 'tis."

The pause again.

"Niver."

"Please."

A long, pulsing interval.

"Impidence!" she murmured, and looked up, her face all rain-washed, and ripe lips tilted to taste of his.

"Ay," he answered, drinking deep.

"I wonder at ye, Davie!" she whispered.

Then for a while was silence only broken by the low whispering of the lips of love.

. . . .

And thus they were situated when a low, rapt voice arrested them—

"'A dear-lov'd lad, convenience snug,
A treacherous inclination.'

Oh, Wullie, I wush you were here!"

It was little M'Adam. He was leaning in at the window, leering at the young pair.

"The creetical moment! and I interfered. . . . David, ye'll never forgie me."

The boy jumped round with an oath; Maggie, her face flaming, started to her feet. The tone, the words, the air of the little man at the window were alike insufferable.

"Odswinge! I'll learn thee to come spyin' on me!" roared the lad. Above him on the mantelpiece blazed

Shepherds' Trophy. Searching any missile in his
/, he reached up a hand for it.

 Ay, gie it me back. Ye robbed me o' it," the little
 ɔ cried, and held out his arms as if to receive his
ɪsure back.

 Dunnot, Davie!" pleaded Maggie, with restraining
d on her lover's arm.

 Od quite him! I'll give him summat!" yelled the boy.
:lose by there stood a pail of water. He seized it,
ɪng it, and slashed its contents at the leering face
:he window.

 ːhe little man started back; but the dirty torrent
ght him and soused him through. The bucket
ɔwed, struck him full on the chest, and rolled him
r in the mud. After it with a rush came David.

 I'll let him know spyin' on me!" he yelled.

 Ɪaggie, whose face was as white as it had been
nson, clung to him, hampering him.

 Dunnot, David, dunnot!" she implored. "He's
 own father."

 I'll father him! I'll larn him!" roared the boy,
[-through the window.

 ʌt the moment Sam'l came floundering furiously
nd the cart shed, followed by 'Enry and oor Job.

 Is he dead?" shouted Sam'l, seeing the prostrate form.

 Ho! ho!" went the other two.

 ːhey picked up the draggled little man and hustled
ɪ out of the yard like a thief, a man on either side
ɪ a man behind.

 ʌs they forced him through the gate he struggled round.

 By Him that made ye! ye shall pay for this, David
ʌdam, you and yer"— But Sam'l's big hand
cended on his mouth, and he was borne away before
t last ill word had flitted into being.

CHAPTER XXIII

HORROR OF DARKNESS

IT was long past dark that night when M'Adam staggered home.

All that evening at the Sylvester Arms his imprecations against David had made the hardest shudder: James Moore, the grey dog, Red Wull's peril, were for once forgotten as in his passion he cursed his son.

The Dalesmen gathered fearfully away from the little dripping madman. For once these men, whom no such geyser outbursts were wont to quell, were dumb before him; only now and then they shot furtive glances at one another, as though on the brink of some desperate enterprise of which he was the objective. But M'Adam noticed nothing, suspected nothing.

When, at length, he lurched into the kitchen of the Grange there was no light and the fire burned low. So dark was the room that a white riband of paper on the table escaped his remark.

The little man sat down heavily, his clothes still sodden, and resumed his tireless anathema.

"I've tholed mair fra' him, Wullie, than Adam M'Adam ever thocht to thole from ony man; and noo it's gane past bearin'. He struck me, Wullie! struck his ain father. Ye see it yersel', Wullie! Na; ye werena there. Oh, gin ye had but bin, Wullie! Him and his madam! But I'll gar him ken Adam M'Adam!"

He sprang to his feet, and, reaching up, took down the old bell-mouthed blunderbuss that hung above the mantelpiece.

"We'll mak' an end to't, Wullie, so we will—aince and for a'!" and he banged the weapon down upon the table. It lay right athwart that slip of still, condemning paper, and still the little man saw it not. Resuming his seat, he prepared to wait.

His hand sought the pocket of his coat and fingered tenderly a small stone bottle. He pulled it out, uncorked it and took a long draught; then placed it on the table by his side.

Gradually the grey head lolled; the shrivelled hand dropped and hung limply down, finger-tips brushing the floor; and he dozed off into a heavy sleep; while Red Wull watched at his feet.

. . . .

It was not till an hour later that David returned home. He was happy as a man is only once in a long life—returning, triumphant, from the winning of his love. His night had passed away; light reigned supreme; the glory of his love victorious flushed his veins; and he brimmed over with large charity. Ay, at Maggie's instigation, he had determined even to interview his father, and ask pardon for that blow, telling him the whole story; and surely if one spark of humanity yet flickered in the old man's breast, he would be moved to forgive.

The lightless house stood in the darkness like a body with a spirit fled. Entering, he groped to the kitchen-door, and opened it; then struck a match and stood at the threshold, peering in.

"Not home, eh?" he muttered, the tiny light above his head. "Ma sarty! 'twas a lucky thing I didna lay ma clutches on him this evenin'—I med ha' kill't him."

He held the match above his head.

Two yellow eyes, glowing like cairngorms in the gloom, and a small dim figure bunched in a chair, told him his surmise was wrong. Many a time had he seen his father in such case before, and now he muttered contemptuously,

"Drunk, the lil swab! sleepin' it aff, I reck'n."

Then he saw his mistake. The hand that hung above the floor twitched and was still again.

There was a clammy silence. A mouse, emboldened by the quiet, scuttled across the hearth. One mighty paw moved: a lightning tap; and the tiny beast lay dead.

Again that hollow stillness: no sound, no movement; only those two unwinking eyes fixed on him immovable.

Then a small voice from the fireside broke the quiet.

"Drunk—the—leetle—swap!"

Again a clammy silence, and a lifelong pause.

"I thowt ye' was sleepin'," said David, at length, lamely.

"Ay, so ye said—'sleepin' it aff'; I heard ye." Then, still in the same small voice, now quivering imperceptibly, "Wad ye obleege me, Sir, by leetin' the lamp? . . . Or d'ye think, Wullie, 'twad be soilin' his dainty fingers? They're mair used, I'm tell't, to danderin' wi' the bonnie brown hair o' his"—

"I'll not ha' ye talk o' ma Maggie so!" interposed the boy passionately.

"*His* Maggie, mark ye, Wullie—*his*! I thocht 'twad soon get that far."

"Tak' care, dad! I'll stan' little mair!" the boy warned him in choking voice; and began to trim the lamp with trembling fingers.

M'Adam forthwith addressed himself to Red Wull.

"I suppose no man iver had sic a son as him, Wullie. Ye ken what I've done for him, and ye ken hoo he's repaid it. He's set himsel' agin me; he's misca'd me; he's robbed me o' ma Cup; last of all, he struck me—struck me afore them a'. We've toiled for him, you and I, Wullie; we've slaved to keep him in hoose and hame, and he's passed his time, the while, in riotous leevin'; carousin' at Kenmuir, amusin' himsel' wi' his"—

He broke off short. The lamp shone out: that strip of paper, pinned on to the table naked and glaring, caught his eye.

"What's this?" he muttered, and unloosed the nail that clamped it down.

This is what he read—

"Adam Mackadam yer warned to mak an end to yer Red Wull will be best for him and Sheep. This is the first yoll ave two mare the third will be the last."

It was written in pencil; the only signature a dagger, rudely limned in red.

M'Adam read the paper once, twice, thrice. As he slowly assimilated its meaning, the blood faded from his face. He stared at it and still stared, with whitening cheeks and pursed lips. Then he stole a glance at David's broad back.

"What d'ye ken o' this?" he asked, at length, in dry thin voice, reaching forward in his chair.

"O' what?"

"O' this,"—holding up the slip. "And ye'd obleege me by the truth for onst."

David turned, took the paper, read it, and laughed harshly.

"It's coom to this, has it?" he said, still laughing, and yet with blenching face.

"Ye ken what it means—I daresay ye pit it there aiblins writ it. Ye'll explain it." The little man spoke still in the same small, even voice, and his eyes never moved off his son's face.

"It's plain as day. Ha' ye not hard?"

"I've heard naethin'. . . . I'd like the truth, David—if ye can tell it."

The boy smiled a forced, unnatural smile, looking from his father to the paper in his hand.

"Ye shall have it, but ye'll not like it. It's this: Tupper lost a sheep to the Killer last neet."

"And what if he did?"

The little man rose smoothly to his feet. Each noticed the other's face—dead-white.

"Why, he—lost—it—on—Wheer d'ye think?" He drawled the words out, dwelling lovingly on each.

"Where?"

"On—the—Red—Screes."

The crash was coming—inevitable now. David knew it, knew that nothing could avert it, and braced himself for the shock. The smile had fled from his face, and his breath fluttered in his throat like the wind before a thunderstorm.

"What of it?" The little man's voice was calm as a summer sea.

"Why, your Wullie was on t' Screes last neet."

"Go on, David."

"And this"—holding up the paper—"tells you that they ken, as I've kent long, that your Wullie—Red Wull—the Terror"—

"Go on."

"—Is"—

"Yes."

"The Black Killer!"

It was spoken. The frayed string was snapped at last. The little man's hand flashed to the bottle that stood before him.

"Ye—liar!" he shrieked, and hurled it with all his strength.

David dodged, ducked, and the bottle hurtled across his shoulder.

Crash! it whizzed into the lamp behind, and broke on the wall beyond. For a moment, darkness; then the spirits met the lamp's smouldering wick and flared high.

By the sudden light David saw his father across the table, pointing with crooked fore-finger. By his master's side Red Wull was standing alert, hackles up, yellow fangs bared; and at his feet lay the wee brown mouse, still and lifeless.

"Oot o' ma hoose! Back to Kenmuir! Back to yer"—

The unpardonable word hovered on his lips like some foul bubble; and never burst.

"No mother this time!" panted David, racing round the table.

"Wullie!"

The Terror leaped to the attack, but David overturned the table as he ran—the blunderbuss crashing to the floor: it fell, opposing a momentary barrier in the dog's path.

"Stan' aff, ye ——!" screeched the little man, seizing a chair in both hands. "Stan' aff, or I'll brain ye!"

David was on him.

"Wullie, Wullie, to me!"

Again the Terror came with a roar like the sea. But

David with a mighty kick, catching him full on the jaw, repelled the attack.

He gripped his father round the waist and lifted him from the ground. The little man, struggling in those iron arms, screamed, cursed, and battered at the face above him.

"The Killer! wad ye ken wha's the Killer? Go and ask 'em at Kenmuir! Ask yer"—

David swayed slightly, crushing the body in his arms till it seemed every rib must break; then hurled it from him with all the might of passion. The little man fell with a thud and a groan.

The blaze in the corner flared, flickered, and died. There was hell-black darkness; silence of the dead.

David stood against the wall, panting, every nerve tightstrung as the hawser of a straining ship.

In the corner lay the body of his father, limp and still; and in the room one other living thing was moving.

He clung close to the wall, pressing it with wet hands. The horror of it all; the darkness; the man in the corner; that moving something, petrified him.

"Father!" he whispered.

There was no reply. A chair creaked at an invisible touch. Something was creeping, stealing, crawling closer.

David was afraid.

"Father!" he cried in hoarse agony, "art' hurt?"

The words were stifled in his throat. A chair overturned with a crash; a great body struck him on the chest; a pestilent breath volleyed in his face; and wolfish teeth were reaching for his throat.

"Come on, Killer!" he screamed.

The horror of suspense was past. *It* had come, and with it he was himself again.

Back, back, back, along the wall he was borne. His hands entwined themselves around a hairy throat; he forced a great head with liquid lightsome eyes away and away; he braced himself for an effort, lifted the huge body at his breast, and heaved it from him. It struck the wall and fell with a soft thud.

As he recoiled, a hand clutched his ankle and sought to trip him. He kicked back and down with all his strength: there was one dreadful groan, and he staggered against the door and out.

There he paused against the wall to breathe.

Striking a match, he lifted his foot to see where the hand had clutched him.

God! there was blood on his heel.

Then a great fear laid hold on him. A cry was suffocated in his breast by the panting of his heart.

He crept back to the kitchen door and listened.

Not a sound.

Fearfully he opened it.

Silence of the tomb.

He banged it to. It opened behind him; and the fact lent wings to his feet.

Turning, he plunged out into the night, and ran through the blackness for his life. And a great owl swooped softly by and hooted mockingly—

"For your life! for your life! for your life!"

Part V

Owd Bob o' Kenmuir

CHAPTER XXIV

A MAN AND A MAID

IN the village even the Black Killer and the murder on the Screes were forgotten in this new sensation. The mystery in which the affair was wrapped, and the ignorance as to all its details, served to whet the general interest. There had been a fight; M'Adam and the Terror had been mauled; and David had disappeared : those were the facts. But what was the origin of the affray no one could say. One or two of the Dalesmen had, indeed, a shrewd suspicion : Tupper looked guilty ; Jem Burton muttered, " I knoo hoo 'twud be " ; while as for Long Kirby he vanished entirely.

Injured as he had been, M'Adam was yet sufficiently recovered to appear in the Sylvester Arms on the Saturday following the fight. He entered the tap-room silently with never a word to a soul ; one arm was in a sling and his head bandaged He eyed every man present critically ; and all except Tammas, who was brazen, and Jim Mason, who was innocent, fidgeted beneath the stare. Maybe it was well for Long Kirby he was not there.

"Anythin' oop?" asked Jem, at length, rather lamely in view of the plain evidences of battle.

"Na, na ; naethin' oot o' the ordinar'," the little man replied, giggling. "Only David set on me and me sleepin'. And"—with a shrug—"here I am noo."

He sat down, wagging his bandaged head and grinning.

"Ye see he's sae playfu', is Davie. He wangs ye o'er the head wi' a chair, kicks ye in the jaw, stamps on yer wame, and all as merry as May." And nothing further could they get from him, except that if David reappeared it was his firm resolve to hand him over to the police for attempted parricide.

"'Brutal assault on an auld man by his son !' 'Twill look well in the *Argus*—he ! he ! They couldna let him off under two years, I'm thinkin'."

M'Adam's version of the affair was received with quiet incredulity. The general verdict was that he had brought his punishment entirely on his own head. Tammas, indeed, who was always rude when he was not witty—and, in fact, the difference between the two is only one of degree—told him straight—

"It sarved thee gaily weel reet. An' I nobbut wish he'd made an end on thee."

"He did his best, puir lad," M'Adam reminded him gently.

"We've had enough o' thee," continued the uncompromising old man. "I'm fair grieved he didna slice thy gizzern while he was at it."

At that M'Adam raised his eyebrows, stared, and then broke into a low whistle.

"That's it, is it ?" he muttered, as though a new light was dawning on him. "Ah ! noo I see."

. . . . . .

The days passed on. There was still no news of the missing one, and Maggie's face became pitifully white and haggard.

Of course she refused to believe that David had attempted to murder his father, desperately tried as she knew he had been. Still it was a terrible thought to her that he might, at any moment, be arrested; and her girlish imagination was perpetually conjuring up horrid pictures of a trial, conviction, and the things that followed.

Then Sam'l started a wild theory that the little man had murdered his son, and thrown the mangled body down the dry well at the Grange. The story was, of course, preposterous; and coming from such a source, might well have been discarded with the ridicule it deserved. Yet it served to set the cap on the girl's fears; and she resolved, at whatever cost, to visit the Grange, beard M'Adam, and discover whether he would not allay her gnawing apprehension.

Her intent she concealed from her father, knowing well that were she to reveal it, he would gently but firmly forbid the attempt; and on an afternoon, some fortnight after David's disappearance, choosing her opportunity, she picked up a shawl, threw it over her head, and fled with palpitating heart out of the farm and down the slope to the Wastrel.

The little plank-bridge rattled as she tripped across it; and she fled faster lest anyone should hear and come to look. And, indeed, at the moment it rattled again, and she started guiltily round. It proved, however, to be only Owd Bob sweeping after her; and she was glad.

"Comin' wid me, lad?" she asked, as the old dog cantered up; thankful to have that grey protector with her.

Round Langholm How fled the two conspirators, over the summer-clad slopes of the Pike, until, at length, they reached the Stony Bottom. Down the bramble-covered bank of the ravine the girl slid, picked her way from stone to stone across the streamlet tinkling there, and scrambled up the opposing bank.

At the top she halted and looked back. The smoke from Kenmuir was wreathing slowly up against the sky; to her right the low grey cottages of the village huddled in the bosom of the Dale; far away over the Marches towered the gaunt Scaur; before her rolled the swelling slopes of the Muir Pike; while behind—and she glanced timidly across her shoulder — was the range squatting on the hilltop like some monster toad.

Her heart failed her. In her whole life she had never spoken to M'Adam; yet she knew him well enough from all David's accounts, ay, and hated him for David's sake. She hated him and feared him too, feared him mortally — this terrible little man. And with a shudder she recalled the dim face at the window, and thought of his notorious hatred of her mother. But even M'Adam could hardly harm a girl coming, broken-hearted, to seek her lover. Besides, was not Owd Bob with her?

And turning, she saw the old dog standing up the hill looking back at her as though he wondered why she waited.

"Am I not enough?" the faithful grey eyes seemed to say.

"Lad, I'm afear't!" was her spoken reply.

Yet that look determined her. She clenched her teeth, drew the shawl about her, and set off running up the hill.

Soon the run dwindled to a walk; the walk to a

crawl; and the crawl to a halt. Her breath was coming painfully, and her heart pattered against her side like the beatings of an imprisoned bird.

Again her grey guardian looked up, encouraging her forward.

"Keep close, lad!" she whispered, starting forward afresh. And the old dog ranged up beside her, shoving into her skirt, as though to let her feel his presence.

So they reached the top of the hill. The house stood before them, grim, unfriendly.

The girl's face was now quite white, yet set: the resemblance to her father was plain to see. With tight lips and breath quick-coming she crossed the threshold, treading softly as though in a house of the dead. There she paused, lifted a warning finger at her companion, bidding him halt without; then turned to the door on the left and tapped.

She listened, her head buried in the shawl, close to the wood panelling. There was no answer: she could only hear the drumming of her heart.

She knocked again. From within came the scraping of a chair cautiously shoved back; then a deep-mouthed cavernous growl.

Her heart stood still, but she turned the handle and entered, leaving a crack wide behind.

Across the room a little man was sitting. His head was swathed in dirty bandages, and a bottle was on the table by his side. He was leaning forward; his face was grey; there was a stare of naked horror in his eyes. One hand grasped the great dog, who stood with head thrown forward and muzzle hideously wrinkled; the other pointed a palsied finger at her.

"Ma God! wha are ye?" he cried hoarsely.

The girl stood hard against the door, fingers still

upon the handle, trembling like a leaf at the aspect of
that uncannie pair.

That look in the little man's eyes petrified her: the
swollen pupils; lashless lids, yawning wide; the broken
range of teeth in that gaping mouth, froze her very
soul. Rumours of the man's insanity tided back upon
her.

"I'm—I"— the words trembled forth.

At the first utterance that shivering hand dropped;
the little man leant back in his chair and gave a soul-
bursting sigh of relief.

No woman had crossed that threshold since his wife
had died; and, for a moment, when first the girl had
entered, silent-footed, aroused from dreaming of the
long ago, he had thought this shawl-clad figure, with the
pale face and peeping hair, no earthly visitor; the spirit,
rather, of one he had loved long since and lost, come to
reproach him with a broken troth.

"Speak up—I canna hear," he said, in tones mild
compared with those last wild words.

"I—I'm Maggie Moore," the girl quavered.

"Moore! Maggie Moore, d'ye say?" he cried, half
rising from his chair, a flush of colour dull upon his
cheek. "The dochter o' James Moore?" He paused,
glowering at her; and she shrank, trembling against
the door.

The little man leant back again. Gradually a grim
smile crept across his countenance.

"Weel, Maggie Moore," he said, half amused, "ony
gate ye're a good pluck'd 'un." And his wizened
countenance looked at her almost kindly from beneath
its dirty crown of bandages.

At that the girl's courage flooded back. After all
this little man was not so very terrible. Perhaps he

would be kind. And in the relief of the moment, the blood swept into her face.

There was not to be peace yet, however. The blush was still hot upon her cheek, when she caught the patter of soft steps in the passage without. A dark muzzle, flecked with grey, pushed in at the crack; two anxious grey eyes followed.

Before she could wave him back, Red Wull had marked the intruder. With a bellow he tore himself from his master's restraining hand, and launched across the room.

"Back, Bob!" screamed the girl; and the dark head withdrew.

The door slammed with a crash as the great dog flung against it, and Maggie was hurled, breathless and white-faced, into a corner.

M'Adam was on his feet, pointing with shrivelled finger, his face distorted.

"Did you bring him? did you daur bring *that* to ma door?"

Maggie huddled in the corner in a palsy of trepidation. Red Wull was now beside her, snarling horribly. With nose to the bottom of the door and busy paws, he was trying to get out. While, on the other side, Owd Bob, snuffling also at the crack, scratched and pleaded to get in. Only two miserable wooden inches divided the blood-foes.

"I browt him to protect me. I—I was afear't."

M'Adam sat down and laughed abruptly.

"Afear't? I wonder ye werena afear't to bring him here. It's the first time he's bin here this three year, and t' had best be the last." He turned to the great dog. "Wullie, Wullie, wad ye?" he called. "Come here. Lay ye doon—so—under ma chair—good lad!

oo's no' the time to settle wi' him. We can wait. /ullie,· we can wait."

Then, turning to Maggie, " Gin ye want him to mak· show at the Trials two months hence, he'd best no' ome here agin. Gin he does, he'll no' leave ma land ive—Wullie'll see to that. . . . Noo, what is't ye ant o' me?"

The girl in the corner, scared out of her senses by tis last incident, remained dumb.

M'Adam marked her hesitation, and grinned sardonic- ly.

" I see hoo 'tis," said he: "yer dad's sent ye. Aince ore he wanted somethin' o' me, and did he come to tch it hissel', like a man? . . . Not he. He sent the on to rob the father." Then, leaning forward in his 1air and glaring at the girl—" Ay, and mair than that! le night the lad set on me he cam'"—with hissing nphasis—" straight from Kenmuir!" He paused and ared at her, intent; and she was still dumb before him. Gin I'd bin killed, Wullie'd ha' bin disqualified from ompetin' for the Cup. With Adam M'Adam's Red Wull ot o' the way . . . noo d'ye see? noo d'ye onderstan'?"

She did not, and he saw it and was satisfied.

What he had been saying she neither knew nor cared. 1e only remembered the object of her mission; she only w before her the father of the man she loved; and a ave of emotion surged up in her breast. She advanced nidly towards him, holding out her hands.

" Eh, Mr. M'Adam," she pleaded, " I com' to ask ye ter David." The shawl had slipped from her head, id lay loose upon her shoulders; and she stood before m with her sad face, her pretty hair all tossed, and 'es big with unshed tears—a touching suppliant. Will ye not tell me wheer he is? I'd not ask it, I'd not trouble ye, but I've bin waitin' a waefu' while, it seems, and eh! I'm wearyin' for news o' him."

The little man regarded her curiously.

"Ah, noo I mind me,"—this to himself. "You're the lass as is thinkin' o' marryin' him?"

"We're promised," the girl answered simply.

"Weel," the other remarked, "as I said afore, ye're a good pluck'd 'un." Then, in a tone in which, despite the cynicism, a certain indefinable sadness was blended, "Gin he mak's you as good a husband as he mad' son to me, ye'll ha' made a maist remarkable match, my dear."

Maggie fired in a moment.

"A good father mak's a good son," she answered almost pertly; and then, with infinite tenderness, "and I'm prayin' a good wife 'll mak' a good husband."

He smiled scoffingly. But the girl never heeded the unspoken sneer, so set was she on her purpose. She had heard of the one tender place in the heart of this little man with the tired face and mocking tongue, and she resolved to attain her end by appealing to it.

"Ye loved a lass yersel' once, Mr. M'Adam. Hoo would you ha' felt had she gan away and left ye? Ye'd ha' bin mad and a', ye know ye would. And, Mr. M'Adam, I love t' lad yer wife loved!" She was kneeling at his feet, her hands upon his knees, looking up at him. Her sad face and quivering lips pleaded for her more eloquently than any words.

The little man was touched.

"Ay, ay, lass, that's enough," he said, trying to avoid those big, beseeching eyes which would not be avoided.

"Will ye not tell me?" she pleaded.

"I canna tell ye, lass, for why, I dinna ken," he

swered querulously. In truth he was moved to the art by her misery.

The girl's last hopes were dashed. She had played r last card, and failed. She had clung with the vour of despair to this last resource; and now it was n from her. She had hoped; and now there was hope. In the anguish of her disappointment she nembered that this was the man who, by his persistent ielty, had driven her love into exile.

She rose to her feet and stood back.

"Nor ken nor care!" she cried bitterly.

At that all the softness fled from the little man's face.

"Ye do me a wrang, lass, ye do indeed," he said,)king up at her with an assumed ingenuousness which, d she known him better, would have warned her to ware. "Gin I kent where the lad was I'd be the iry first to let you—and the p'lice, ken it—eh, Wullie, ! he!" He chuckled and rubbed his knees, regard- ss of the contempt blazing in the girl's face.

"I canna tell ye where he is noo, but ye'd aiblins care hear o' when I saw him last." He turned his chair e better to address her. "'Twas like so: I was sittin' in this vairy chair it was—asleep, when he crep' up int and lep' on me back. I knew naethin' o't ava, l I found masel' on the floor and him kneelin' on me. 'our time's come, dad,' says he, ' I'm fair set on finish- g ye.' 'Spare me!' says I, 'spare me, dear Davie,— r yer neck's sake!' 'Don't ye wish it?' says he, and gan hammerin' me head agin the floor. 'Gimme ne for a bit prayer, dear lad,' says I"—

The girl waved to him, superbly contemptuous.

"Ye're leein', ivery word o't."

The little man hitched his trousers, crossed his legs,

"An honest lee for an honest purpose is a matter ony man may be proud of, as you'll ken when you've my years, ma lass."

The girl crossed the room. At the door she turned.

"Then ye willna tell me wheer he is?" she asked, with a heart-breaking trill in her voice.

"On ma word, lass, I dinna ken!" he cried, half passionately.

"On your word, M'Adam!" she said, with a quiet scorn in her voice that might have stung Iscariot.

The little man spun round, an angry red dyeing his cheeks. In another moment he was suave and smiling again.

"I canna tell ye where he is noo," he said; "but, aiblins, I could let ye know where he's gaein' to."

"Cansta'? · Wilta'?" cried the simple girl; and in a moment was across the room and at his knees.

"Closer, and I'll whisper."

The little ear, peeping from its nest of brown, tremblingly approached his lips.

M'Adam leant forward and whispered — one short, sharp word; then sat back, grinning, to watch the effect of his disclosure.

He had his revenge—an unworthy revenge on such a victim. And watching the girl's face, the cruel disappointment merging in the heat of her indignation, he had yet enough nobility to regret his triumph.

She sprang from him as though he were unclean.

"And you his father!" she cried in burning tones.

She crossed the room again. At the door she paused. Her face was white and she was quite composed.

"If David did strike you, you drove him to it," she said, speaking in calm, gentle accents. "You ken— none so well—whether you've bin a good father to him

—and him no mother, poor laddie; whether you've
in to him what she'd ha' had ye be. Ask yer con-
cience, Mr. M'Adam. An' if he was a bit aggravatin'
t times, had he no reason? He'd a heavy cross to
ear, had David, and you ken best if you helped to ease
t for him."

The little man pointed to the door; but the girl
eld on.

"Doesta' think when you were cruel to him, jeerin'
nd fleerin', he niver felt it—because he was ower proud
o show ye? He'd a big, saft heart, had David, anonder
he varnish. Many's the time when mother was alive,
've seen him throw himself into her arms greetin', and
ry, 'Eh, if I'd nobbut mother! 'Twas different like
vhen mother was alive—he was kinder to me then.
An' noo I've no one—I'm aloan.' And he'd sob and
ob in mother's arms, and she, greetin' sair hersel',
vould comfort him, while he, bit laddie, would no' be
omforted, cryin' broken-like, 'There's noan to care for
ne noo—I'm aloan. Mother's left me, and, eh! I'm
prayin' to be wid her.'"

The clear, girlish voice shook. M'Adam, sitting with
ace averted, waved to her, mutely ordering her to be
;one. But she continued, gentle, sorrowful, relent-
ess—

"An' what will you say to his mother when you meet
ier, as ye must soon noo, and she asks you, 'An' what
' David? What o' t' lad I left wid you, to guard and
keep for me, faithful and true, till this day?' And then
ye'll hae to speak the truth—God's truth; and ye'll hae
o answer, 'Sen' the day ye left me I niver said a kind
vord to the lad; I niver bore wid him, and niver tried
o; and in the end I drove him by persecution to try
ind murder me.' Then mebbe she'll look at ye—you

best ken hoo; and she'll say, 'Adam, Adam! is this what I deserved fra' thee?'"

The gentle, implacable voice ceased. The girl slipped softly out of the room; and M'Adam was left alone to his thoughts and his dead wife's memory.

"Mither and father, baith! Mither and father, baith!" rang remorselessly in his ears.

CHAPTER XXV

THE CHASE IN THE DARK

THE summer was passing, marked throughout with the bloody trail of the Killer.

Nightly you might still hear at the Arms that assertion stamped home with dogmatic fist, "It's t' Terror, I tell thee!" and as often that irritating, inevitable retort, "Ay; but wheer's t' proof?" While often at the same moment, in a house not far away, a little lonely man sat before a low-burnt fire, rocking to and fro, biting his nails, and muttering to the great dog whose head lay between his knees—

"If we had but the proof, Wullie! if we had but the proof! I'd give ma right hand aff my arm if we had the proof to-morrow."

Sometimes there would be a cessation in the crimes; then a shepherd, going his rounds, would notice his sheep packing in unaccustomed squares. A raven, gorged to the crop, would rise before him, and flap wearily away; and in a little bloody-dabbled hollow he would come on the murderer's latest victim.

The Dalesmen were in despair. There was no proof; no hope; no seeming likelihood that the end was near. While as for the Tailless Tyke, the only evidence to incriminate him had flown with David. Every effort had proved futile alike: the one hundred pounds reward had brought no issue; the police had done nothing; a special

Commissioner from the Board of Agriculture had been equally successful; after the affair in the Witch's Lap the Killer never ran a risk, yet never missed a chance.

Then, as a last resource, Jim Mason tried his hand. He took a holiday from his duties and disappeared into the wilderness. Three days and three nights no man saw him. On the morning of the fourth he reappeared, haggard, unkempt, a furtive look haunting his eyes, sullen for once, irritable, who had never been irritable before—to confess his failure. Cross-examined further, he answered with unaccustomed fierceness, " I seed nowt, I tell thee. Whaur's the liar as said I did?"

But that night his missus heard him in his sleep conning over something in slow, fearful whisper, " Two—on—'em: one—ahint—t'udder. The first—big—bull-like; t' second "—at which point Mrs. Mason smote him a smashing blow in the ribs, and he woke in a sweat, crying terribly, " Who said I seed "—

. . . .

The days were slipping away; the summer was hot upon the land, and with it the Black Killer was forgotten; David was forgotten; everything sank into oblivion before the all-absorbing interest of the coming Trials.

The long-anticipated battle for the Shepherds' Trophy was looming close; soon everything that hung upon the issue of that struggle would be decided finally. For ever the justice of Th' Owd 'Un's claim to his proud title would be settled. If he won, he won outright—a thing unprecedented in the annals of the Cup; if he won, the place of Owd Bob o' Kenmuir as first in his profession was assured for all time. Above all, it was the last event in the six years' struggle 'twixt Red and Grey. It was the last time those two great rivals would meet in battle. The supremacy of one would be decided finally. For win or lose it was the last public appearance of the Grey Dog of Kenmuir.

And as every hour brought the great day nearer, the ferment in the countryside surpassed all precedent. The heat of the Dalesmen's enthusiasm was only intensified by the fever of their apprehension. Many a man would lose more than he cared to contemplate were Th' Owd 'Un beat. But he'd not be! Nay; owd, indeed, he was—two years older than his great rival; there were a hundred risks, a hundred chances; still, "What's the odds agin Owd Bob o' Kenmuir? I'm takin' 'em. Who'll lay agin Th' Owd 'Un?"

And with the air saturated with this perpetual talk of the old dog; these everlasting references to his certain victory; his ears drumming with the often boast that the grey dog was the best in the North, M'Adam became the silent, ill-designing man of six months since—morose, brooding, suspicious, muttering of conspiracy, plotting revenge.

At the Sylvester Arms he would sit alone in a far corner, silent, glowering, shunning companions like a dog in the first stage of rabies. Sometimes he would burst into a paroxysm of insane giggling, slapping his thigh as at some huge jest, and muttering, "Ay; it's likely they'll beat us, Wullie. Yet aiblins there's a wee somethin'—a somethin' we ken and they dinna—eh, Wullie, he! he! he!"

He seemed like one hatching eternally some secret enterprise. Now he babbled low and rapid in Red Wull's ear; now he exploded into a clatter of hushed tittering; then clapped into sudden silence, casting stealthy eyes around, glaring, and nibbling at his nails in a fury of apprehension.

He resumed his ancient practice of haunting Kenmuir. The women dared hardly leave the yard for fear of him. Now from behind a wall, now through the bars of a gate, now down through a veil of branches, the yellow mask would peer. Sam'l informed Maggie that doubtless the little man was looking for the ghost of his murdered son.

The Master at first inclined to scoff at these reports. But soon he had cause to change his tone. Passing the larch copse in the doubtful dusk of a summer evening, there struck on his ear a click as of a cocking trigger.

He looked round: nothing could he see. He hearkened: silence. He peered into the darkness of the wood; and at length discerned a still face screwing round a tree-boll to watch him.

" M'Adam ! " he called, amazed.

Detected, the little man emerged. His hands were behind him; but the stock of a protruding gun did not escape the Master's eye.

" What's ta' doin' here wid t' goon ? " he asked sharply.

" Waitin'."

" For what ? "

" The Black Killer."

The Master stared.

" To shoot him ? "

" Ay."

The Master was ill-pleased.

" I'd liefer ye waited elsewhere. Ye med shoot ma Bob here by accident."

" Ye need fear no accident, James Moore. When I shoot, it'll be deleeberate."

The Master turned to go.

" Ye'll not catch Killer here, I tell ye. He's not ower fond o' Kenmuir."

" That seems so, James Moore," the little man replied

THE CHASE IN THE DARK

topping him. "And hoo d'you count for yer luck—hat you alane should escape him?"

The Master swung round and pointed at the grey log who stood close by listening in the half-night.

"There's my luck!" he said.

M'Adam laughed harshly.

"So I thought, so I thought. And I suppose ye're hinkin' that yer luck"—nodding at the grey dog—will win ye the Cup for sure a month hence?"

"I hope so."

"Strange if he should not!" mused the other.

The Master's eyes flashed. He recalled the many umours he had heard; M'Adam's perpetual presence bout Kenmuir; and the attempt on the old dog early n the year.

"I canna think ony one'd be coo'ard enough to nurder him!" he cried, his voice thrilling.

M'Adam leant forward: his eyes were glittering.

"Ye'd no' think ony one'd be coo'ard enough to set he son to murder the father. Yet someone did set he lad on to 'sassinate me. He failed at me, and noo, suppose, he'll try at Wullie." The thin voice rang vindictive in the gloom. "One way or t'ither, fair or oul, Wullie or me, ain or baith, has got to go afore Cup Day—eh, James Moore, eh?"

The Master shoved past him.

"I'll stop to hear no more, M'Adam, else, mebbe, I'd yet fine and angry wid ye. Noo, hod bye!" And he passed away into the night.

Yet the interview served to rouse his alarm. And when two days later Sam'l reported that, having been up atop of the big stack, he had found in the hay a orm, clearly defined, as of where a man had lain, he ooked grave.

In the thick of the following night, Watch, the black crossbred chained in the yard, challenged raucously It was as though the Master had been waiting the signal; for while the night still echoed he emerged from the house, lantern in hand.

At the same moment, Tammas and Sam'l came down the steps from the loft.

" Owd 'Un ! " the Master called.

There came no answering form.

" Owd 'Un ! " again.

No reply.

"Wheeriver's he gotten to?" whispered Tammas, peering into the porch where the old dog was wont to sleep.

"Not far, I'll lay," said the Master, and turned to the business in hand. " Noo, oop wid t' ladder ! "

They leaned it against the stack. The Master began to ascend, lantern in mouth. His head on a level with the top of the stack, he peered round, casting the rays of light over the floor of hay.

"Sitha' owt, Master?" asked Tammas in anxious whisper.

The other made no reply; he was climbing cautiously on to the stack.

" Th' Owd 'Un com' back yet ? " came his voice from above, after an interval.

" Nay."

" Then gang t' top o' croft and ca'."

Tammas obeyed. Thrice his whistle pierced the night; then he returned.

"Owd 'Un ! Owd 'Un ! " he called—" Wheeriver arta' gotten to ? "

The answer came from an unexpected quarter. Far

THE CHASE IN THE DARK

...ay over the Marches there resounded a deep booming ...ttle-cry.

Tammas gasped. Sam'l gaped. The lantern flashed ...wnward through the night and crashed to the ground. The two men below looked at one another. Neither ...oke. It was the Grey Dog's Ca'.

"Mebbe—mebbe," began Tammas, and stayed, at ...ter loss for explanation.

The Master was creaking down the ladder.

"Nowt theer," he said shortly; and his voice seemed steady.

He joined the others. The three stood silent at the ...ot of the stack. The night was as still as a cathedral. Then of a sudden there sounded a crash in the ...stance, and, hard on top of it, a second, as of two ...eplechasers bursting through a hedge.

The three listened. Another moment, and there ...uck on their ears, clear in the calm of night, the ...ttle of feet hounding furiously towards them.

Sam'l was shaking.

"Two on 'em!"

"Ma wud! and in a rare pooder too. Hark!"

The words were barely out when the yard-gate ...ttled and rattled again as if struck by flying feet. ...wo phantom shapes, one on the other's heels, slung ... them. Across the yard they flung like a storm of ...il, hound and hounded; flashed away over the wall; ...en a terrific slatter on the hard slope, as of drums ...ating a charge; the plank-bridge clanged and clanged ...ain: then silence.

Watch was waking the night. The three men were ...embling. The thing had burst on them like a ...rnado; swept past and gone. Barely a minute had ...apsed since that first thunder-call upon the Marches.

"Whativer?" gasped Tammas.

"Bogles baith!" Sam'l hazarded.

Only the Master stayed silent.

Sam'l shuffled away; the others followed. Doors banged; bolts rang: and the small figure, hanging rat-wise in the crevice between two stacks, dropped to the ground and pattered away.

CHAPTER XXVI

A SHOT IN THE NIGHT

'T was only three short weeks before Cup Day that one afternoon Jim Mason brought a letter to nmuir. The Master opened it as the postman still od in the door.

It was from Long Kirby—still in retirement—begging n for mercy's sake to keep Th' Owd 'Un safe within ors at nights, at least till after the Trials.

This was how the smith concluded his ill-spelt note—

'Look out for M'Adam i tell you, i *know* hel tri at)wd un afore cup day—failin im you, if the ole dog's :e i'm a ruined man i say, so for the luv o God keep r eyes wide."

The Master read the letter and handed it to the stman, who perused it carefully.

"Sitha' here noo," said Jim at length, speaking with earnestness that made the other stare, "I wish)o'd do what he asks thee: keep Th' Owd 'Un in o' ets that is."

The Master shook his head.

"Nay," said he, "M'Adam or no M'Adam, Cup or Cup, Th' Owd 'Un has the run o' ma land same as 's had sen' a puppy. Why, Jim, the first neet I shut n up, that neet the Killer comes, I'll lay!"

The postman turned wearily away, and the Master

stood looking after him, wondering what had come of late to his former cheery friend.

Those two were not the only warnings James Moore received. During the weeks immediately preceding the Trials, the danger signal was perpetually flaunted beneath his nose.

Twice again, did Watch hurl a brazen challenge on the night air. Twice did the Master, with lantern, Sam'l, and Owd Bob, sally forth and search every hole and corner on the premises—to find nothing. Vi'let Thornton, the dairymaid, gave notice, avowing that the farm was haunted; that, on several occasions in the early morning, she had seen a bogle flitting down the slope to the Wastrel—a sure portent, Sam'l declared, of an approaching death in the house. While once a shearer, coming up from the village, reported having seen, in the twilight of dawn, a little ghostly figure, haggard and startled, stealing silently from tree to tree in the coppice by the lane. The Master, however, irritated by these constant vain alarms, dismissed the story summarily. "One thing I'm sartin o'," said he: "There's not a crittur moves on Kenmuir at neets but Th' Owd 'Un kens it."

Yet, even as he said it, a little man, draggled, weary-eyed, smeared with dew and dust, was limping in at the door of a house barely a mile away.

"Nae luck, Wullie, curse it!" he cried, throwing himself into a chair, and addressing someone who was not there—"nae luck. An' yet I'm sure o't as I am that there's a God in heaven."

.   .   .   .   .   .

M'Adam was an old man now. But little more than fifty, yet he looked to have reached man's allotted years. His sparse hair was quite white; his body shrunk and

owed; and his thin hand shook like an aspen as it
groped to the familiar bottle.

In another matter, too, he was altogether changed.
Formerly, whatever his faults, there had been no harder
working man in the countryside. At all hours, in all
weathers, you might have seen him with his gigantic
attendant going his rounds. Now all that was different:
he never put his hand to the plough, and with none to
help him the land was left utterly uncared; so that men
said that, of a surety, there would be a farm to let on
the March Mere estate come Michaelmas.

Instead of working, the little man sat all day in the
kitchen at home, brooding over his wrongs, brewing
vengeance. Even the Sylvester Arms knew him no
more; for he stayed where he was with his dog and his
bottle. Only, when the shroud of night had come down
to cover him, he slipped out and away on some errand
on which not even Red Wull accompanied him.

So the time fled on, till the Sunday before the Trials
came round.

All that day M'Adam sat in his kitchen, drinking,
muttering, hatching revenge.

"Curse it, Wullie! curse it! The time's slippin'—
slippin'—slippin'. Thursday next—but three days
mair! and I haena the proof—I haena the proof!" and
he rocked to and fro, biting his nails.

All day long he never moved. Long after sunset he
sat on; long after the dark had eliminated the features
of the room.

"They're all agin us, Wullie. It's you and I alane,
lad. M'Adam's to be beat somehow, onyhow; and
Moore's to win. So they've settled it, and so 'twill be—
onless, Wullie, onless—but curse it! I've no' the proof!"
and he hammered the table in the agony of his impotence.

At midnight he arose, a mad, desperate plan looming through his fuddled brain.

"I swore I'd pay him, Wullie, and I will. If I hang for it, I'll be even wi' him. I haena the proof, but I *know*—I *know*!" He groped his way to the mantelpiece with blind eyes and swirling brain. Reaching up fumbling hands, he took down the old blunderbuss from above the fireplace.

"Wullie," he whispered, chuckling hideously, "Wullie, cóme on! You and I—he! he!" But the Tailless Tyke was elsewhere. At nightfall he had slouched silently out of the house on business he best wot of.

So his master crept out of the room alone, on tiptoe, still chuckling.

The cool night air refreshed him, and he stepped stealthily along, his quaint weapon across his shoulder: down the hill, across the Bottom, skirting the Pike, till he reached the plank-bridge over the Wastrel.

He crossed it safely, that Providence whose care is drunkards placing his footsteps. Then he stole up the slope like a hunter stalking his prey.

Arrived at the gate, he raised himself, and peered over into the moon-lit yard. There was no sign or sound of living creature. The little grey house slept peacefully in the shadow of the Pike, all unaware of the man with murder in his heart laboriously climbing the yard-gate.

The door of the porch was wide, the chain hanging limply down unused; and the little man could see within, the moon shining on the iron studs of the inner door and the blanket of him who should have slept there, and did not.

"He's no' there, Wullie! he's no' there!"

He jumped down from the gate. Throwing all

lution to the winds, he reeled recklessly across the
yard. The drunken delirium of battle was on him.
The fever of anticipated victory flushed his veins. At
length he would take toll for the injuries of years.

Another moment and he was before the good oak
door, battering it madly with clubbed weapon, yelling,
dancing, screaming vengeance.

"Where is he? what's he at? Come and tell me that,
James Moore! Come doon, I say, ye coward! Come
and meet me like a man!

> 'Scots, wha hae wi' Wallace bled,
> Scots, wham Bruce has aften led—
> Welcome to your gory bed,
>   Or to victorie—e!'"

The soft moonlight streamed down on the white-
haired madman screaming his war-song.

The quiet farmyard, startled from its sleep, awoke
in an uproar. Cattle shifted in their stalls; horses
whinnied; fowls chattered, aroused by the din and dull
thudding of the blows; and above the rest, loud and
piercing, the shrill cry of a terrified child.

Maggie, wakened from a vivid dream of David
chasing the police, hurried a shawl around her, and in a
minute had the baby in her arms and was comforting
her; vaguely fearing the while that the police were
after David.

James Moore flung his window up. Leaning out, he
looked down on the dishevelled, dancing figure below
him.

M'Adam heard the noise, glanced up, and saw his
enemy. Straightway he ceased his attack on the door,
and running beneath the window, shook his weapon at
his foe.

"There ye are, are ye! Curse ye for a coward! curse ye for a liar! Come doon, I say, James Moore! come doon—I daur ye to it! Aince and for a' let's settle oor account."

The Master, looking down from above, conjectured that at length the little man's brain had gone.

"What doesta' want?" he asked, as calmly as he could, hoping to gain time.

"What is't I want?" screamed the madman. "Heark to him! He crosses me in ilka thing; he plots agin me; robs me o' ma Cup; he sets ma son agin me and pits him on to murder me. And in the end he"—

"Coom then, coom! I'll"—

"Gie me back the Cup ye stole, James Moore! Gie me back ma son ye've took from me! And there's anither thing: what's yer Grey Dog doin'? where's yer"—

The Master interposed again.

"I'll coom doon and talk things ower wid ye," he said soothingly. But before he could withdraw M'Adam had jerked his weapon to his shoulder, and aimed it full at his enemy's head.

The threatened man looked down the thing's great quivering mouth, wholly unmoved.

"Ye mun hold it steadier, little man, if ye'd hit," he said grimly. "There, I'll coom help ye." He withdrew slowly; and all the time was wondering where the grey dog was.

In another moment he was downstairs, unbarring the door. On the other side stood M'Adam, blunderbuss at shoulder, finger trembling on the trigger.

"Hi, Master! hod back or thoo's dead!" roared a voice from the loft.

"Father! Father! back wid thee!" screamed

A SHOT IN THE NIGHT

aggie, who saw it all from the window above the
,or.

The warnings came too late: the blunderbuss went
" with a roar, belching out a storm of sparks and
ioke. The shot peppered the door like hail, and the
iole yard seemed for a moment wrapped in flame.

"Aw! ah! ma gummy! 'Elp! Murder! Eh! Oh!"
llowed a lusty voice, and it was not James Moore's.

The little man, the cause of the uproar, lay quite
ll upon the ground, with another figure standing
er him. As he had stood, finger on trigger, waiting
· that last bolt to be drawn, a grey form, shooting
ne knew whence, had silently attacked him from
hind, and jerked him backwards to the ground.
ith the shock of the fall the blunderbuss had gone

The last bolt was thrown back with a clatter, and
ɛ Master emerged. In a glance he took in the whole
ne: the fallen man; the grey dog; the still smok-
3 weapon.

"Thee was't, Bob, lad?" he said. "I was wonderin'
1eer you were. Ye com' just at the reet moment, as
 aye do." Then, in loud voice, addressing the dark-
ss, "Ye're not hurt, Sam'l Todd—I can tell that by
r noise: it was nobbut t' shot aff t' door warmed thee.
)om away doon and gie me a hand."

He walked up to M'Adam, who still lay gasping on
e ground. The shock of the fall and recoil of the
ɛapon had knocked the breath out of the little man;
yond that he was barely hurt.

The Master stood over his fallen enemy, and looked
ernly down at him.

"I've put up wid mair fra' thee, M'Adam, than I
ɔuid from ony other man," he said. "But this is

far ower mickle—comin' here at neet wi' loaded arms, scarin' t' women and childer oot o' their lives, and I can but think meanin' worse. If ye were half a mak' o' man I'd gie ye the finest bangin' ever ye had; but as you ken weel, I could no more hit you than I could a woman. Why ye've gotten this doon on me you ken best. I niver did you or any other man a harm. As to the Cup, I've got it and I'm goin' to do ma best to keep it—it's for you to win it fra' me if ye can o' Thursday. As for what ye say o' David, it's a lee. As for what ye're drivin' at wid yer hints and mysteries, I've no more idee than a babe unborn. . . . Noo I'm goin' to lock ye up—ye're not safe abroad. I'm thinkin' I'll hae to hand ye ower to the p'lice."

With the help of Sam'l, he dragged the stunned little man across the yard; and shoved him into a tiny coal-hole at the end of the cowhouse.

"You think it ower that side, ma lad," he called, as he turned the key, "and I will this." And with that he retired to bed.

Early in the morning, he went to release his prisoner. He was a minute too late; for scuttling down the slope and away, was a little black-begrimed, tottering figure· with white hair blowing in the wind.

"Happen it's as well," thought the Master, watching the flying figure. Then, "Hi, Bob, lad!" he called; for the grey dog, ears back, tail streaming, was hurling down the slope after the fugitive.

On the bridge M'Adam turned, and seeing his pursuer hot upon him, screamed, missed his footing, and fell with a loud splash into the stream—almost in that identical spot into which, years before, he had plunged to save Red Wull.

On the bridge Owd Bob halted and looked down at

the man struggling beneath him. He made a half move as though to leap in to the rescue of his enemy; then, seeing there was no necessity, he turned and trotted back to his master.

"Ye nobbut served him reet, lad, I'm thinkin'," said the Master. " Like as not he com' here wi' the intent to mak' an end to ye. Weel, after Thursday, I pray God we'll ha' peace. It's gettin' above a joke."

The two turned back into the yard.

But down below them, along the edge of the stream, for the second time in this story, a little dripping figure was tottering homewards. The little man was crying; the hot tears mingling on his cheeks with the undried waters of the Wastrel.

CHAPTER XXVII

THE SHEPHERDS' TROPHY

CUP Day.

It broke calm and beautiful, no cloud on the horizon, no threat of storm in the air; a fitting day on which the Shepherds' Trophy must be won outright.

And well it was so. For never since the founding of the Dale Trials, had such a concourse been gathered together on the north bank of the Silver Lea. From the Highlands they came; from the far Campbell country; from the Peak; from the county of many acres; from all along the silver fringes of the Solway, assembling in that quiet corner of the earth to see the famous Grey Dog of Kenmuir fight his last great battle for the Shepherds' Trophy.

From the break of day, the good pike-road from Grammoch-town groaned with traffic. By noon, the gaunt Scaur looked down on such a gathering as it had never seen. The paddock at the back of the Dalesman's Daughter was packed with a clammering, chattering, multitude: animated groups of farmers; bevies of stolid rustics; sharp-faced townsmen; loud-voiced bookmakers, thrown together like toys in a sawdust bath; whilst here and there, on the outskirts of the crowd, a lonely man and wise-faced dog, come from afar to wrest his proud title from the best sheep-dog in the North.

At the back of the enclosure was drawn up a formid-
e array of carts and carriages, varying as much in
ility and character as did their owners. There was
 Squire's landau, rubbing axle-boxes with Jem
rton's modest moke-cart; and there Viscount
dsaye's flaring barouche side by side with the red-
eeled waggon of Kenmuir.
n the latter, Maggie, sad and sweet in her simple
nmer garb, leaned over to talk to Lady Eleanour;
ile golden-haired Wee Anne, delighted with the
ging crowd, trotted about the waggon, waving to her
nds, and shouting from very joyousness.
Close by was the gathered host of Dalesmen. Long
·by was there, returned from his retirement; Jim
son, sallow-faced and dull-eyed; Tammas, cynical
l self-contained; Sam'l, prophesying defeat; while
Ned Hoppin, centre of the thickest knot, was telling
v, on the Saturday previous, he had lost a sheep to
 Killer, and asseverating his conviction as to the
ntity of the criminal.
Across the Silver Lea was a little group of judges,
pecting the course.
The line laid out ran thus. The sheep must first be
nd on the Fells to the right of the starting flag;
n up the slope and away from the spectators, round
lag and obliquely down the hill again; through a
) in the wall; along the hillside, parallel to the
ver Lea; abruptly to the left through a pair of
gs—the trickiest turn of them all; then down the
pe to the pen, which was set up close to the plank-
dge over the stream.
The proceedings began with the Local Stakes, won
Rob Saunderson's veteran, Shep. There followed the
en Juveniles', carried off by Ned Hoppin's young

dog. It was late in the afternoon when at length the great event of the meeting came on.

In the enclosure behind the Dalesman's Daughter the clamour of the crowd increased tenfold, and the yells of the bookmakers redoubled.

"Here I am, gen'lemen! here I am! ole Jack, the man you know. Liberal odds and you'll get your money... Bob! what price Bob? I'll take seven to four Grey—even money Red. Five to one bar two! Any money some on 'em!"

. . . . . .

Across the stream is clustered about the starting-flag the finest array of sheep-dogs ever seen together.

"I've never seen such a field, and I've seen fifty!" is Parson Leggy's verdict.

There, beside his master, stands Owd Bob, observed of all. With curtseying quarters, silver-waving brush, and dark head proudly high, he scans his challengers. Over against him that mean, light-limbed, terrier-like black is the unbeaten Pip, winner of the Cambrian Stakes at Llangollen—as many hold, the best of all the good dogs that have come from sheep-dotted Wales. Beside him, the splendid sable collie, with the tremendous coat and slash of white on throat and face, is the famous MacCallum More, fresh from his victory at the Highland meeting. The grizzled bob-tail with high curt quarters and blue eyes staring through their shaggy veil, is the champion of the Southern Downs—Sir Galahad. That wolfish black-and-tan is Jess, on whom the Yorkshiremen are laying as though they loved her: she, they affirm, can catch a hare in a fair course. Besides these, Tupper's big blue Rasper is there, Londesley's Lassie, and many more—too many

nention : big and small, grand and mean, smooth and
gh—and not a bad dog amongst them.

And alone, his back to the others, stands a little,
ved, conspicuous form—Adam M'Adam ; while the
at dog beside him, scowling incarnation of defiance,
?ed Wull, the Terror o' th' Border.

The Tailless Tyke had already run up his fighting
ours. For MacCallum More, advancing to examine
; forlorn great adversary, had conceived for him a
lent antipathy, and straightway had spun at him
h all the fury of the Highland cateran, who attacks
t and explains afterwards. Red Wull had turned
him with savage, silent gluttony; bob-tailed Rasper
; racing up to join the attack, and in another second
three would have been locked inseparably ; but just
ime M'Adam intervened.

Then one of the judges came hurrying up.

"Mr. M'Adam," he cried angrily, "if that brute of yours
s fighting again, hang me if I don't disqualify him!"

A dull flush of passion swept across the little man's
e. "Come here, Wullie!" he called. "Gin you
elant tyke attacks ye agin, ye're to be disqualified."

He was unheeded. The battle for the Cup had
;un, little Pip leading the dance.

On the opposite slope the babel had subsided now.
cksters left their wares, and bookmakers their stools,
watch the struggle. Every eye was intent on the
ving figures of man and dog and three sheep across
stream.

One after one the competitors ran their course and
ined their sheep : there was no single failure. And
received their just meed of applause save only Adam
Adam's Red Wull.

Last of all, when Owd Bob trotted out to uphold his

title, there went up such a roar as made Maggie's wan cheeks to blush with pleasure, and Wee Anne to scream right lustily.

His was an incomparable exhibition. Sheep should be humoured rather than hurried; coaxed rather than coerced. And that sheep-dog has attained the summit of his art, who subdues himself and leads his sheep in pretending to be led. Well might the bosoms of the Dalesmen swell with pride as they watched; well might Tammas pull out that hackneyed phrase—" the brains of a man and the way of a woman"; well might the crowd bawl their enthusiasm, and Long Kirby puff his cheeks, and rattle the money in his trouser pockets.

But of this part it is enough to say that in the end Pip, Owd Bob, and Red Wull were selected to fight out the struggle afresh.

The course was altered and stiffened. Beyond the stream it remained unchanged: up the slope; round a flag; down the hill again; through a gap in the wall; along the hillside; down through the two flags; turn, and to the stream again. But the pen was now moved from its former position, carried over the bridge, up the near slope, and the hurdles put together at the very foot of the multitude.

A stiff course if ever there was one; and the time allowed, ten short minutes.

The spectators hustled and elbowed in endeavours to obtain posts of vantage. And well they might; for about to begin was the finest exhibition of sheep-handling any man there was ever to behold.

Evan Jones and little Pip led off.

Those two, who had won on many a hard-fought
[fie]ld, worked together as they had never worked before.
[S]mooth and swift, like a yacht in Southampton Water;
[ro]und the flag; through the gap; down between the two
[fla]gs—accomplishing right well that awkward turn; and
[ba]ck to the bridge.

There they halted: the sheep would not face that
[na]rrow way. Once, twice, and again, they broke; and
[ea]ch time the gallant Pip, his tongue out and tail
[qu]ivering, brought them back to the bridge-head.

At length one faced it; then another and—it was too
[lat]e. Time was up. The judges signalled; and the
[W]elshman called off his dog and withdrew.

Out of sight of mortal eye, in a dip of the ground,
[Ev]an Jones sat down and took the small dark head
[be]tween his knees; and you may be sure the dog's
[he]art was heavy as the man's. "We did our best,
[Pi]p," he cried brokenly, "but we're beat—the first time
[ev]er we've been."

No time to dally.

James Moore and Owd Bob were off on their last run.
No applause this time; not a voice was raised:
[an]xious faces; twitching fingers; the whole crowd tense
[as] a stretched wire. A false turn, a wilful sheep, a
[ca]ntankerous judge, and the grey dog would be beat.
[An]d not a man there but knew it.

Yet over the stream master and dog went about their
[bu]siness, never so quiet, never so collected; for all the
[wo]rld as though rounding up a flock on the Muir Pike.

The old dog found his sheep in a twinkling; and from
[the] first it was evident they were a wild, scared trio.
[Ro]unding the first flag, one bright-eyed wether made a
[da]sh for the open. He was quick; but the grey dog

was quicker: a splendid recover, and a sound like a sob from the thousands on the hill.

Down the slope for the gap in the wall. Below the opening James Moore took his stand to stop and turn them. A distance behind loitered Owd Bob, seeming to follow rather than to drive, yet watchful of every movement and anticipating it, one eye on his master the other on his sheep; never hurrying them, never flurrying them, yet bringing them rapidly along.

No word was spoken; barely a gesture made; yet they worked, master and dog, like one divided.

Through the gap, along the hill parallel to the spectators, playing into one another's hands like men at polo.

A wide sweep for the turn at the flags, and the sheep wheeled as though at the word of command dropped through them, and travelled rapidly for the bridge.

"Steady!" whispered the crowd.

"Steady, man!" muttered Parson Leggy.

"Hold 'em for God's sake!" croaked Kirby huskily Ah-h-h! d——... I knew it. I seed it comin'!"

The pace down the hill had grown quicker—too quick Close on the bridge the three sheep made an effort to break. A dash, and two were checked; but the third went away like the wind, and after him Owd Bob, a grey streak against the green.

Tammas was cursing silently; Kirby white to the lips; and in the stillness you could plainly hear the Dalesmen's sobbing breath.

"Gallop! they say he's old and slow," muttered the Parson. "Dash! Look at that!" For the grey dog racing like the Nor' Easter over the sea, had already retrieved the fugitive.

Man and dog were coaxing the three a step at a time
wards the bridge.

One ventured; the others followed.

In the middle the leader stopped and tried to turn;
d time was flying—flying, and the penning alone must
ke minutes. Many a man's hand was at his watch,
t no one could take his eyes off the group below to
ok.

"We're beat. I've won bet, Tammas," groaned
m'l. The two had a long-standing wager on the
atter. "I olas knoo hoo 'twud be. I olas tell't thee
t' owd tyke,"—then breaking into a bellow, his honest
:e crimson with enthusiasm,—"Coom on, Master!
od for thee, Owd 'Un! Yon's t' style!"

For the grey dog had leapt on the back of the hind-
ost sheep; it had surged forward against the next,
d they were over, and making up the slope amidst a
under of applause.

At the pen it was a sight to see shepherd and dog
orking together. The Master, his face stern and a
tle whiter than its wont, casting forward with both
nds, herding the sheep in; the grey dog, eyes big
d bright, dropping to hand, crawling and creeping,
oser and closer.

"They're in!—Nay—Ay—dang me! Stop 'er!—
od Owd 'Un! Ah-h-h, they're in!" and the last
eep reluctantly passed through on the stroke of time.

A roar went up from the crowd; Maggie's white face
rned pink; and the Dalesmen mopped wet brows.
ne mob surged forward, but the stewards held them
ck.

"Back, please! Don't encroach! M'Adam's to
me."

From the far bank the little man watched the scene.

His coat and cap were off; his hair gleamed white in the sun; his sleeves were rolled up; and his face was twitching as he stood ready.

The hubbub over the stream at length subsided. One of the judges nodded to him.

"Noo, Wullie! noo or niver!" and they were off.

"Back, gentlemen! back! He's off; he's coming! M'Adam's coming!"

They might well shout and push; for the great dog was on to his sheep almost before they knew it; and they went away with a rush and Red Wull right on their backs. Up the slope they swept and round the first flag, already galloping. Down the hill for the gap, and M'Adam was flying ahead to turn them. But they passed him like a hurricane, and Red Wull was in front with a plunge and turned them alone.

"M'Adam wins! Five to four M'Adam! I lay agin Bob!" rang out a clear voice in the silence.

Through the gap they rattled, ears back, feet twinkling like the wings of driven grouse.

"He's lost 'em! They'll break! They're away!" was the cry.

Sam'l was half up the wheel of the Kenmuir waggon; every man was on his toes; ladies standing in their carriages; even Jim Mason's face flushed with momentary excitement.

The sheep were tearing along the hillside, all together, like a white scud. After them, galloping like a Waterloo winner, raced Red Wull. And last of all, leaping over the ground like a demoniac, making not for the two flags but the plank-bridge, the white-haired figure of M'Adam.

"He's beat! The Killer's beat!" roared a strident voice.

"M'Adam wins! Five to four M'Adam! I lay agin
vd Bob!" rang out the clear reply.
Red Wull was now racing parallel to the fugitives
d above them. All four were travelling at a terrific
e; and the two flags were barely twenty yards in
nt. To effect the turn a change of direction must be
ıde through a right angle.
"He's beat! he's beat! M'Adam's beat! Can't make
ıohow!" was the roar.
From over the stream a yell—
"Turn 'em, Wullie!"
At that the great dog swerved down on the flying
ee. They wheeled, still at the gallop, like a troop of
ralry, and dropped, clean and neat, between the flags;
d down to the stream they rattled, passing M'Adam
the way as though he were standing.
"Weel done, Wullie!" came a scream from the far
nk; and from the crowd an involuntary burst of
plause.
"Ma wud!"
"Did ta' see that?"
"By gob!"
It was a turn, indeed, of which the smartest team in
: galloping horse-gunners might have been proud: a
ıde later and they must have overshot the mark, a
ıde sooner and a miss.
"He's not been two minutes so far. We're beaten;
n't you think so, Uncle Leggy?" asked Muriel
lvester, looking up piteously into the Parson's face.
"It's not what I think, my dear, it's what the judges
nk," the Parson replied testily.
Right on to the centre of the bridge the leading sheep
loped, and stopped abruptly.
Up above in the crowd there was utter silence; staring

eyes; rigid fingers. The sweat was dripping off Long Kirby's face; and, at the back, a green-coated bookmaker slipped his notebook in his pocket, and glanced behind him. James Moore, standing in front of them all, was the calmest there.

Red Wull was not to be denied. Like his forerunner he leapt on the back of the hindmost sheep. But the red dog was heavy where the grey was light. The sheep staggered, slipped, and fell.

Almost before it had touched water, M'Adam, his face afire and eyes flaming, was in the stream. In a second he had hold of the struggling creature and had half-thrown, half-shoved it on to the bank.

Again a tribute of admiration, led by James Moore.

The little man scrambled, panting, on to the bank and raced after sheep and dog. His face was white beneath the perspiration; his breath came in quavering gasps; his trousers were wet and clinging to his legs; he was trembling in every limb and yet indomitable.

They were up to the pen, and the last wrestle began.

The crowd, silent and motionless, craned forward to watch the uncannie pair working so close below them. M'Adam's eyes were staring, unnaturally bright; his bent body was projected forward; and he tapped with his stick on the ground like a blind man, coaxing the sheep in. And the Tailless Tyke, tongue out, flanks heaving, crept and crawled and worked up to the opening, patient as he had never been before.

They were in at last.

There was a lukewarm, half-hearted cheer: then silence.

Exhausted and trembling, the little man leant against the pen, one hand upon it; while Red Wull, his flanks still heaving, gently licked the other. Quite close stood

/ ames Moore and the grey dog; above, was the black wall of people, utterly still; below, the judges comparing notes. In the silence you could almost hear the panting of the crowd.

Then one of the judges approached the Master and shook him by the hand.

The grey dog had won. Owd Bob o' Kenmuir had won the Shepherds' Trophy outright!

A second's palpitating silence; a woman's hysterical laugh; and a deep-mouthed bellow rent the expectant air: shouts, screams, hat-tossings, back-clappings, blending in a din that made the many-winding waters of the Silver Lea quiver and quiver again.

Owd Bob o' Kenmuir had won outright.

Maggie's face flushed scarlet; Wee Anne flung fat arms towards her triumphant Bob and screamed with the best; Squire and Parson, each red-cheeked, were boisterously shaking hands; Long Kirby, who had not prayed for thirty years, ejaculated with heartfelt earnestness — "Thank God!" Sam'l Todd bellowed in Tammas's ear, and almost slew him with his mighty buffets; while amongst the Dalesmen some laughed like drunken men; some cried like children; all joined in that roaring song of victory.

To little M'Adam, standing with his back to the crowd, that storm of cheering came as the first announcement of defeat.

A wintry smile, like the sun over a March sea, crept across his face.

"We might ha' kent it, Wullie," he muttered softly.

The tension loosed, the battle lost, the little man almost broke down. There were red dabs of colour in his face; his eyes were big; his lips pitifully quivering: he was near to sobbing.

An old man—utterly alone—he had staked his all on a throw—and lost.

Lady Eleanour marked the forlorn little figure standing solitary on the fringe of the uproarious mob. She noticed the expression on his face; and her tender heart went out to the little lone man in his defeat.

She went up to him and laid a hand upon his arm.

"Mr. M'Adam," she said timidly, "won't you come and sit down in the tent? You look *so* tired."

The little man wrenched roughly away. The unexpected kindness, coming at that moment, was almost too much for him.

A few paces off he turned again—

"It's real kind o' yer Leddyship," he said huskily; and tottered away to be alone with Red Wull.

Meanwhile the victors stood like rocks in the tideway. About them surged a continually changing throng, shaking the man's hand, patting the dog.

Maggie had carried Wee Anne to tender her congratulations; Long Kirby had come, Tammas, Saunderson, Hoppin, Tupper, Londesley, Parson Leggy—all but Jim Mason; and now, elbowing through the press, came the Squire.

"Well done, James! well done, indeed! Knew you'd win! told you so—eh, eh!" then facetiously to Owd Bob, "Knew you would, Robert, old man! Ought to —Robert the Dev—mustn't be a naughty boy—eh, eh! And oh! by-the-by, James, I've fixed the Manor dinner for to-day fortnight. Tell Saunderson and Tupper, will you? Want all the tenants there." He disappeared into the crowd, but in a minute had fought his way back. "I'd forgotten something," he shouted. "Tell our Maggie perhaps you'll have news for her after it h! eh!" and he was gone again.

Last of all, James Moore was aware of a blotchy, rinning face at his elbow.

"I maun congratulate ye, Mr. Moore. Ye've beat us— ou and the gentlemen-judges."

"'Twas a close thing, M'Adam," the other answered. An' ye made a gran' fight. In ma life I never saw a ner turn than yours by the two flags yonder. I hope e bear no malice."

"Malice! Me? Is it likely? Na, na. 'Do onto ery man as he does onto you—and somethin' ever,' 1at's my motter. Na, na; there's nae gude fech'in gin fate—and the judges. Weel, I wush you well o' er victory. Aiblins 'twill be oor turn next."

Then a rush, headed by Sam'l, roughly hustled the ne away, and bore the other off on its shoulders it oisterous triumph.

In presenting the Cup, Lady Eleanour made a rettier speech than ever. Yet all the while she was aunted by a white miserable face; and all the while he was conscious of two black moving dots in the aurk Muir Pass opposite her—solitary, desolate, a ontrast to the huzzaing crowd around,

That is how the Champion Challenge Dale Cup—the orld-known Shepherds' Trophy—came to wander no 1ore; won outright by the last of the Grey Dogs of Kenmuir—Owd Bob, son of Battle.

Why he was the last of his line is now to be told.

Part VI

The Black Killer

CHAPTER XXVIII

RED-HANDED

THE sun was hiding behind the Pike. Over the lowlands the breath of night hovered still; and the hillside was shivering in the chillness of dawn.

Down on the sward beside the Stony Bottom there lay the ruffled body of a dead sheep. All about the victim the dewy ground was dark and patchy like dishevelled velvet; bracken trampled down; stones displaced as though by striving feet; and the whole spotted with the all-pervading red.

A score yards up the hill, in a writhing confusion of red and grey, two dogs at death-grips. While yet higher, a pack of wild-eyed hill-sheep watched, fascinated, the bloody drama.

The fight raged. Red and grey, blood-spattered, murderous-eyed, the crimson froth dripping from their jaws; now rearing high with arching crests and wrestling paws; now rolling over in tumbling, tossing, worrying disorder, the two fought out their blood-feud.

Above, the close-packed flock huddled and stamped,

ver edging nearer to watch the issue. Just so must
ie women of Rome have craned round the arenas to
;e two men in death-struggle.

The first cold flicker of dawn stole across the green.
'he red eye of the morning peered aghast over the
1oulder of the Pike. From the sleeping Dale there
rose the yodling of a man driving his cattle home.
Day was upon them.

James Moore was waked by a whimpering cry
eneath his window. He leaped out of bed and rushed
) look; for well he knew 'twas not for nothing that the
ld dog was calling.

"Lord o' me! What'n's gotten to thee, Owd 'Un?"
e cried in anguish. And, indeed, his favourite, war-
aubed past recognition, presented a pitiful spectacle.

In a moment the Master was downstairs and out,
xamining him.

" Poor owd lad, ye've fair cop't it this time!" he cried.
'here was a ragged tear on the dog's cheek; a deep
ash in his throat from which the blood still welled,
:aining the white escutcheon on his chest; while head
nd neck were clotted with the red.

Hastily the Master summoned Maggie. After her,
indrew came hurrying down. And a little later, a
ny, night-clad, naked-footed figure appeared in the
oor, wide-eyed, and then fled, screaming.

They doctored the old warrior on the table in the
itchen. Maggie tenderly bathed his wounds, and
ressed them with gentle, pitying fingers; and he stood
ll the while grateful yet fidgeting, looking up into his
iaster's face as if imploring to be gone.

"It mun ha' bin a rousan bout—eh, dad?" said the
irl as she worked.

"Ay; and wi' whom? 'Twarn't for nowt he got fightin', I warrant. Nay; he's a tale to tell has Th' Owd 'Un, and— Ah-h-h! I thowt as mickle! Sitha' noo?" For bathing the bloody jaws, he had come upon a cluster of tawny red hair, hiding in the corners of the lips.

The secret was out. Those few hairs told their own accusing tale. To but one creature in the Daleland could they belong—the Tailless Tyke.

"He mun ha' bin trespassin'!" cried simple Andrew.

"Ay, and up to some o' his bloody wark, I'll lay," the Master answered. "But Th' Owd 'Un shall show us."

The old dog's hurts proved less serious than had at first seemed possible. His good grey coat, forest-thick about his throat, had never served him in such good stead. And, at length, the wounds washed and sewn up, he leaped down all in a hurry from the table and made for the door.

"Noo, owd lad, ye may show us," said the Master, and, with Andrew, hurried after him down the hill, along the stream, and over Langholm How. And as they neared the Stony Bottom, the sheep, herding in groups, raised frightened heads to stare.

Of a sudden, a cloud of poisonous flies rose buzzing up before them; and there in a dimple of the ground lay a murdered sheep. Deserted by its comrades; the glazed eyes staring upwards; the throat horribly gaping, it slept its last sleep.

The matter was plain to see. At last the Black Killer had visited Kenmuir.

"I guessed sae mickle," said the Master, standing over the mangled body. "Weel, it's the worst neet's work ever the Killer done. I reck'n Th' Owd 'Un com'

RED-HANDED

on him while he was at it; and then they fowt. And, na sarty! it mun ha' bin a fight too." For all around were traces of that terrible struggle: the earth torn up and tossed; bracken uprooted; and, throughout, little dabs of wool and tufts of tawny hair, mingling with dark-stained iron-grey wisps.

James Moore walked slowly over the battlefield; stooping as though he were gleaning. And gleaning he was. A long time he bent so, and at length raised himself.

"The Killer has killed his last," he muttered; "Red Wull has run his course." Then, turning to Andrew, " Run ye home, lad, and fetch the men to carry yon away," pointing to the carcase. "And, Bob, lad, you've done your work for to-day, and gay weel too, gang home wid him. I'm off to see to this."

He turned and crossed the Stony Bottom. His face was set like a rock. At length the proof was in his hand. Once and for all the hill-country should be rid of its scourge.

As he stalked up the hill, a dark head appeared at his knee. Two big grey eyes, half-doubtful, half-penitent, wholly wistful, looked up at him; and a silvery brush signalled a mute request.

"Eh, Owd 'Un, but ye should ha' gone wi' Andrew!" he said. "Hooiver, as ye are here, coom along." And he strode away up the hill, gaunt and menacing, with the grey dog at his heels.

As they approached the house, M'Adam was standing in the door, sucking his eternal twig.

The Master eyed him closely as he came; but the sour face framed in the door betrayed nothing. Sarcasm, surprise, challenge, were all writ there, plain to read, but no guilty consciousness of the other's errand, no storm of passion to hide a failing heart. If it was acting it was splendidly done.

As man and dog passed through the gap in the hedge, the expression on his face changed again. He started forward.

"James Moore, as I live!" he cried, and advanced with hands extended, as though welcoming a long-lost brother. "'Deed and it's a weary while sin' ye've honoured ma puir hoose;" and, in fact, it was nigh twenty years. "I tak' it gey kind in ye to look in on a lonely auld man. Come ben and let's ha' a crack: James Moore kens weel hoo welcome he aye is in ma bit biggin'."

The Master ignored the greeting.

"One o' ma sheep been killed dyke-back," he announced shortly, jerking his thumb over his shoulder.

"The Killer?"

"The Killer."

The cordiality beaming in every wrinkle of the little man's face was absorbed in a wondering interest; and that again gave place to sorrowful sympathy.

"Dear, dear! it's come to that has it--at last?" he said gently, and his eyes wandered to the grey dog and dwelt mournfully upon him. "Man, I'm sorry—I canna tell ye I'm surprised. Masel', I kent it all alang. But gin Adam M'Adam had tell't ye, ye'd no' ha' believed him. . . . Weel, weel, he's lived his life, gin ony dog iver did; and noo he maun gang where he's sent a-many before him. Puir man! puir tyke!" He heaved a sigh, profoundly melancholy, tenderly sympathetic. Then, brightening a little, "Ye'll ha' come for the gun?"

James Moore listened, at first puzzled. Then he caught the other's meaning and his eyes flashed.

"Thou fool, M'Adam! did ye iver tell o' a sheep-dog worryin' his master's sheep?"

The little man was smiling and suave, rubbing his hands softly together.

"Ye're right—I niver did. But your dog is not as ither dogs—'there's none like him—none,' I've heard ye say so yersel', mony a time. An' I'm wi' ye. There's none like him—for devilment." His voice began to quiver and his face to blaze. "The dog has a devil—I've tell't ye so. It's his cursed cunning that's deceived everyone but me—whelp o' Satan that he is!" He shouldered up to his tall adversary. "If not him, wha else had done it?" he asked, looking up into the other's face as if daring him to speak.

The Master's shaggy eyebrows lowered. He towered above the other like the Muir Pike above its surrounding hills.

"Wha, ye ask?" he replied coldly; "and I answer you—Your Red Wull, M'Adam, your Red Wull! It's your Wull's t' Black Killer! it's your Wull's bin the plague o' the land these months past! it's your Wull's killed ma sheep back o' yon!"

At that, all the little man's affected good-humour fled.

"Ye lee, man! ye lee!" he cried in dreadful scream, dancing up to his antagonist. "I knoo hoo 'twad be! I said so! I see what ye're at! Ye've found at last—blind that ye've been!—that it's yer ain hell's tyke that's the Killer, and ye think by yer leein' impitations to throw the blame on ma Wullie. Ye rob me o' ma cup; ye rob me o' ma son; ye wrang me in ilka thing: there's but ae thing left me—Wullie. And now ye're set on takin' him awa'. But ye shall not—I'll kill ye

He was all a-shake, bobbing up and down like a stopper in a soda-water bottle; almost sobbing.

"Ha' ye no' wranged me enough wi'oot that? ye lang-leggit liar, wi' yer skulkin' murderin' tyke!" he cried. "Ye say it's Wullie. Where's yer proof?" and he snapped his fingers in the other's face.

The Master was now as calm as his enemy was passionate.

"Wheer?" he replied sternly; "why, theer!" holding out his right hand. "Yon's proof enough to hang a huner'd." For lying in his broad palm was a little bundle of that damning red hair.

"Where?"

"Theer."

"Let's see it."

The little man bent to look closer.

"There's for yer proof!" he cried; and spat deliberately down into the other's naked palm. Then he stood back, facing his enemy, in a manner to have done credit to a nobler deed.

James Moore strode forward. It looked as if he was about to make an end of his miserable adversary, so strongly was he moved. His chest heaved, and the blue eyes blazed. But just as one had thought to see him take his foe and crush him, who should come stalking round the corner of the house but the Tailless Tyke.

A droll spectacle he made, laughable even at that moment. He walked all stiff and slow; his button-tail was shut down; his head and neck were swathed in bandages, and beneath their ragged fringe the red-shot eyes gleamed up molten murder.

Round the corner he came, unaware of strangers; then, straightway recognising his visitors, halted abrupt-

RED-HANDED

...is hackles ran up; each individual blade leapt to the gage; and a snarl, like a rusty brake shoved hard ...wn, escaped in jarring thunder from the port-holes ...his lips. Then he trotted heavily forward, his head ...king low and lower as he came.

And Owd Bob, eager to take up the gage of battle, ...vanced, glad and gallant, to meet him. Daintily he ...:ked his way across the yard, head and tail erect, ...rfectly self-contained; only the long grey hair about ... neck stood up like the ruff of a courtier of Queen ...izabeth.

But the war-worn warriors were not to be allowed ...eir will.

"Wullie, Wullie, wad ye?" cried the little man.

"Bob, lad, coom in!" called the other. Then he ...rned and looked down at the man beside him, ...ntempt flaunting in every feature.

"Well?" he said shortly.

M'Adam's hands were opening and shutting; his ...:e was quite white beneath the tan; but he spoke ...lmly.

"I'll tell ye the whole story, and it's the truth," he ...id. "I was up there the morn"—pointing to the ...ndow above—" and I see Wullie crouchin' down ...angside the Stony Bottom. (Ye ken he has the ...n o' ma land o' neets the same as your dog.) In a ...init' I see anither dog squatterin' alang on your side ...e Bottom. He creeps up to the sheep on the hillside, ...ases 'em, and doons one. The sun was risen by then, ...d I see the dog clear as I see you now. *It was that ...g there—I swear it!*" His voice rose as he spoke ; ...d he pointed a damning finger at the grey dog.

"Noo, Wullie, thinks I! And afore ye could clap ...r hands. Wullie was over the Bottom and on to him as he gorged, the bloody-minded murderer. They fought and fought—I could hear the roarin' o't where I stood. I watched till I could watch nae langer, and, all in a sweat, I rin doon the stairs and oot. When I got there, there was yer tyke makin' fu' split for Kenmuir, and Wullie comin' up the hill to me. . . . It's God's truth, I'm tellin' ye. Tak' him hame, James Moore, and let his dinner be an ounce o' lead. 'Twill be the best day's work iver ye done."

The little man was lying—there could be no doubt of it. Yet he spoke with an earnestness, a seeming belief in his own story, that might have convinced one who knew him less well.

But the Master only looked down on him with a great scorn.

"It's Monday to-day," he said coldly; "I gie ye till Saturday. If ye've not done your duty by then—and well ye ken what 'tis—I shall come do it for ye. Ony gate I shall come and see. I'll mind ye agin o' Thursday—ye'll be at the Manor dinner, I suppose. Noo I've warned ye, and ye ken best whether I'm in earnest or no'. Bob, lad!"

He turned away, but turned again.

"I'm sorry for ye, but I've ma duty to do—so've you. Till Saturday I shall breathe no word to ony soul o' this business, so that if ye see good to put him oot o' t' way widoot bodderment no one need iver ken as hoo Adam M'Adam's Red Wull was the Black Killer."

He turned away for the second time. But the little man sprang after him, and clutched him by the arm.

"Look ye here, James Moore!" he cried in thick, shaky, horrible voice. "Ye're big, I'm sma'; ye're strang, I'm weak; ye've ivery one to your back; I've

RED-HANDED

er a one; you tell your story, and they'll believe —for ye go to church; I'll tell mine, and they'll ɔk I lee—for I dinna. But a word in your ear! ver agin I catch ye on ma land, by ——!" he swore a at oath—" I'll no' spare ye. . . . Ye ken best if I'm earnest or no.' " And his face was dreadful to see in hideous seriousness.

CHAPTER XXIX

FOR THE DEFENCE

THAT night a vague story was whispered in the Sylvester Arms. But Tammas, on being interrogated, pursed his lips and replied, " Nay; A'm sworn to say nowt." Which was the old man's way of putting that he knew nowt.

On Thursday morning James Moore and Andrew came down arrayed in all their best. It was the day of the Squire's annual dinner to his tenants.

The two, however, were not allowed to start upon their way, until they had undergone a critical inspection at Maggie's hands: she brushed up Andrew; tied his scarf; saw his boots and hands were clean; and tittivated him generally till she had converted the ungainly hobbledehoy into a thoroughly likely young man.

And all the while she was thinking of that other boy for whom on such gala days she had been wont to perform like offices. And her father, marking the tears in her eyes, and mindful of the Squire's mysterious hint, said gently—

"Cheer oop, lass. Happen I'll ha' news for thee the neet."

The girl smiled wanly.

"Happen so, dad," she said. But in her heart she doubted.

Nevertheless it was with a cheerful countenance that
stood in the door with Wee Anne and Owd Bob
I waved the travellers God-speed; while the golden-
red lassie, fiercely gripping the old dog's tail with
: hand and her sister with the other, screamed them
ordless farewell.

The sun had reached its highest when the two way-
rs passed through the grey portals of the Manor.

n the stately entrance hall, imposing with all the
dences of a long and honourable line, were gathered
v the many tenants throughout the wide March
re Estates. Weather-beaten, rent-paying sons of
soil; most of them native-born; many of them like
nes Moore, whose fathers had for generations owned
l farmed the land they now leased at the hands
the Sylvesters, there in the old hall they were
embled, a mighty host; statesmen no longer, good
n and true yet.

And apart from the others, standing as though in
y beneath the frown of one of those steel-clad
riors who held the door, was little M'Adam, puny
ays, paltry now, mocking his manhood.

The door at the far end of the hall opened, and the
ire entered, beaming on everyone.

Here you are—eh, eh! How are you all? Glad
see ye. Good-day, James! good-day, Saunderson!
d-day to you all! Bringin' a friend with me—eh,
" And he stood aside to let by his agent, Parson
ggy, and last of all, shy and blushing, a fair-haired
ing giant.

Eh, if it isna David!" was the cry. "Eh, lad, we's
l to see thee!" And they thronged about the boy
king him by the hand, and asking him his story.

Twas but a simple tale. After his flight on the

eventful night he had gone south, drovering. He had written to Maggie and been surprised and hurt to receive no reply. In vain he had waited, and, too proud to write again, had remained ignorant of his father's recovery, neither caring nor daring to return. Then, by mere chance, he had met the Squire at the York cattle-show; and that kind man had eased his fears and obtained from him a promise to return as soon as the term of his engagement had expired. And there he was.

The Dalesmen gathered round the boy, listening to his tale, and in return telling him the home news and chaffing him about Maggie, while the Squire, his jolly face red with pleasure and mirth, stood by, chuckling. "Eh, James, what d'you think of my surprise—eh, eh? What'll your Maggie say?"

Of all the people present only one seemed unmoved; and that was M'Adam. When first David had entered, he had started forward, a flush of colour warming his thin cheeks; but no one had noticed his emotion, and now, back again beneath his armoured friend, he watched the scene, a sour smile playing about his lips.

"I think the lad might ha' the grace to come and say he's sorry for 'temptin' to murder me. Hooiver,"—with a characteristic shrug,—"I suppose I'm onraisonable."

Then the gong rang out, and the Squire led the way into the great dining-hall. At the one end of the long table, heavy with all the solid delicacies of such a feast, he took his seat with the Master of Kenmuir upon his right. At the other end was Parson Leggy. While down the sides the stalwart Dalesmen were arrayed, with M'Adam a little lost figure in the centre.

At first they talked but little, awed like children: knives plied; glasses tinkled; the carvers had all their work; only the tongues were at rest. But the Squire's

ging laugh and the Parson's cheery tones soon put
'm at their ease; and a babel of voices rose and
xed.

Of them all only M'Adam sat silent. He talked to no
n, and you may be sure no one talked to him. His
id crept oftener to glass than plate, till the sallow
e began to flush, and the dim eyes to grow un-
turally bright.

Towards the end of the meal there was loud tapping
the table, calls for silence, and men pushed back their
airs. The Squire was on his feet to make his speech.
He started by telling them how glad he was to see
'm there. He made an allusion to Owd Bob and the
epherds' Trophy which was heartily applauded. He
iched on the Black Killer, and said he had a remedy
propose: that Th' Owd 'Un should be set upon the
minal's track—a suggestion which was received with
mendous cheering, while M'Adam's cackling laugh
ild be heard high above the rest.

From that he dwelt upon the existing condition of
riculture, the depression in which he attributed to the
e Radical Government. He said that now with the
nservatives in office, and a Ministry composed of
onourable men and gentlemen," he felt convinced that
ngs would brighten. The Radicals' one ambition
s to set class against class, landlord against tenant.
ell, during the last five hundred years, the Sylvesters
d rarely been—he was sorry to have to confess it—
od men (laughter and dissent); but he never yet
ard of the Sylvester, though he shouldn't say it, who
s a bad landlord (loud applause).

This was a free country, and any tenant of his who was
t content (a voice—"'Oo says we's not?")—"thank
u, thank you!"—well, there was room for him outside

(cheers). He thanked God from the bottom of hi heart that, during the forty years he had been re sponsible for the March Mere Estate, there had neve: been any friction between him and his people (cheers) and he didn't think there ever would be (loud cheers) "Thank you, thank you," and his motto was—"Shun a Radical as you do the Devil!" and he was very glad to see them all there—very glad : and he wished to give them a toast—" The Queen, God bless her!" and—wait a minute!—with Her Majesty's name to couple—he was sure that Gracious Lady would wish it—that of "Owd Bob o' Kenmuir!" Then he sat down abruptly amidst thundering applause.

The toasts duly honoured, James Moore, by pre scriptive right as Master of Kenmuir, rose to answer He began by saying that he spoke "as representing al the tenants," but he was interrupted.

"Na," came a shrill voice from half-way down the table; "ye'll except me, James Moore. I'd as lief be represented by Judas."

There were cries of—" Hod tongue o' thee, lil man !' and the Squire's voice—" That'll do, Mr. M'Adam!"

The little man restrained his tongue, but his eyes were burning ; and the Master continued his speech.

He spoke briefly and to the point, in short stilted phrases. And all the while M'Adam kept up a low voiced, running commentary. At length the little man could control himself no longer. Half rising from his chair, he leaned forward with hot face, and cried, "Si down, James Moore! Hoo daur ye stan' there like an honest man, ye whitewashed sepulchre? Sit down, say, or"—threateningly—" wad ye hae me come to ye?"

At that the Dalesmen laughed uproariously, and even

Master's grim face relaxed. But the Squire's voice
[ran]g out sharp and stern—
"Keep silence and sit down, M'Adam! D'you hear
[me], Sir? If I have to speak to you again it will be to
[ord]er you to leave the room."

The little man obeyed, sullen and vengeful, like a
[beat]en cat.

The Master concluded his speech by calling on all
[pre]sent to give three cheers for the Squire, her ladyship,
[and] the young ladies.

The call was responded to enthusiastically, every man
[sta]nding. Just as the noise was at its zenith, Lady
[Eleanour] herself, with her two fair daughters, glided
[into] the gallery at the end of the hall; whereat the
[che]ering became deafening.

Slowly the clamour subsided. One by one the
[occup]ants sat down. At length there was left standing
[onl]y one solitary figure. His face was set, and he
[gri]pped his chair with thin, nervous hands.

"Mr. Sylvester," he began, in low yet clear voice, "ye
[sai]d this is a free country and we're a' free men. And
[tha]t bein' so I'll tak' the liberty, wi' yer permission, to
[say] a word. It's maybe the last time I'll be wi' ye, so I
[hop]e ye'll listen to me."

The Dalesmen looked surprised, and the Squire
[un]easy. Nevertheless he nodded assent.

The little man straightened himself. His face was
[ten]se as though strung up to some high resolve. All
[the] passion had fled from it, all the bitterness was gone,
[an]d left behind was a strange, ennobling earnestness.
[Sta]nding there in the silence of that great hall, with
[eve]ry eye upon him, he looked like some prisoner at the
[ba]r about to plead for his life.

"Gentlemen," he began, "I've been amang ye noo a

score years, and I can truly say there's not a man in this room I can ca' 'Friend.'" He looked along the ranks of upturned faces. "Ay, David, I see ye; and you, Mr. Hornbut; and you, Mr. Sylvester—ilka ain o' you, and not one as 'd back me like a comrade gin a trouble came upon me." There was no rebuke in the grave little voice, it merely stated a hard fact.

"There's, I doot, no one amang ye but has someone —friend or blood—to wham he can turn when things are sair wi' him. I've no one.

'I bear alane my lade o' care'—

alane wi' Wullie, who stands to me, blaw or snaw, rain or shine; and whiles I'm feared he'll be took from me." He spoke this last half to himself, a grieved, puzzled expression on his face, as though lately he had dreamed some ill dream.

"Forbye Wullie I've no friend on God's earth. And, mind ye, a bad man aften mak's a good friend—but there! ye've never given me the chance. It's a sair thing that, gentlemen, to ha' to fight the battle o' life alane: no one to pat ye on the back, no one to say 'Weel done!' It hardly gies a man a chance. Forgin he does try and fails, men never mind the tryin', they only mark the failin'.

"I dinna' blame ye. There's somethin' bred in me, it seems, as sets iveryone agin me. It's the same wi' Wullie and the tykes—they're doon on him same as men are on me. I suppose we was made so. Sin' I was a lad it's aye bin the same. From schooldays I've had iveryone agin me."

There was a moment's pause; then the voice began again—

"In ma life I've had three friends. Ma mither—and

went; then ma wife"—he gave a great swallow—d she's awa; and I may say they're the only two 1an bein's as ha' lived on God's earth in ma time : iver tried to bear wi' me;—and Wullie. A man's her—a man's wife—a man's dog! it's aften a' he has his warld; and the more he prizes them the more they are to be took from him."

'he little earnest voice shook, and the dim eyes kered and filled.

Sin' I've bin amang ye—twenty odd years—can man here mind speakin' ony word that wasna ill ne?"

Ie paused: there was no reply.

I'll tell ye. All the time I've lived here I've had kindly word spoke to me, and that a fortnight ne, and not by a man then—by her Leddyship, God s her!"

Ie glanced up into the gallery. There was no one ole there: but a curtain at one end shook as though ere sobbing.

Weel, I'm thinkin' we'll be gaein' in a wee while , Wullie and me, alane and thegither, as we've aye e. And it's time we went. Ye've had enough o' us, it's no' for me to blame ye. And when I'm gone .t'll ye say o' me?—'He was a drunkard.' I am. : was a sinner.' I am. 'He was ilka thing he 1ldna be.' I am. 'We're glad he's gone.' That's .t ye'll say o' me. And it's but ma deserts."

'he gentle condemning voice ceased, and began in.

That's what I am. Gin things had been differ', ins I'd ha' bin differ'. D'ye ken Robbie Burns? ... it's a man I've read—and read—and read. D'ye ken ' I love him as some o' you do yer Bibles?—Because

there's a humanity about the man. A weak m
himsel', aye slippin', slippin', slippin', and tryin' to ha
up; sorrowin' ae minute, sinnin' the next; doin'
deeds and wishin' 'em undone — just a plain hum
man, a sinner. And that's why, I'm thinkin', h
tender for us as is like him:—*he understood.* It's wl
he wrote—after ain o' his tumbles, I'm thinkin'—tl
I was goin' to tell ye—

> 'Then gently scan yer brither man,
> Still gentler sister woman,
> Tho' they may gang a kennin' wrang,
> To step aside is human:'—

the doctrine o' Charity. Gie him his chance, sa
Robbie, tho' he be a sinner. Mony a man 'd be diff
mony bad 'd be gude, gin they but had their chan
Gie 'em their chance, says he, and I'm wi' him. As '
ye see me here—a bad man wi' still a streak o' good
him. Gin I'd had ma chance aiblins 'twad be—a go
man wi' just a spice o' the devil in him. The difl
between what is and what ought to ha' hin."

CHAPTER XXX.

THE DEVIL'S BOWL

HE sat down. In the great hall was silence, save for a tiny sound from the gallery like a sob
[sup]pressed.

[T]he Squire rose hurriedly and left the room. After [him], one by one, trailed the tenants.

[A]t length, two only remained: M'Adam, sitting [sol]itary, with a long array of empty chairs on either [han]d; and, at the far end of the table, Parson Leggy, [gri]m, rigid, motionless.

[W]hen the last man had left the room the Parson [rose], and, with lips tight set, strode across the silent hall. ["]M'Adam," he said rapidly and almost roughly, "I've [liste]ned to what you've said, as I think we all have, with [so]re heart. You hit hard; but I think you were [jus]t. And if I've not done my duty by you as I [mig]ht—and I fear I've not—it's now my duty as God's [min]ister to be the first to say I'm sorry." And it [was] evident from his face what an effort the words [cost] him.

[T]he little man tilted back his chair, and raised his [hea]d. It was the old M'Adam who looked up. The [thin] lips were curled; a grin was crawling across the [moc]king face; and he wagged his head gently as he [look]ed at the speaker through the slits of half-closed [eye]s.

"Mr. Hornbut, I believe ye thocht me in earnest deed and I do!" He leaned back in his chair and laughed softly. "Ye swallered it all doon like best butter. Dear, dear! to think o' that!" Then, stretching forward, "Mr. Hornbut, I was playin' wi' ye!"

The Parson's face, as he listened, was ugly to watch. He shot out a hand and grabbed the scoffer by the coat; then dropped it again and turned abruptly away.

As he passed through the door a little sneering voice called after him—

"Mr. Hornbut, I ask ye hoo you, a minister o' the Church of England, can reconcile it to your conscience to think—tho' it be but for a minute—that there can be ony good in a man, and him no church-goer? Si ye're a heretic—not to say a heathen!" He sniggered to himself, and his hand crept to a half-emptied wine decanter.

An hour later, James Moore, his business with the Squire completed, passed through the hall on his way out. Its only occupant was now M'Adam. The Master walked straight up to his enemy.

"M'Adam," he said gruffly, holding out a sinewy hand, "I'd like to say"—

The little man brushed aside the token of friendship.

"Na, na. No cant, if ye please, James Moore. That'll aiblins go down wi' the parsons, but not wi' me. I ken you and you ken me, and all the whitewash i' the warld 'll no' deceive us."

The Master turned away, and his face was hard as the nether millstone. But the little man pursued him.

"I was nigh forgettin'," he said. "I've a surprise for ye, James Moore. But I hear it's yer birthday o' Sunday, and I'll keep it till then—he! he!"

Ye'll see me afoor Sunday, M'Adam. On Saturday, told ye, I'm coomin' to see if you've done yer duty." Whether ye come, James Moore, is your business; ther ye'll iver go, once there, I'll mak' mine. I've ıed ye twice noo," and the little man laughed that h, cackling laugh of his.

t the door of the hall the Master met David.

Noo, lad, ye're coomin' along o' Andrew and me," aid; "Maggie 'll niver forgie us if we dunnot bring home."

Thank you kindly, Mr. Moore," the boy replied. e to see Squire first; and then ye may be sure I'll fter you."

he Master faltered a moment.

David, have ye spoken to yer father yet?" he asked w voice. " I think ye should, lad."

he boy made a gesture of dissent.

I canna," petulantly.

I would, lad," the other advised. "If ye don't, ye be sorry after."

s he turned away, he heard the boy's steps, dull and len, crossing the hall; and then a thin would-be ial voice in the emptiness—

I declar' if 'tisna David! The return o' the leegal—he! he! So ye've seen yer auld dad at and *the* last: the proper place, say ye, for yer er—he! he! Eh, lad, but I'm blithe to see ye. : mind when we was last thegither? Ye was :lin' on ma chest—'Your time's come, dad,' says and wangs me ower the face—he! he! I mind it ' 'twas yesterday. Weel, weel, we'll say nae mair it it. Boys will be boys. Sons will be sons. dents will happen. And if at first ye don't succeed, , try, try again."

Dusk was merging into darkness when the Master and Andrew reached the Dalesman's Daughter. It had long been dark when they emerged from the cosy parlour of the inn, and plunged out into the night. As they crossed the Silver Lea and trudged over that familiar ground where a fortnight since had been fought out the battle of the Cup, the wind fluttered past them in spasmodic gasps.

"Theer's trouble in t' wind," said the Master.

"Ay," answered his laconic son.

All day there had been no breath of air, and the sky dangerously blue. Now a world of black was surging up from the horizon, smothering the star-lit night. Small dark clouds, like puffs of smoke, detaching themselves from the main body, were driving tempestuously forward, the vanguard of the storm. In the distance was a low rumbling like heavy tumbrils on the floor of heaven. All about, the wind sounded hollow like a mighty scythe in corn. The air was oppressed with a leaden blackness—no glimmer of light on any hand; and as they began the ascent of the Pass they reached out blind hands to feel the rock-face.

A sea fret, cool and wetting, fell. A few big raindrops splashed heavily down. The wind rose with a leap and roared past them. And the water-gates of heaven were flung wide.

Wet and weary, they battled on; thinking sometimes of the cosy parlour behind, sometimes of the home in front; wondering whether Maggie, in flat contradiction of her father's orders, would be up to welcome them or whether only Owd Bob would come out to meet them.

The wind volleyed past like salvoes of artillery. The rain stormed at them from above; 'spat at them from the rock-face; and leaped at them from their feet.

THE DEVIL'S BOWL

)nce they halted for a moment, finding a miserable
lter in a crevice of the rock.

It's a Black Killer's neet!" panted the Master. "I
<'n he's oot."

Reck'n he is," the boy gasped.

Jp and up they climbed through the blackness,
;d and buffeted. The eternal thunder of the rain
; all about them, the clamour of the gale above, and
beneath, the roar of angry waters.

)nce, in a lull in the storm, the Master turned and
<ed back into the blackness along the path they
come.

Did ye hear owt?" he roared above the muffled
ghing of the wind.

Nay," Andrew shouted back.

I thowt I hard a step!" the Master cried, peering
/n.

}ut nothing could he see.

"hen the wind leaped to life again like a giant from
sleep, drowning all sound with its hurricane voice;
they turned and bowed to their task again.

Jearing the summit, the Master turned once more.

Theer it was again!" he called; but his words were
pt away on the storm; and they buckled to the
iggle afresh.

!ver and anon the moon gleamed down through the
of tossing sky. Then they could see the wet wall
ve them, with the water tumbling down its sheer
:; and far below, in the roaring gutter of the Pass,
rown-stained torrent. Hardly, however, had they
e to glance around when a mass of cloud would,
ry jealously up; and all again was blackness and
;e.

\t length, nigh spent, they topped the Neck of the

Pass and emerged into the Devil's Bowl. There, overcome with their exertions, they flung themselves on to the ground to draw breath.

Behind them, the wind rushed with a sullen roar up the funnel of the Pass. It screamed above them as though ten million devils were a-horse; and blurted out on to the Marches beyond.

As they lay there, still panting, the moon gleamed down in pallid graciousness. In front, through the lashing rain, they could discern the hillocks that squat, hag-like, around the Bowl; and lying in its bosom, its waters ploughed now into a thousand white-tipped furrows, the Lone Tarn.

The Master raised his head and craned forward at the ghostly scene. Of a sudden he reared himself on his arms, and stayed motionless awhile; then he dropped as though dead, forcing down Andrew with an iron hand.

"Lad, did ye see?" he whispered.

"Nay; what was't?"

"Theer!"

But as the Master pointed, a blurr of cloud intervened, and all was dark. Quickly it passed; and again the lantern of the night shone down. Then Andrew, looking with all his eyes, saw indeed.

There, in front, by the fretting waters of the Tarn, packed in a solid phalanx, with spurting breaths and every head turned in the same direction, was a flock of sheep. They were motionless; all-intent; staring with horror-bulging eyes. A column of steam rose from their bodies into the rain-pierced air. Panting and palpitating, yet they stood with their backs to the water, as though determined to sell their lives dearly.

Beyond them, not fifty yards away, crouched a hump-backed boulder, casting a long, misshapen shadow in the moonlight. And beneath it were two black objects, one still struggling feebly.

"T' Killer!" gasped the boy, and, all ablaze with excitement, began forging forward.

"Steady, lad, steady!" urged the Master, dropping a restraining hand on the boy's shoulder.

Above them a huddle of clouds flung in furious rout across the night, and the moon was veiled.

"Follow, lad!" ordered the Master, and began to crawl silently forward. As stealthily Andrew pursued. And over the sodden ground they crept, one behind the other, like two night-hawks on some foul errand.

On they crawled, prone during the blinks of moon, stealing forward in the dark. At length, the swish of the rain on the waters of the Tarn, and the sobbing of the flock in front, warned them they were near.

They skirted the trembling pack, passing so close as to brush against the flanking sheep; yet they were unnoticed, for the sheep were soul-absorbed in the tragedy in front; only, when the moon was in, Andrew could hear them huddling and stamping in the night; and again, as it shone out, fearfully they edged closer to watch the bloody play.

Along the Tarn edge the two crept. And still the gracious moon hid their approach, and the drunken wind drowned with its revelry the sound of their coming.

So they stole on, on hands and knees, with hearts aghast and fluttering breath; until, of a sudden, in a lull of wind, they could hear, right before them, the smack and slobber of bloody lips, chewing their bloody meal.

"Say thy prayers, Red Wull. Thy last minute's coom!" muttered the Master, rising to his knees; then, in Andrew's ear, "When I rush, lad, follow!" For he thought, when the moon rose, to jump in on the great dog, and, surprising him as he lay gorged and unsuspicious, to deal him one terrible swashing blow, and end for ever the lawless doings of the Tailless Tyke.

The moon flung off its veil of cloud. White and cold, it stared down into the Devil's Bowl; on murderer and murdered.

Within hand's cast of the avengers of blood humped the black boulder. On the border of its shadow lay a dead sheep; and standing beside the body, his coat all ruffled by the hand of the storm—Owd Bob—Owd Bob o' Kenmuir.

Then the light went in, and darkness covered the land.

CHAPTER XXXI

THE DEVIL'S BOWL

IT was Owd Bob. There could be no mistaking. In the wide world there was but one Owd Bob o' Kenmuir. The silver moon gleamed down on dark head and rough grey coat, and lit the white escutcheon on his chest.

And in the darkness James Moore was lying with his face pressed downwards that he might not see.

Once he raised himself on his arms: his eyes were shut and face uplifted, like a blind man praying. He passed a weary hand across his brow; his head dropped again; and he moaned and moaned like a man in everlasting pain.

Then the darkness lifted a moment, and he stole a furtive glance at the scene in front.

It was no dream: clear and cruel in the moonlight, the hump-backed boulder; the dead sheep; and that grey figure, beautiful, motionless, damned for all eternity.

The Master turned his face and looked at Andrew, a dumb, pitiful entreaty in his eyes; but in the boy's white horror-stricken countenance was no comfort. Then his head lolled down again, and the strong man was whimpering.

"He! he! he! 'Scuse ma laffin', James Moore—he! he! he!"

A little man, all wet and shrunk, sat hunching on a

mound above them, rocking his shrivelled form in the agony of his merriment.

"Ye raskil—he! he! Ye rogue—he! he!" and he shook his fist waggishly at the unconscious grey dog.

"I owe ye anither grudge for this—ye've anticipated me!" and he leant back and shook this way and that in convulsive mirth.

The man below him rose heavily to his feet, and tumbled towards the mocker, his great figure swaying from side to side as though in blind delirium, moaning still as he went. And there was that on his face which no man can mistake. Boy that he was, Andrew knew it.

"Father! father!" he pleaded, laying impotent hands upon him.

But the strong man shook him off and rolled on, swaying and groaning, with that awful expression plain to see in the moonlight.

In front the little man squatted in the rain, bowed double still; and took no thought to flee.

"Come on, James Moore! come on!" he laughed, malignant joy in his voice; and something gleamed bright in his right hand, and was hid again. "I've bin waitin' this a weary while noo."

Then had there been done something worse than sheep-murder in the dreadful lonesomeness of the Devil's Bowl upon that night; but, of a sudden, there sounded the splash of a man's foot, falling heavily behind. A hand like a falling tree smote the Master on the shoulder; and a voice roared above the noise of the storm, "Mr. Moore! Look, man! look!"

The Master tried to shake off that detaining grasp. It pinned him where he was, immovable.

"Look, I tell thee!" cried that great voice again.

A hand pushed past him and pointed; and sullenly he turned and looked.

The wind had dropped suddenly as it had risen; the little man on the mound had ceased to chuckle; Andrew's sobs were hushed; and in the background the huddled flock edged closer. The world hung balanced on the pin-point of the moment. Every eye was in the one direction.

With dull uncomprehending gaze James Moore stared as bidden. There was the grey dog naked in the moonlight, heedless still of any witnesses; there the murdered sheep, lying within and without that distorted shade; and there the hump-backed boulder.

He stared into the shadow and still stared. Then he started as though struck: *the shadow of the boulder had moved.*

Motionless, with head shot forward and bulging eyes, he gazed.

Ay, ay, ay; he was sure of it: a huge dim outline, as of a lion *couchant*, in the very thickest of the blackness. At that he was seized with such a palsy of trembling that he must have fallen but for the strong arm encircling him.

Clearer every moment grew that crouching figure. At length they plainly could discern the line of arching loins, the crest thick as a stallion's, the massive, wagging head.

No mistake this time. There he lay in the deepest black, gigantic, revelling in his horrid debauch—the Black Killer.

And they watched him at his feast. Now he burrowed into the spongy flesh; now turned to lap the dark pool glittering at his side like claret in a silver cup; now lifting his head, he snapped irritably at the rain, and the moon caught his wicked, rolling eye, and the red shreds of flesh dripping from his jaw; and again, raising his great muzzle as if about to howl, he let the delicious nectar trickle down his throat to ravish his palate.

So he went on, all unsuspicious, wisely nodding in slow-mouthed gluttony. And in the stillness, between the claps of wind, they could hear the smacking of his lips. While all the time the grey dog stood before him, motionless as though carved in stone.

At last, as the murderer rolled his great head, he saw that still figure. At the sight he leaped back, dismayed. Then with a deep-mouthed roar that shook the waters of the Tarn, he was up and across his victim with fangs bared, coat standing erect in wet rigid furrows from top-knot to tail.

So the two stood, face to face, with perhaps a yard of rain-pierced air between them.

The wind hushed its sighing to listen. The moon stared down, white and dumb. Away at the back the sheep edged closer. Save for the everlasting thunder of the rain there was stillness.

An age, it seemed, they waited so. Then a voice, clear yet low and far-away, like a bugle in a distant city, broke the silence.

"Eh, Wullie!"

There was no anger in the tones, only an incomparable reproach: the sound of the cracking of a man's heart.

At the call the great dog leaped round, snarling in hideous passion. He saw the small familiar figure, clear-cut against the tumbling sky; and for the only time in his life Red Wull was afraid.

His blood-foe was forgotten; the dead sheep was

THE DEVIL'S BOWL

forgotten; everything was forgotten in the agony of that moment. He cowered upon the ground, and a cry like that of a lost soul was wrung from him: it rose on the still night air and floated, wailing, away—out of the lonely hollow, over the desolate Marches, into the night.

On the mound above stood his master. The little man's white hair was naked to the night; the rain poured down his face; and his hands were folded behind him. He stood there, looking down into the dell below him, as a man may stand at the tomb of his late-buried wife. And there was such an expression on his face as could not be described.

"Wullie, Wullie, to me!" he cried at length; and his voice sounded weak and far like a distant memory.

At that, the huge brute crawled towards him on his belly, whimpering as he came, very pitiful in his distress. He knew his fate as every sheep-dog knows it. That troubled him not. His pain, insufferable, was that this, his friend and father, who had trusted him, should have found him in his sin.

So he crept to his master's feet; and the little man never moved.

"Wullie, ma Wullie!" he said very gently. "They've aye bin agin me—and noo you. A man's mither, a man's wife, a man's dog! they're all I've iver had, and noo ain o' they three has turned agin me. Indeed I am alone!"

At that the great dog raised himself, and placing his forepaws on his master's chest, tenderly, lest he should hurt him who was already hurt past healing, he stood towering above him; while the little man laid his two cold hands on the dog's shoulders.

So they stood, looking at one another, like a man and his love.

At M'Adam's word, Owd Bob looked up and for the first time saw his master.

He seemed in no wise startled, but trotted over to him. There was nothing fearful in his carriage, no haunting blood-guiltiness in the deep grey eyes which never told a lie, which never, dog-like, failed to look you in the face. Yet his tail was low, and, as he stopped at his master's feet, he was quivering. For he too knew and was not unmoved.

For weeks he had tracked the Killer; for weeks he had followed him as he crossed Kenmuir, bound on his bloody errands; yet always had lost him on the Marches. Now, at last, he had run him to ground; yet his heart went out to his enemy in his distress.

"I thowt t'had bin thee, lad!" the Master whispered his hand on the dark head, "I thowt t'had bin thee!"

Rooted to the ground, the three watched the scene between M'Adam and his Wull.

In the end the Master was whimpering; Andrew crying; and David turned his back.

At length, silent, they moved away.

"Had I—should I go to him?" asked David hoarsely, nodding towards his father.

"Nay, nay, lad," the Master replied. "Yon's not a matter for a man's friends."

So they marched out of the Devil's Bowl, and left those two alone together.

A little later, as they tramped along, James Moore heard pattering, staggering footsteps behind.

He stopped: the other two went on.

"Man!" a voice whispered, and a face, white and pitiful as a mother's pleading for her child, looked into his, "Man! ye'll no' tell them a'? I'd no' like 'em to ken 'twas ma Wullie. Think an t'had bin yer ain dog."

"You may trust me," the other answered thickly.

The little man stretched out a palsied hand.

"Gie us yer hand on't. And G-God bless ye, James Moore."

So those two shook hands in the moonlight, with none to witness it but the God who made them.

And that is why the mystery of the Black Killer is still unsolved in the Daleland. Many have surmised: besides those three only one other knows—knows now which of the two he saw upon a summer's night was the guilty, which the innocent. And Postie Jim tells no man.

CHAPTER XXXII

THE KILLER AT BAY

ON the following morning there was a sheep-auction at the Dalesman's Daughter.

Early as many of the farmers arrived there was one earlier. Tupper, the first man to enter the sand-floored parlour, found M'Adam before him.

He was sitting a little forward in his chair; his thin hands rested on his knees; and on his face was a gentle dreamy expression such as no man had ever seen there before. All the harsh wrinkles seemed to have fled in the night; and the sour face, stamped deep with the bitterness of life, was softened now, as if at length at peace.

"When I com' doon this mornin'," said Teddy Bolstock in a whisper, "I found 'im sittin' just so. And he's nor moved nor spoke since."

"Wheer's t' Terror, then?" asked Tupper, awed somehow into like hushed tones.

"In t' paddock at back," Teddy answered, "marchin' hoop and doon, hoop and doon, for a' the world like a sentry-soger. And so he was when I looked oot o' window when I woke."

Then Londesley entered, and after him, Ned Hoppin, Rob Saunderson, Jim Mason, and others, each with his dog. And each as he came in and saw the little lone figure, for once without its huge attendant genius put the same question; while the dogs sniffed about the little man, as though suspecting treachery. And all the time M'Adam sat as though he neither heard nor saw, lost in some sweet sad dream; so quiet, so silent that more than one thought he slept.

After the first glance the farmers paid him little heed, clustering round the publican at the farther end of the room to hear the latest story of Owd Bob.

It appeared that a week previously, James Moore with a pack of sheep had met the new Grammoch-town butcher at the Dalesman's Daughter. A bargain concluded, the butcher started with the flock for home. As he had no dog, the Master offered him Th' Owd 'Un. "And he'll pick me up i' t' toon to-morrow," said he.

Now the butcher was a stranger in the land. Of course he had heard of Owd Bob o' Kenmuir; yet it never struck him that this handsome gentleman with the quiet, resolute manner, who handled sheep as he had never seen them handled, was that hero, the best sheep-dog in the North.

Certain it is that by the time the flock was penned in the enclosure behind the shop, he coveted the dog—ay, would even offer ten pounds for him!

Forthwith he locked the old dog in an outhouse—summit of indignity; resolving to make his offer on the morrow.

When the morrow came, he found no dog in the outhouse, and, worse, no sheep in the enclosure. A sprung board showed the way of escape of the one, and a displaced hurdle that of the other. And as he was making the discovery, a grey dog and a flock of sheep, travelling along the road towards the Dalesman's Daughter, met the Master.

From the first Owd Bob had mistrusted the man

The attempt to confine him set the seal on his suspicions. His master's sheep were not for such a rogue; and he worked his own way out and took the sheep along with him. (A year later, the old dog's judgment was proved correct; for the man absconded.)

The story was told to a running chorus of—" Ma wud! —Good Owd 'Un!—Ho! ho! did he that?"

Of them all, only M'Adam sat strangely silent.

Rob Saunderson, always glad to draw the little man, remarked it.

"And what doesta' think o' that, Mr. M'Adam, for a wunnerfu' tale of a wunnerfu' tyke?" he asked.

"It's a gude tale, a vera gude tale," the little man answered dreamily. "And James Moore didna invent it: he had it from the Christmas number o' the *Flockkeeper* in saxty." (On the following Sunday, old Rob, from sheer curiosity, reached down the specified number of the paper. To his amazement he found the little man was right. There was the story almost identically. None the less is it also true of Owd Bob o' Kenmuir.)

"Ay, ay," the little man continued, "and in a day or twa James Moore 'll ha' anither tale to tell ye—a better tale, ye'll think it—mair laffable. And yet—ay—no'— I'll no' believe it. I niver loved James Moore, but I think, as Mr. Hornbut aince said, he'd rather die than lie. . . . Owd Bob o' Kenmuir!" he continued in a whisper; "up till the end I canna shake him aff. Hafflins I think that where I'm gaein' to there'll be grey dogs sneakin' around and around me in the twilight. And they're aye behind and behind and I canna, canna "—

Teddy Bolstock interrupted, lifting his hand for silence.

"Heark! thunder."

They listened. From without came a gurgling, jarring roar, dreadful to hear.

"It's coomin' nearer."

"Nay, it's gangin' away."

"No thunder that."

"Mair like t' Lea in flood. And yet— Eh, Mr. M'Adam, what is it?"

The little man had moved at last. He was on his feet, staring about him, wild-eyed.

"Where's yer dogs?" he screamed.

"Here's mi— Nay, by thunder! but he's not," was the astonished cry.

In the interest of the story no man had noticed that his dog had risen from his side; no one had noticed a file of shaggy figures creeping out of the room.

"I tell ye it's the tykes! I tell ye it's the tykes! They're on ma Wullie—fifty to one they're on him! My God! my God! and me not there! . . . Wullie, Wullie!" in a scream, "I'm wi' ye!"

At the same moment, Bessie Bolstock rushed in, white-faced.

"Hi! father! Mr. Saunderson! all o' you! T' tykes fightin' mad! Hark!"

There was no time for that. Each man seized his stick and rushed for the door; and M'Adam led them all.

A rare thing it was for the little man and his Red Wull to be apart. So rare that others besides the men in that little tap-room noticed it.

Saunderson's old Shep walked quietly to the back-door and looked out. There on the slope below him he saw what he sought, stalking up and down, gaunt and grim, like a lion at feeding-time. And as the old dog watched, his tail was slowly swaying as though he were well pleased.

He walked back into the tap-room just as Teddy began his tale. Twice he made the round of the room, silent-footed. From dog to dog he went, stopping at each as though urging him on to some great enterprise; then he made for the door again, looking back to see if any followed.

One by one the others rose and trailed out after him: big blue Rasper; Londesley's Lassie; Ned Hoppin's young dog; Grip and Grapple, the publican's bull-terriers; Jim Mason's Gyp, foolish and flirting even now; others there were; and last of all, waddling in the rear, that scarred Amazon, the Venus.

Out of the house they pattered, silent and unseen, with murder in their hearts. At last they had found their enemy alone. And slowly, in a black cloud, like the Shadow of Death, they dropped down the slope upon him.

And he saw them coming, knew their errand, as who should better than the Terror of the Border, and was glad. Death it might be, and such an one as he would wish to die; at least distraction from that long-drawn, haunting pain. And he grinned as he looked at the approaching crowd and saw there was not one there but he had humbled in his time.

He ceased his restless pacing, and awaited them. His great head was high as he scanned them contemptuously, daring them to come on.

And on they came, marching slow and silent like soldiers at a funeral: young and old; bob-tailed and bull; terrier and collie, flocking like vultures to the dead. And the Venus, heavy with years, rolled after them on her bandy legs, panting in her hurry lest she should be late: for had she not the blood of her blood to avenge?

So they came about him, slow, certain, murderous, opening out to cut him off on every side.

There was no need. He never thought to move. Long odds 'twould be—crushingly heavy; yet he loved them for it, and was trembling already with the glory of the coming fight.

They were up to him now; the sheep-dogs walking round him on their toes, stiff and short like cats on coals; their backs a little humped, heads averted, yet eyeing him askance.

And he remained stock still, nor looked at them. His great chin was cocked, his muzzle wrinkled in a dreadful grin. As he stood there, shivering a little, eyes rolling back, breath grating in his throat to set every bristle on edge, he looked infernal.

The Venus ranged alongside him. No preliminary stage for her: she never walked where she could stand or stood where she could lie. But stand she must now, breathing hard through her nose, never taking her eyes off that pad she had marked for her own. Close beside her were crop-eared Grip and Grapple, looking up at the line above them where hairy neck and shoulder joined. Behind was big Rasper, and close to him, Lassie. Of the others each had marked his place, each taken up his post.

Last of all, old Shep took his stand full in front of his enemy, their shoulders almost rubbing, head past head.

So the two stood a moment, as though whispering; each diabolical, each rolling back red eyes to watch the other; while from the little mob there rose a snarling, bubbling snore, like giants wheezing in their sleep.

Then like lightning each struck. Rearing high, they

wrestled with striving paws and the expression of fiends incarnate. Down they went, Shep underneath, and the great dog with a dozen of these wolves of hell upon him. Rasper, devilish, was riding on his back; the Venus—well for him—had struck and missed; but Grip and Grapple had their hold; and the others, like leaping demoniacs, were plunging into the whirlpool vortex of the fight.

And there, where a fortnight before he had fought and lost the battle of the Cup, Red Wull now battled for his life.

Long odds: but what cared he? The long-drawn agony of the night was drowned in that glorious delirium; the hate of years came bubbling forth. In that supreme moment he would avenge his wrongs on humanity. And he went in to fight, revelling like a giant in the red lust of killing.

Long odds. Never before had he faced such a galaxy of foes. His one chance lay in quickness: to prevent the swarming crew getting their hold till at least he had diminished them.

Then it was a sight to see the great brute, huge as a bull-calf, strong as a bull, rolling over and over and up again, quick as a kitten; leaping here, striking there; shaking himself free; swinging his quarters; fighting with feet and body and teeth—every inch of him at war. More than once he broke through the ruck; only to turn again. No flight for him, nor thought of it.

Up and down the slope the dark mass tossed, like some hulk the sport of waves. Black and white, sable and grey, worrying at that great centrepiece; up and down, roaming wide, leaving everywhere a trail of red.

Gyp he had pinned and hurled across his shoulder.

Grip followed: he shook her till she rattled, then flung her afar; and she fell with a horrible thud, not to rise; while Grapple, the death to avenge, hung tighter. In a scarlet soaking patch of the ground lay Kirby's lurcher, doubled up in a dreadful ball. And Hoppin's young dog, who three hours before had been playing tenderly with the children, now fiendish to look on, dragged after the huddle up the hill. Back the mob rolled on her. When it was passed, she lay quite still, grinning, a handful of tawny hair and flesh in her dead mouth.

So they fought on. And ever and anon a great figure rose up from the inferno all around, rearing to his full height, his head all ragged and bleeding, the red foam dripping from his jaws. Thus he would appear momentarily, like some dark rock amidst a raging sea; and down he would go again.

Silent now they fought, dumb and determined. Only you might have heard the rend and rip of tearing flesh; a hoarse gurgle as some dog went down; the panting of dry throats; and now and then a sob from that central figure. He was fighting for his life. The Terror of the Border was at bay.

All who meant it were on him now. The Venus had her hold at last; and never but once in a long life of battles had she let go; Rasper, his breath coming in dreadful rattles, clipped him horribly by the loins; while a dozen other devils with hot eyes and wrinkled nostrils clung still.

Long odds. And down he went, smothered beneath the weight of numbers, yet struggled up again; his great head torn and dripping, eyes a gleam of rolling red and white, the little tail stern and stiff like the stump of a flagstaff shot away. He was desperate but indomitable; and he sobbed as he fought doggedly on.

Long odds: it could not last. And down he went at length, silent still—never a cry should they wring from him in his agony: the Venus glued to that mangled pad; Rasper beneath him now; three at his throat; two at his ears; a crowd on flanks and body.

The Terror of the Border was overwhelmed at last.

"Wullie! ma Wullie!" screamed M'Adam, bounding down the slope a crook's length in front of the rest. "Wullie! Wullie! to me!"

At the cry the huddle below was convulsed. It heaved and swayed and dragged to and fro, like the sea lashed into life by some dying Leviathan.

A gigantic figure, tawny and red, fought its way to the surface. A great tossing head, gory past recognition, flung out from the ruck. One quick glance he shot from ragged eyes at the little flying figure in front; then with a roar like a waterfall plunged towards it, shaking off the bloody leeches as he went.

"Wullie! Wullie! I'm wi' ye!" cried that little voice, now so near.

Through — through — through! an incomparable effort, and his last.

They hung to his throat, they clung to his muzzle, they were round and about him.

Down he went again with a sob and a little suffocating cry, shooting up at his master one quick beseeching glance as the sea of blood closed over him—worrying, smothering, tearing, like foxhounds at the kill.

They left the dead, and pulled away the living. And it was no light task; for the pack were mad for blood.

THE KILLER AT BAY

At the bottom of the wet mess of hair and red and flesh was old Shep, stone-dead. And as Saunderson pulled the body out, his face was working; for no man can lose in a crack the friend of a dozen years and remain unmoved.

The Venus lay there, her teeth clenched still in death; smiling that her vengeance was achieved. Big Rasper, blue no longer, was gasping out his life. Two more came crawling out to find a quiet spot where they might lay them down to die. Before the night had fallen another had gone to his account; while not a dog who fought upon that day but carried the scars of it to his grave. The Terror o' th' Border, terrible in his life, like Samson, was yet more terrible in his dying.

Down at the bottom lay that which once had been Adam M'Adam's Red Wull.

At the sight the little man neither raved nor swore: it was past that for him. He sat down, heedless of the soaking ground, and took the mangled head in his lap, very tenderly.

"They've done ye at last, Wullie — they've done ye at last," he muttered, convinced that the attack had been organised while he was detained in the tap-room.

On hearing that little voice, the dog gave one weary wag of his stump-tail. And with that, the Tailless Tyke, Adam M'Adam's Red Wull, the Black Killer, went to his long home.

One after one the Dalesmen bore away their dead, and the little man was left alone with the body of his last friend.

Dry-eyed he sat there, nursing the dead dog's head; hour on hour; alone; crooning to himself—

> "'Monie a sair daurk we twa hae wrought,
> An' wi' the weary warl' fought!
> An' monie an anxious day I thought
> We wad be beat'—

An' noo we are, Wullie—noo we are!"

So he went on, repeating the lines over and over again, always with the same sad termination.

"A man's mither — a man's wife — a man's dog! they three are a' little M'Adam iver had to back him. D'ye mind the auld mither, Wullie? and her 'Niver be doon-hearted, Adam; ye've aye got your mither' —and ae day I had not. And Flora, Wullie (ye remember Flora, Wullie? Na, na; ye dinna), wi' her laffin' daffin' manner, cryin' to me, 'Adam, ye say ye're alane. But ye've me—is that no' enough for ony man?' And God kens it was—while it lasted." He broke down, and sobbed awhile. "And you, Wullie—and you! the only man friend iver I had." He sought the dog's bloody paw with his right hand.

> "'And here's a hand, my trusty fier',
> And gie's a haud o' thine;
> And we'll tak' a right guid willie-waught,
> For auld lang syne.'"

He sat there, stroking the poor head upon his lap, bending over it like a mother over a sick child.

"They've done ye at last, lad—done ye sair. And noo I'm thinkin' they'll no' rest content till I'm gone. And oh, Wullie!" he bent down and whispered, "I dreamed sic an awfu' thing: that ma Wullie— But there! 'twas but a dream."

So he sat on, crooning to the dead dog; and no man

roached him. Only Bessie of the inn watched the
lone figure from afar.

It was long past noon when at length he rose, laying
the dog's head reverently down, and tottered away
towards that bridge which once the dead thing on the
ice had held against a thousand.

He crossed it and turned: there was a look upon his
face, half hopeful, half fearful, very piteous to see.

"Wullie, Wullie, to me!" he cried; only the accents,
formerly so fiery, were now weak as a dying man's.

He waited: in vain.

"Are ye no' comin', Wullie?" he asked at length, in
quavering tones. "Ye're not used to leave me."

He walked away a pace, then turned again and
whistled his shrill sharp call; only now it sounded like
a broken echo of itself.

"Come to me, Wullie!" he implored very pitifully.
"'Tis the first time iver I kent ye not come and me
whistlin'. What ails ye, lad?"

He recrossed the bridge, walking blindly like a
sobbing child; and yet dry-eyed.

Over the dead body he stooped.

"What ails ye, Wullie?" he asked again. "Will you
leave me?"

Then Bessie, watching fearfully, saw him bend, sling
the great body on to his back, and stagger away.

Limp and hideous, the carcase hung down from his
shoulders. The huge head, with grim, wide eyes and
lolling tongue, jolted and swagged with the motion,
seeming to grin a ghastly defiance at the world it had

And the last Bessie saw of them was that bloody,
grinning mask, with the puny legs staggering beneath their
load, as the two passed out of the world's ken.

.   .   .   .

In the Devil's Bowl, next day, they found the pa[ir]
Adam M'Adam and his Red Wull, face to face; de[ad]
not divided; each save for the other alone. The d[ead]
his saturnine expression glazed and ghastly in the fixe[d]
ness of death, propped up against that hump-back[ed]
boulder beneath which, a while before, the Bla[ck]
Killer had dreed his weird; close by, his master, lyi[ng]
on his back, his dim dead eyes staring up at the heav[en]
where now he had appeared, one hand still clasping
crumpled photograph: the weary body at rest at la[st]
the mocking face—mocking no longer—alight with
whole-souled, transfiguring happiness.

POSTSCRIPT

ADAM M'ADAM and his Red Wull lie buried
together; one just within, the other just without,
consecrated pale.

The only mourners at the funeral were David, James
[Mo]re, Maggie, and a grey dog peering through the
gate.

During the service, a carriage stopped at the church-
[yard], and a lady with a stately figure and a gentle face
[step]ped out and came across the grass to pay a last
[tribu]te to the dead. And Lady Eleanour, as she joined
[the] group about the grave, seemed to notice a more
[than] usual solemnity in the Parson's voice as he intoned
["e]arth to earth—ashes to ashes—dust to dust—in sure
[and] certain hope of the Resurrection to eternal life."

When you wander in the grey hill-country of the
[Nort]h, in the loneliest corner of that lonely land you
[may] chance upon a hoar farmhouse lying in the shadow
[of th]e Muir Pike.

[En]tering, a tall old man comes out to greet you—the
[Mas]ter of Kenmuir. His shoulders are bent now; the
[hair] that was so dark is frosted; but the blue-grey eyes
[meet] you as proudly in the face as of yore.

[A]nd while the girl with the glory of golden hair is
[prep]aring food for you—they are hospitable to a fault,
[thes]e Northerners—you will notice on the mantelpiece,
[stan]ding solitary, a massive silver Cup, dented. That

is the world-known Shepherds' Trophy, won outrigh[t] as the old man will tell you, by Owd Bob, last and be[st] of the Grey Dogs of Kenmuir. The last because he i[s] the best; because once, for a long-drawn unit of tim[e] James Moore had thought him to be the worst.

When, at length, you take your leave, the old ma[n] will accompany you to the top of the slope to point th[e] way.

"Ye cross the stream; ower Langholm How, yonde[r] past the Bottom; and oop t' hill on far side. Ye' happen on t' hoose o' top. And mebbe ye'll me[et] Th' Owd 'Un on t' road.—Good-day to you, sir, goo[d] day."

So you go as he has bidden you: across t[he] stream, skirting the How, over the gulf, and up t[he] hill again.

On the way, as the Master has foretold, you com[e] upon an old grey dog, trotting soberly along. T[he] Owd 'Un, indeed, seems to spend the evening of h[is] life going thus between Kenmuir and the Grange. T[he] dark muzzle is almost white; the gait, formerly [so] smooth and strong, is very slow; venerable, indeed, he of whom men still talk as the best sheep-dog in t[he] North.

As he passes, he stays to scan you. The noble hea[d] is high, and one foot raised; and you look into tw[o] deep grey eyes such as you have never seen before soft, a little dim, and infinitely sad.

That is Owd Bob o' Kenmuir, of whom the tales a[re] many as the flowers on the may. With him dies t[he] last of the immortal line of the Grey Dogs of Kenmui[r].

You travel on up the hill, something pensive, a[nd] knock at the door of the house on the top.

A woman, comely with the inevitable comeliness

erhood, opens to you. And nestling in her arms
ittle boy with golden hair and happy face, like a
b of Correggio.

u ask the child his name. He kicks and crows
looks up at his mother, and in the end lisps
shly, as if it was the merriest joke in all this
r world, "Adum Mataddum."

www.ingramcontent.com/pod-product-compliance
Lightning Source LLC
Chambersburg PA
CBHW022115230426
43672CB00008B/1396